TOTAL MATH

GRADE 2

AMERICAN EDUCATION PUBLISHING™

An imprint of Carson-Dellosa Publishing
Greensboro, NC

Carson-Dellosa Publishing LLC
P.O. Box 35665
Greensboro, NC 27425 USA

ISBN 978-1-60996-814-4

01-334117784

Table of Contents

Dapper Dog's Campout

Directions: Dapper Dog is going on a camping trip. Draw an **X** on the word in each row that does not belong.

1.	flashlight	candle	radio	fire
2.	shirt	pants	coat	bat
3.	cow	car	bus	train
4.	beans	hot dog	ball	bread
5.	gloves	hat	book	boots
6.	fork	butter	cup	plate
7.	book	ball	bat	milk
8.	dogs	bees	flies	ants

Classifying

Directions: The words in each list form a group. Choose the word from the box that describes each group and write it on the line.

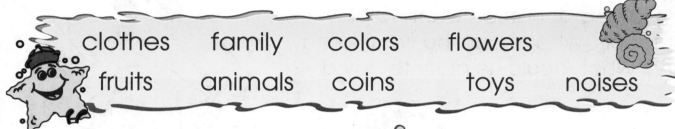

clothes   family   colors   flowers
fruits   animals   coins   toys   noises

rose   crash   mother
buttercup   bang   father
tulip   ring   sister
daisy   pop   brother

_____   _____   _____

puzzle   green   grapes
wagon   purple   orange
blocks   blue   apple
doll   red   plum

_____   _____   _____

shirt   dime   dog
socks   penny   horse
dress   nickel   elephant
coat   quarter   moose

_____   _____   _____

Classifying: A Rainy Day

Directions: Read the story. Then, circle the objects Jonathan needs to stay dry.

It is raining. Jonathan wants to play outdoors. What should he wear to stay dry? What should he carry to stay dry?

Classifying: Outdoor/Indoor Games

Classifying is putting things that are alike into groups.

Directions: Read about games. Draw an **X** on the games you can play indoors. Circle the objects used for outdoor games.

Some games are outdoor games. Some games are indoor games. Outdoor games are active. Indoor games are quiet.

Which do you like best? _____

Classifying: Art Tools

Directions: Read about art tools. Then, color only the art tools.

Andrea uses different art tools to help her design her masterpieces. To cut, she needs scissors. To draw, she needs a pencil. To color, she needs crayons. To paint, she needs a brush.

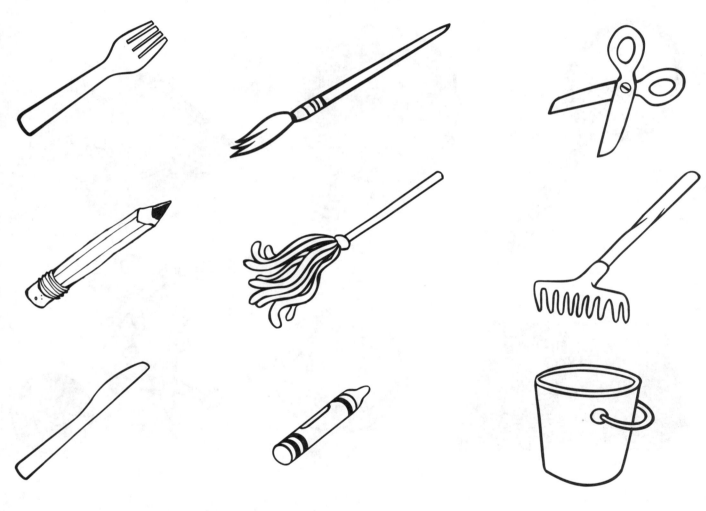

Write which tools are needed to:

draw   color   cut

_____   _____   _____

Classifying: Foods

Darcy likes fruit and things made from fruit. She also likes bread.

Directions: Circle the things on the menu that Darcy will eat.

MENU

apple pie	corn
peas	rolls
beans	banana bread
oranges	grape drink
chicken	

Classifying: Animal Habitats

Directions: Read the story. Then, write each animal's name under **WATER** or **LAND** to tell where it lives.

Animals live in different habitats. A **habitat** is the place of an animal's natural home. Many animals live on land and others live in water. Most animals that live in water breathe with gills. Animals that live on land breathe with lungs.

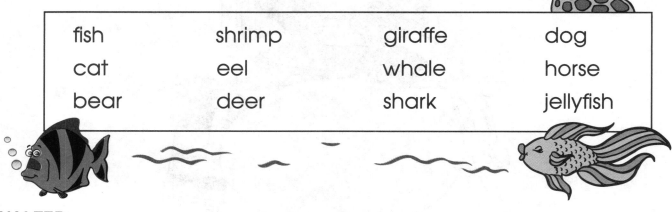

fish	shrimp	giraffe	dog
cat	eel	whale	horse
bear	deer	shark	jellyfish

WATER

1. _____   4. _____

2. _____   5. _____

3. _____   6. _____

LAND

1. _____   4. _____

2. _____   5. _____

3. _____   6. _____

Dot-to-Dot Fun

Directions: Connect the dots. Color the creature.

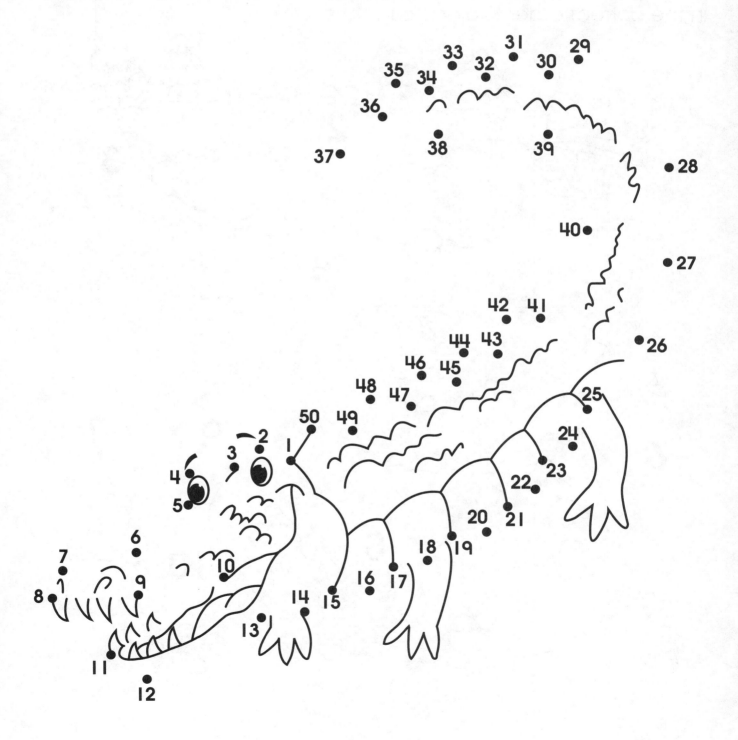

Happy Hikers

Directions: Trace a path through the maze by counting from **1** to **10** in the correct order. Color the picture.

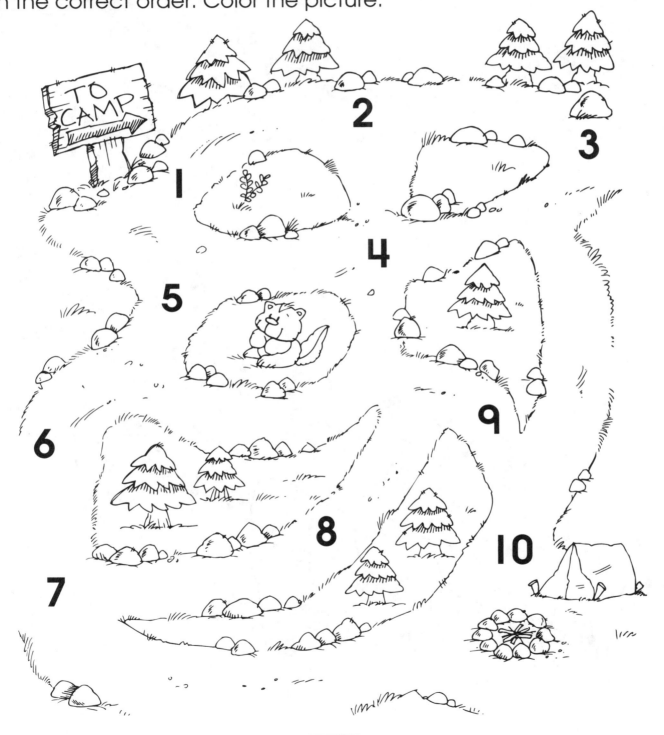

Rainbow-Colored Numbers

Directions: Color the spaces: **1** = **red**, **2** = **blue**, **3** = **yellow**, **4** = **green**, and **5** = **orange**

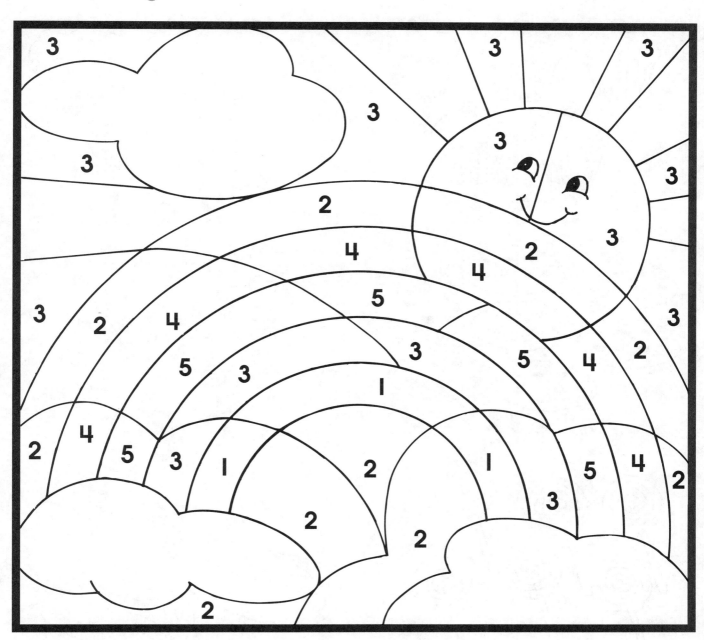

Food Favorites

Directions: Count the pictures in each group. Circle the number. Color the pictures.

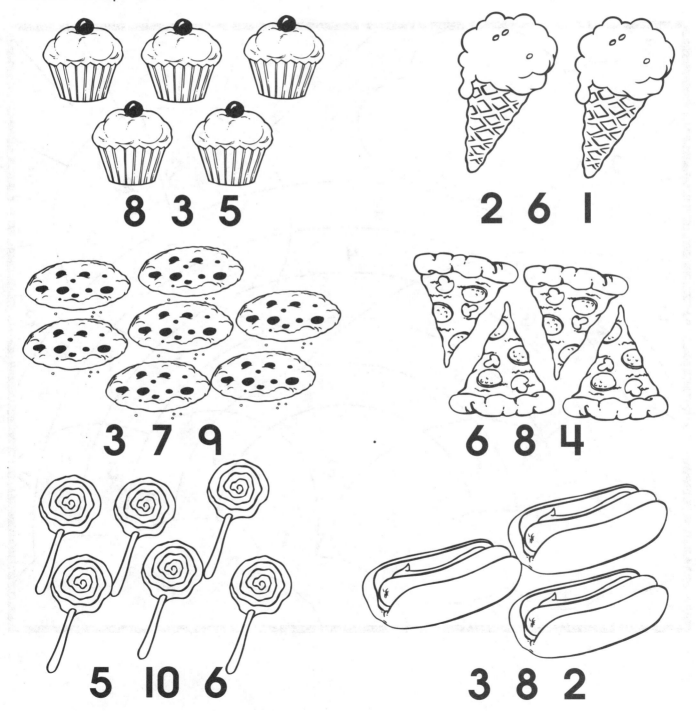

8 3 5

2 6 1

3 7 9

6 8 4

5 10 6

3 8 2

Zany Zoo

Directions: Count and color each group of animals. Cut out the numbers and glue them in the correct boxes.

glue

glue

glue

glue

glue

3 5 1 2 4

This page was left intentionally
blank for cutting activity on
previous page.

Name _____

Clown Capers

Directions: Count the number of each thing in the picture. Write the number on the line.

Take an Animal Count!

Directions: Count each group of zoo animals. Draw a line from the number to the correct number word. The first one shows you what to do.

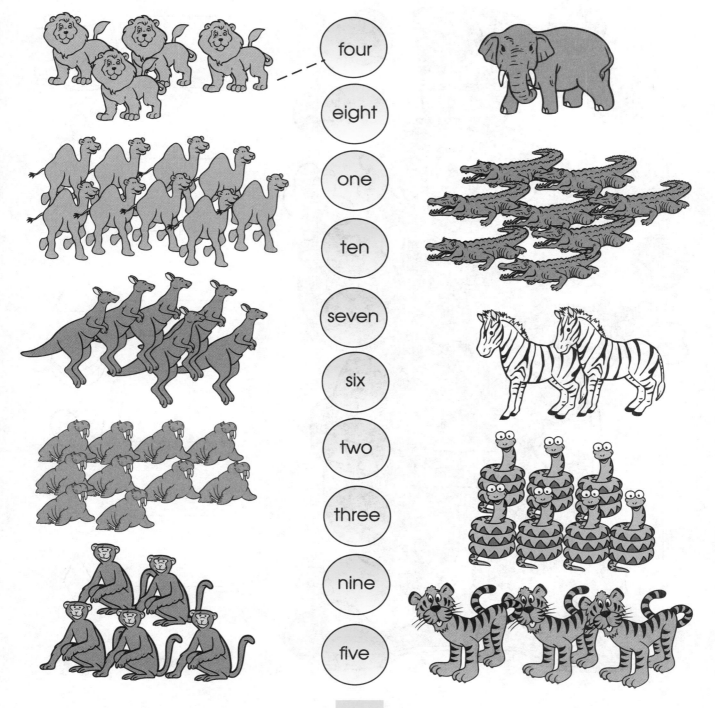

Sheepish Shepherd

Directions: Count the sheep on the hill. Then, write that number on each tree.

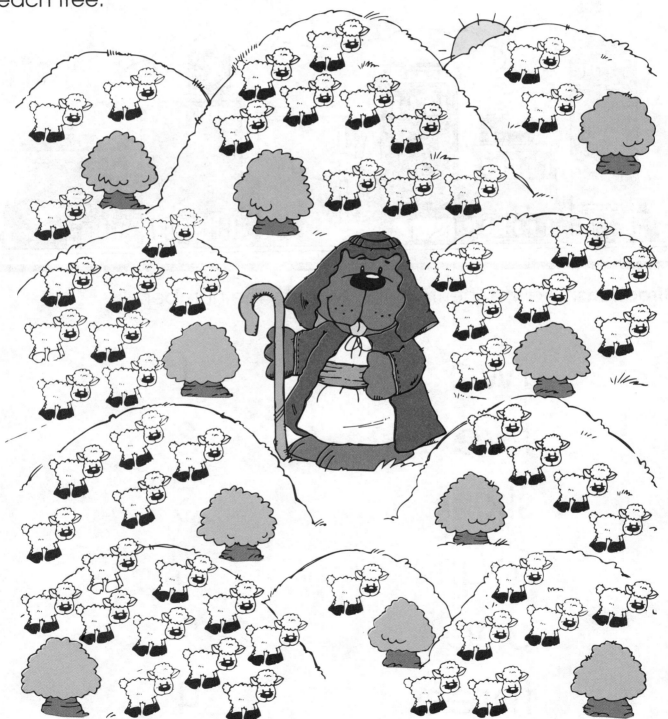

21

Name _____

Number Words

Directions: Number the buildings from one to six.

Directions: Draw a line from the word to the number.

two	1
five	3
six	5
four	6
one	2
three	4

Number Words

Directions: Number the buildings from five to ten.

Directions: Draw a line from the word to the number.

nine	8
seven	10
five	7
eight	5
six	9
ten	6

Number Words

Directions: Write each number beside the correct picture. Then, write it again.

| one | two | three | four | five | six | seven | eight | nine | ten |

Example:

six   six

Sequencing Numbers

Sequencing is putting numbers in the correct order.

Directions: Write the missing numbers.

Example: 4, __5__ , 6

3, _____ , 5   7, _____ , 9   8, _____ , 10

6, _____ , 8   _____ , 3, 4   _____ , 5, 6

5, 6, _____   _____ , 6, 7   _____ , 3, 4

_____ , 9, 10   _____ , 7, 8   2, _____ , 4

2, 3, _____   1, 2, _____   7, 8, _____

2, _____ , 4   _____ , 7, 8   4, _____ , 6

6, 7, _____   2, 3, _____   1, _____ , 3

7, 8, _____   _____ , 3, 4   _____ , 9, 10

Counting

Directions: Write the numbers that are:

next in order	one less	one greater
22, 23, _____ , _____	_____ , 16	6, _____
674, _____ , _____	_____ , 247	125, _____
227, _____ , _____	_____ , 550	499, _____
199, _____ , _____	_____ , 333	750, _____
329, _____ , _____	_____ , 862	933, _____

Directions: Write the missing numbers.

13   14

163   166

821   823

Name _____

Too Much for Mo

Directions: Count the number of each vegetable in the picture. Write the number in the correct box.

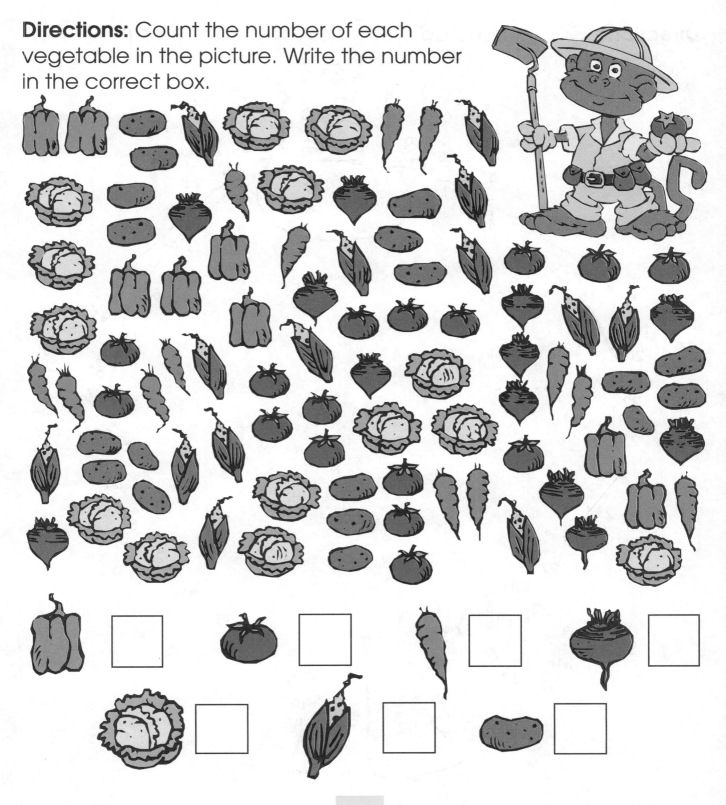

Mystery Animal

Directions: Connect the dots from **1** to **75**. Color the animal.

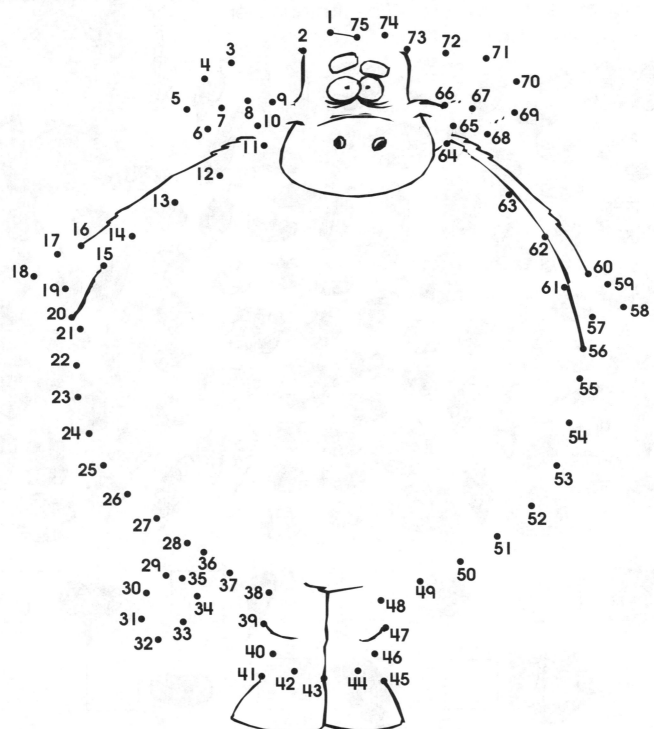

Note the Count

Directions: Count the number of notes on each page of music. Write the number on the line below it. In each box, circle the greater number of notes.

Directions: Color the note in each box that is greater.

Plump Piglets

Directions: Read the clues to find out how many ears of corn each pig ate. Write the number on the line below each pig.

Patsy: I ate the number that comes before **26**.

Horace: I ate the number that comes between **87** and **89**.

Pinky: I ate the number that comes after **92**.

Hilda: I ate the number that comes before **57**.

Porky: I ate the number that comes between **39** and **41**.

Who ate the most? _____ Who ate the least? _____

Teddy Bears in a Row

Directions: Cut out the bears at the bottom of the page. Glue them where they belong in number order.

This page was left intentionally blank for cutting activity on previous page.

Name _____

Counting by Twos

Directions: Count by **2**s to draw the path to the store.

2 4 6 8 10 8 10 12 10 14 16 16 18 20

Two for the Pool

Directions: Count by **2**s. Write the numbers to **30** in the water drops. Begin at the top of the slide and go down.

Cookie Clues

Directions: Find out what holds something good! Count by **5**s to connect the dots. Color the picture.

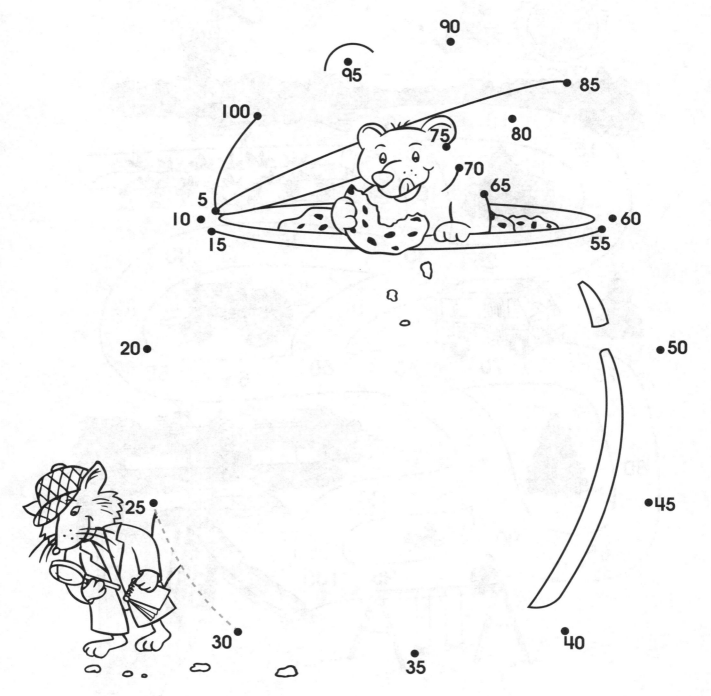

35

Counting by Fives

Directions: Count by **5**s to draw the path to the playground.

I'm Counting on You

Directions: Count by **2**s. Trace and write the numbers below.

2		6							

Directions: Count by **5**s. Trace and write the numbers below.

5		15							

Directions: Count by **2**s.
Connect the dots.
Color the picture.

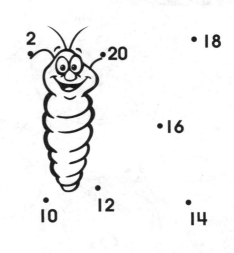

Directions: Count by **5**s.
Connect the dots.
Color the picture.

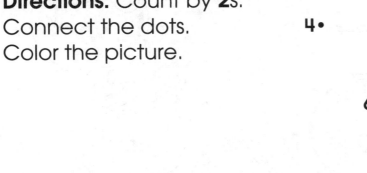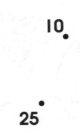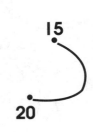

Name _____

Desert Trek

Directions: Count by **10**s. Color each canteen with a **10** to lead the camel to the watering hole.

Caterpillar Count

Directions: Count by **5**s.
Draw a triangle around each number as you count by **5**s.

1	2	3	4	5	6	7	8	9	10
11	12	13	14	15	16	17	18	19	20
21	22	23	24	25	26	27	28	29	30
31	32	33	34	35	36	37	38	39	40
41	42	43	44	45	46	47	48	49	50

Directions: Count by **5**s.

5   10   ___   ___   ___   ___   ___   ___

___   ___

Directions: Count by **10**s.
Draw a box around each number as you count by **10**s.

1	2	3	4	5	6	7	8	9	10
11	12	13	14	15	16	17	18	19	20
21	22	23	24	25	26	27	28	29	30
31	32	33	34	35	36	37	38	39	40
41	42	43	44	45	46	47	48	49	50

Directions: Count by **10**s.   10   ___   ___   ___   ___

Counting by Twos, Fives, and Tens

Directions: Write the missing numbers.

Count by **2**s.

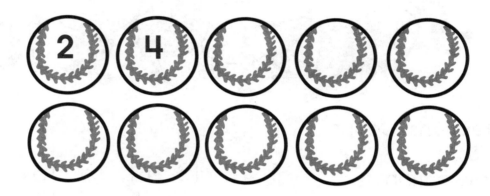

Count by **5**s.

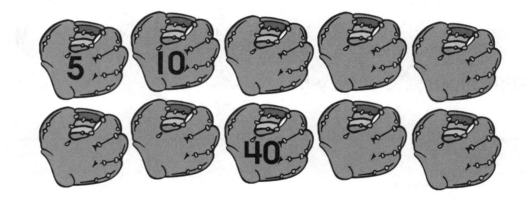

Count by **10**s.

Critter Count

Directions: Count by **2**s, **5**s, and **10**s to find the "critter count."

Each worm = 2. Count by **2**s to find the total.

= _____

= _____

Each turtle = 5. Count by **5**s to find the total.

= _____

= _____

Each ladybug = 10. Count by **10**s to find the total.

= _____

= _____

Hundred Chart

Directions: Count to 100.

1	2	3	4	5	6	7	8	9	10
11	12	13	14	15	16	17	18	19	20
21	22	23	24	25	26	27	28	29	30
31	32	33	34	35	36	37	38	39	40
41	42	43	44	45	46	47	48	49	50
51	52	53	54	55	56	57	58	59	60
61	62	63	64	65	66	67	68	69	70
71	72	73	74	75	76	77	78	79	80
81	82	83	84	85	86	87	88	89	90
91	92	93	94	95	96	97	98	99	100

Largest and Smallest

Directions: In each shape, circle the smallest number. Draw a square around the largest number.

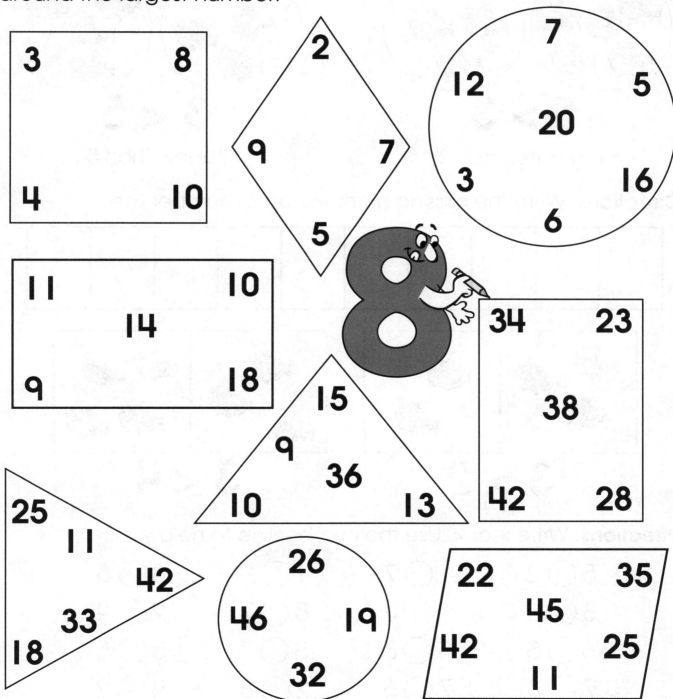

Name _____

Fishing for Answers

5 > 3

5 is greater than 3

3 < 5

3 is less than 5

Directions: Write the missing numbers in the number line.

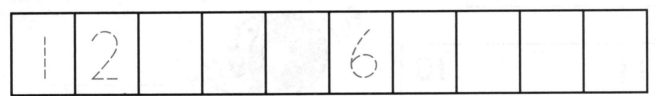

| 1 | 2 | | | | 6 | | | | |

3 > 2

3 < 4

Directions: Write > or <. Use the number line to help you.

5 ◯ 2   1 ◯ 7   1 ◯ 9   8 ◯ 5

3 ◯ 4   9 ◯ 3   8 ◯ 7   2 ◯ 4

6 ◯ 5   5 ◯ 3   5 ◯ 7   3 ◯ 5

7 ◯ 3   7 ◯ 6   2 ◯ 8   4 ◯ 2

"Mouth" Math

Directions: Write < or > in each circle. Make sure the "mouth" is open toward the greater number!

36 ◯ 49   35 ◯ 53

20 ◯ 18   74 ◯ 21

53 ◯ 76   68 ◯ 80

29 ◯ 26   45 ◯ 19

90 ◯ 89   70 ◯ 67

Name _____

Who Has the Most?

Directions: Circle the correct answer.

1. Traci has 3 🐞 s.

   Bob has 4 🐞 s.

   Bill has 5 🐞 s.

   Who has the most 🐞 s?

   Traci   Bob   Bill

2. Pam has 7 🐶 s.

   Joe has 5 🐶 s.

   Jane has 6 🐶 s.

   Who has the most 🐶 s?

   Pam   Joe   Jane

3. Jennifer has 23 🐮 s.

   Sandy has 19 🐮 s.

   Jack has 25 🐮 s.

   Who has the most 🐮 s?

   Jennifer   Sandy   Jack

4. Ali has 19 🐛 s.

   Burt has 18 🐛 s.

   Brent has 17 🐛 s.

   Who has the most 🐛 s?

   Ali   Burt   Brent

5. The boys have 14 🐱 s.

   The girls have 16 🐱 s.

   The teachers have 17 🐱 s.

   Who has the most 🐱 s?

   boys   girls   teachers

6. Rose has 12 🐰 s.

   Betsy has 11 🐰 s.

   Leslie has 13 🐰 s.

   Who has the most 🐰 s?

   Rose   Betsy   Leslie

Who Has the Fewest?

Directions: Circle the correct answer.

1. Pat had 4 ⚽ s.

   Charles had 3 ⚽ s.

   Andrea had 5 ⚽ s.

   Who had the fewest number
   of ⚽ s?

      Pat   Charles   Andrea

2. Jeff has 5 🏀 s.

   John has 4 🏀 s.

   Bill has 6 🏀 s.

   Who has the fewest number
   of 🏀 s?

       Jeff   John   Bill

3. Jane has 7 ⚾ s.

   Susan has 9 ⚾ s.

   Fred has 8 ⚾ s.

   Who has the fewest number
   of ⚾ s?

      Jane   Susan   Fred

4. Charles bought 12 s.

   Rose bought 6 s.

   Dawn bought 24 s.

   Who bought the fewest
   number of ⚪ s?

      Charles   Rose   Dawn

5. John had 9 🏈 s.

   Jack had 8 🏈 s.

   Mark had 7 🏈 s.

   Who had the fewest
   number of 🏈 s?

      John   Jack   Mark

6. Edith bought 12 🎾 s.

   Michelle bought 16 🎾 s.

   Marty bought 13 🎾 s.

   Who bought the fewest
   number of 🎾 s?

      Edith   Michelle   Marty

Less Than, Greater Than

Directions: The open mouth points to the larger number. The small point goes to the smaller number. Draw the symbol **<** or **>** to the correct number.

Example: 5 $\left(\ >\ \right)$ 3   This means that 5 is greater than 3, and 3 is less than 5.

12 $\bigcirc$ 2   16 $\bigcirc$ 6

16 $\bigcirc$ 15   1 $\bigcirc$ 2

7 $\bigcirc$ 1   19 $\bigcirc$ 5

9 $\bigcirc$ 6   11 $\bigcirc$ 13

Name _____

Have a Ball!

Directions: Color the second ball **brown**.

Color the sixth ball yellow.

Color the fourth ball orange.

Color the first ball **black**.

Color the fifth ball **green**.

Color the seventh ball **purple**.

Swimming in Style!

Directions: Color the swimsuits. The first person is wearing a yellow mask.

Color the fourth suit **brown.**

Color the second suit **purple.**

Color the first suit **red.**

Color the seventh suit pink.

Color the third suit **blue.**

Color the eighth suit **green.**

Color the fifth suit orange.

Color the sixth suit yellow.

Orderly Ordinals

Directions: Write each word on the correct line to put the words in order.

| second | fifth | seventh | first | tenth |
| third | eighth | sixth | fourth | ninth |

1. _____   6. _____

2. _____   7. _____

3. _____   8. _____

4. _____   9. _____

5. _____   10. _____

Directions: Which picture is circled in each row? Underline the word that tells the correct number.

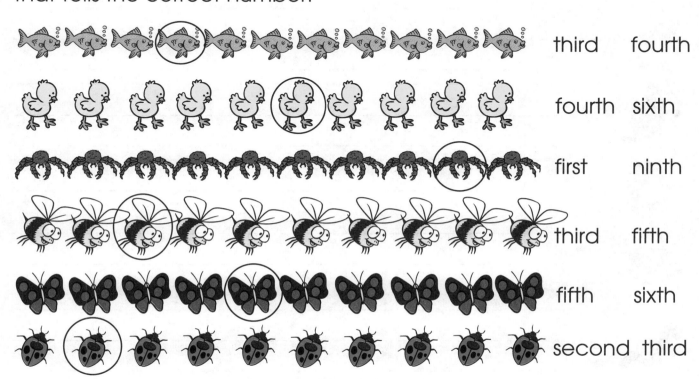

third   fourth

fourth   sixth

first   ninth

third   fifth

fifth   sixth

second   third

Name _____

Which Place in the Race?

Directions: Write the correct word to tell each runner's place in the race.

Flags First

Directions:

Color the ninth flag **red**.
Write **O** on the second flag.
Color the eighth flag **blue**.
Write **D** on the first flag.
Color the sixth flag **yellow**.
Write **G** on the fourth flag.
Color the tenth flag **purple**.
Write **O** on the third flag.
Color the seventh flag **green**.
Color the fifth flag **orange**.
What word did you spell?_____

How Many Robots in All?

Directions: Look at the pictures. Complete the addition sentences.

Example:
How many s are there in all?

$2 + 4 = \underline{6}$

How many s are there in all?

$3 + 5 = \underline{}$

How many s are there in all?

$4 + 3 = \underline{}$

How many s are there in all?

$4 + 1 = \underline{}$

 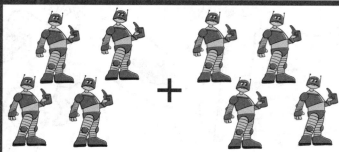

How many s are there in all?

$2 + 5 = \underline{}$

How many s are there in all?

$4 + 4 = \underline{}$

Name _____

How Many Rabbits?

Directions: Look at the pictures. Complete the addition sentences.

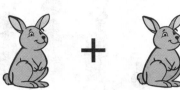

Example:
How many s are there in all?

$$1 + 1 = \underline{2}$$

How many s are there in all?

$$3 + 6 = \underline{}$$

How many s are there in all?

$$6 + 1 = \underline{}$$

How many s are there in all?

$$3 + 4 = \underline{}$$

How many s are there in all?

$$4 + 5 = \underline{}$$

How many s are there in all?

$$2 + 3 = \underline{}$$

Name _____

Alien Problems

Directions: Look at the pictures. Complete the addition sentences.

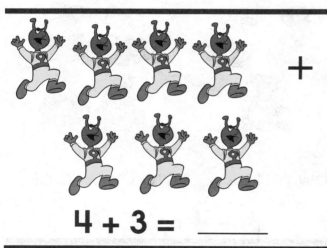

Example:

2 + 3 = _5_

1 + 7 = _____

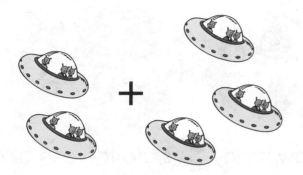

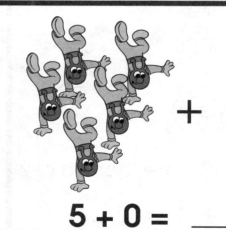

4 + 3 = _____

5 + 0 = _____

3 + 3 = _____

4 + 5 = _____

The Missing Chickens

Directions: Draw the missing pictures. Complete the addition sentences.

Example:

___ + 2 = 3

___ + 3 = 6

5 + ___ = 7

___ + 3 = 5

___ + 4 = 8

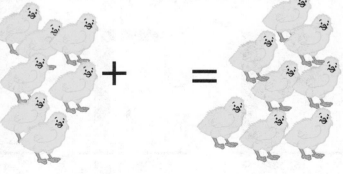

7 + ___ = 8

Signs of Gain

Directions: Roll a die. Write the addend from the die in the top box. Add to find the sum. Roll again to make each sentence different.

How Many in All?

Directions: Count the number in each group and write the number on the line. Then, add the groups together and write the sum.

 _____ strawberries

 _____ strawberries

How many in all? _____

 _____ cookies

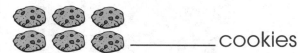 _____ cookies

How many in all? _____

 _____ shoes

 _____ shoes

How many in all? _____

_____ balloons

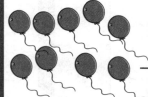 _____ balloons

How many in all? _____

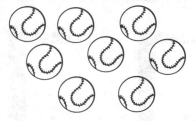 _____ balls

   _____ balls

How many in all? _____

_____ flowers

 _____ flowers

 How many in all? _____

Adding 1

Directions: Write a number in the top box of each problem. Complete the problem. Make each problem different.

Counting Up

Directions: Count up to get the sum. Write the missing addend in each blank.

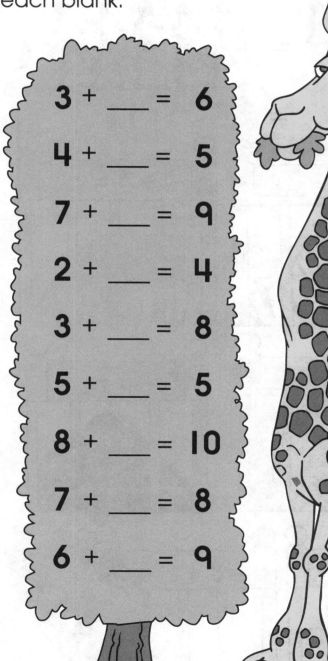

$3 + \underline{} = 6$

$4 + \underline{} = 5$

$7 + \underline{} = 9$

$2 + \underline{} = 4$

$3 + \underline{} = 8$

$5 + \underline{} = 5$

$8 + \underline{} = 10$

$7 + \underline{} = 8$

$6 + \underline{} = 9$

$8 + \underline{} = 9$

$4 + \underline{} = 6$

$6 + \underline{} = 6$

$5 + \underline{} = 7$

$4 + \underline{} = 7$

$9 + \underline{} = 10$

$5 + \underline{} = 8$

$7 + \underline{} = 10$

$6 + \underline{} = 8$

Animal Addition

Directions: Add to find the sum. **Example:**

4 + 7 = 11

3 + 9 = 12

6 + 7 = ___

6 + 5 = ___

5 + 7 = ___

4 + 9 = ___

9 + 6 = ___

7 + 7 = ___

9 + 6 = ___

6 + 8 = ___

It's All the Same

Directions: Count the objects and fill in the blanks. Then, switch the addends and write another addition sentence.

Example:

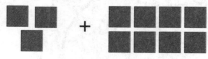 +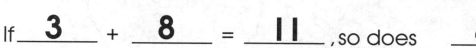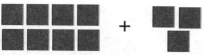

If __3__ + __8__ = __11__ , so does __8__ + __3__ .

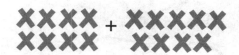

If _____ + _____ = _____ , so does _____ + _____ .

If _____ + _____ = _____ , so does _____ + _____ .

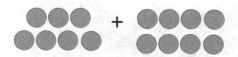

If _____ + _____ = _____ , so does _____ + _____ .

If _____ + _____ = _____ , so does _____ + _____ .

Add the Apples

Directions: Match the addition sentences with their sums.

Target Practice

Directions: Add the numbers from the inside out. The first one has been done for you.

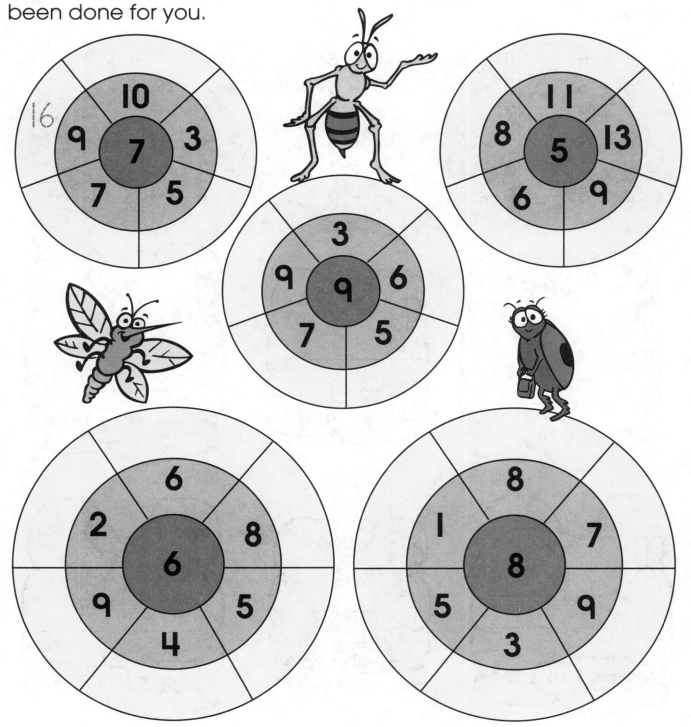

Ride the Rapids

Directions: Write each problem on the life jacket with the correct answer.

8 + 5	8 + 6	7 + 5	8 + 4	4 + 9
6 + 6	9 + 7	9 + 5	6 + 7	5 + 9
7 + 8	7 + 9	8 + 9	8 + 8	
6 + 9	7 + 6	5 + 8	3 + 9	
9 + 3	5 + 7	8 + 7	7 + 7	
6 + 8	9 + 8	9 + 6	9 + 4	

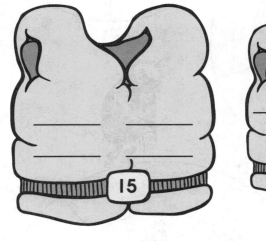

15

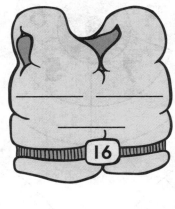

16

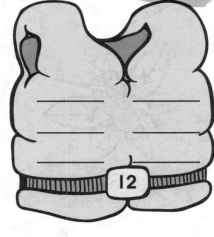

12

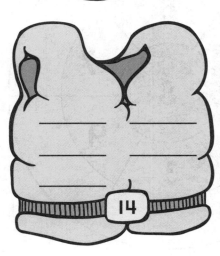

14

17

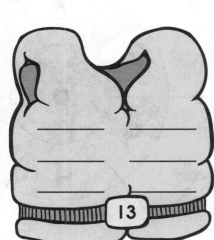

13

Math-Minded Mermaids

Directions: Look at each number. Then, look in each seashell. Circle each pair of numbers that can be added together to equal that number.

12

7	5	3	6
10	2	6	6
9	11	8	4
3	9	1	8

9

1	9	6	3
8	0	4	7
5	9	5	2
3	2	7	5

11

10	7	8	3
5	4	4	8
6	3	6	5
	2	9	
	3	8	

10

3	7	9	1
10	5	5	9
0	8	6	4
8	2		
3	7		

Name _____

Ancient Adding

Directions: Roll a pair of dice. Write the addend from each die on the lines below. Add to find the sum. Roll again to make each sentence different.

___ + ___ = ___   ___ + ___ = ___

___ + ___ = ___   ___ + ___ = ___

___ + ___ = ___   ___ + ___ = ___

___ + ___ = ___   ___ + ___ = ___

___ + ___ = ___   ___ + ___ = ___

___ + ___ = ___   ___ + ___ = ___

___ + ___ = ___   ___ + ___ = ___

Name _____

Lots of Number Partners

Directions: Connect as many pairs as you can to make each sum.

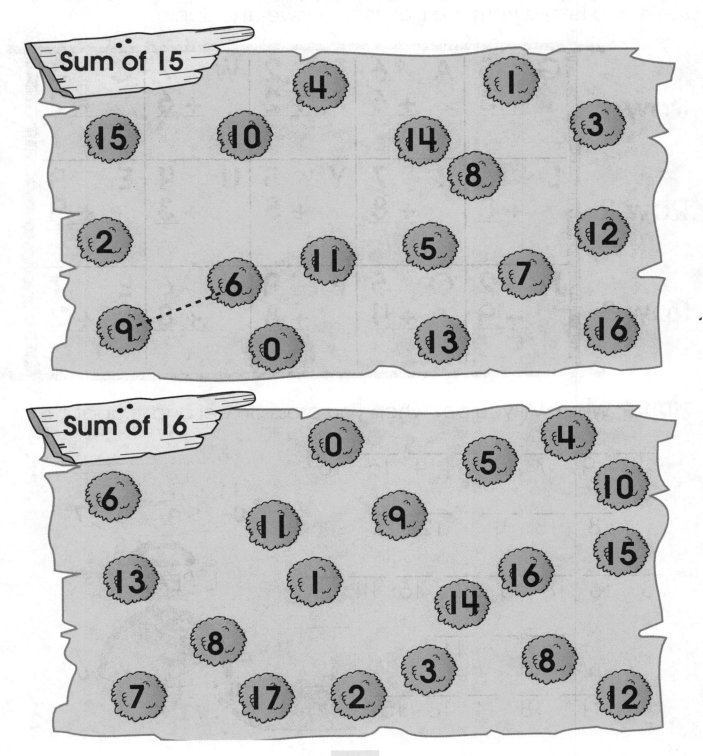

Name _____

Solve the Riddle

Directions: Add to find the sums. Connect the dots in order. Use the sums and letters from the boxes to answer the riddle.

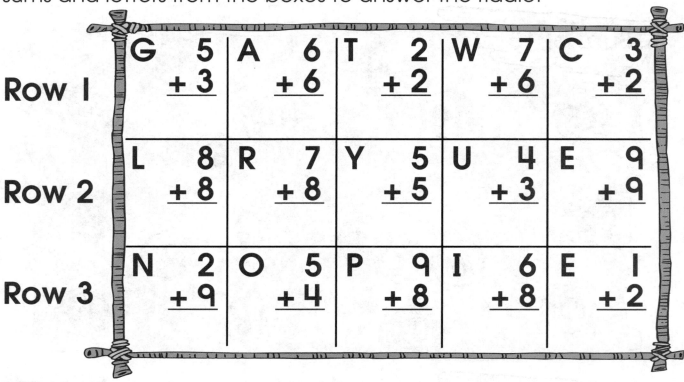

Row 1	G 5 +3	A 6 +6	T 2 +2	W 7 +6	C 3 +2
Row 2	L 8 +8	R 7 +8	Y 5 +5	U 4 +3	E 9 +9
Row 3	N 2 +9	O 5 +4	P 9 +8	I 6 +8	E 1 +2

RIDDLE: What will you get when you cross an eel and a goat?

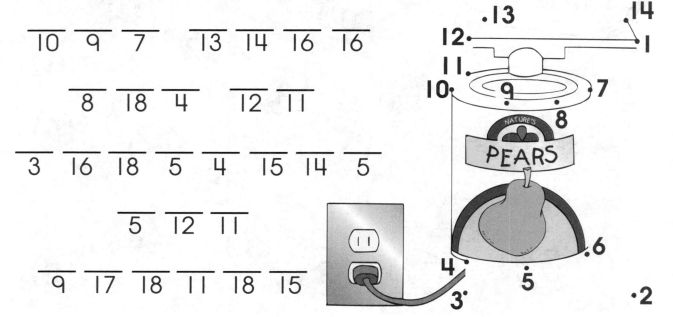

$\overline{10}$ $\overline{9}$ $\overline{7}$ $\overline{13}$ $\overline{14}$ $\overline{16}$ $\overline{16}$

$\overline{8}$ $\overline{18}$ $\overline{4}$ $\overline{12}$ $\overline{11}$

$\overline{3}$ $\overline{16}$ $\overline{18}$ $\overline{5}$ $\overline{4}$ $\overline{15}$ $\overline{14}$ $\overline{5}$

$\overline{5}$ $\overline{12}$ $\overline{11}$

$\overline{9}$ $\overline{17}$ $\overline{18}$ $\overline{11}$ $\overline{18}$ $\overline{15}$

Name _____

Snorkeling Solutions

Directions: Add the numbers in each mask. Write the sums in the bubbles. Color the bubbles of the four largest sums.

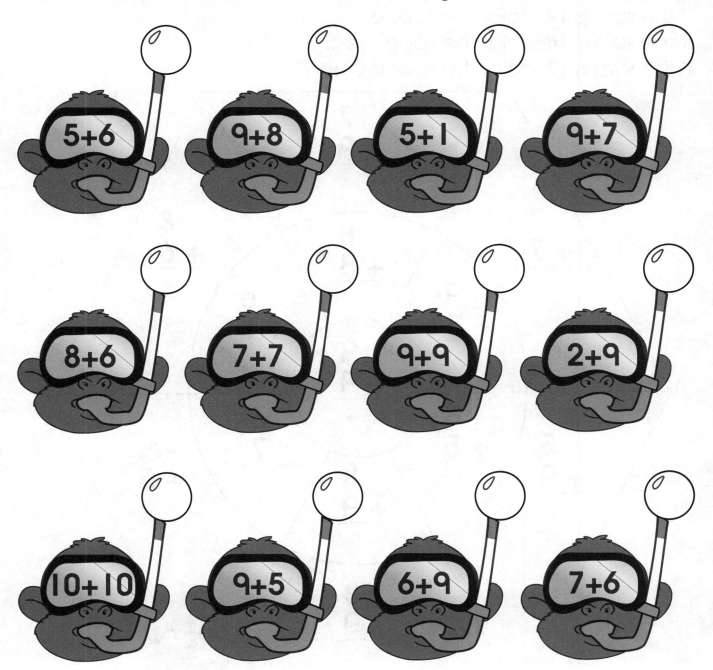

5+6 9+8 5+1 9+7

8+6 7+7 9+9 2+9

10+10 9+5 6+9 7+6

Coloring by Number

Directions: Find each sum.
If the sum is **13**, color the space **brown.**
If the sum is **14**, color the space yellow.
If the sum is **16**, color the space red.
If the sum is **17**, color the space blue.

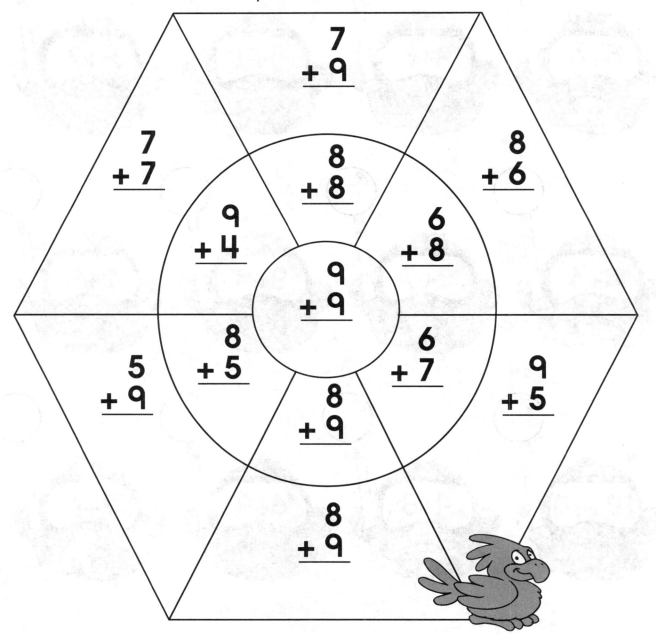

Name _____

Counting Up the Coins

Directions: Solve the problem on each bag. Write the answer on the coin below it. Color the odd sums yellow.

$$9 + 2$$

$$6 + 7$$

$$4 + 7$$

$$8 + 8$$

$$6 + 9$$

$$7 + 5$$

$$5 + 8$$

$$9 + 9$$

$$7 + 4$$

$$8 + 3$$

$$8 + 9$$

$$6 + 5$$

$$8 + 7$$

$$7 + 9$$

$$6 + 6$$

Mys-sss-terious Music

Directions: Solve the problems. Color the spaces using the answers.

ANSWER COLOR KEY:

= 0 – 2

= 3 – 6

= 7 – 9

= 10 – 12

= 13 – 16

= 17 – 20

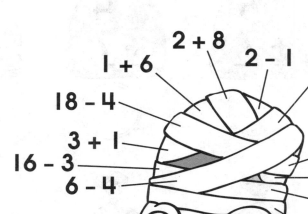

2 + 8

1 + 6

2 – 1

7 – 4

18 – 4

3 + 1

16 – 3

6 – 4

8 + 8

17 – 6

9 + 6

16 – 4

8 + 9

8 + 7

11 + 8

10 + 9

9 + 1

1 – 1

1 + 1

19 + 1

9 + 9

9 – 4

9 + 7

16 – 7

0 – 0

5 + 5

8 + 3

9 + 4

11 – 2

18 + 2

7 + 5

20 – 1

4 + 3

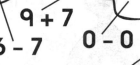
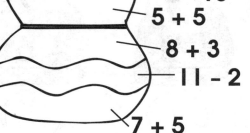

Food Facts

Directions: Draw pictures to show what happens in each story. Solve the problem.

The monkey holds 2 s.

He has 8 s in the jeep.

How many s in all? _____

There are 4 s on the tree.

There are 3 s on the ground.

How many s in all? _____

The monkey picked 2 s.

There are 6 more s left on the vine.

How many s in all? _____

There are 5 s in the bag.

There are 4 s in your hand.

How many s in all? _____

Name _____

Problem Solving

Directions: Solve each problem.

 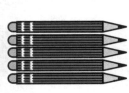

$$\begin{array}{r} 6 \\ + 5 \\ \hline \end{array}$$ pencils in a box
more pencils
pencils in all

grapes on a plate
more grapes
grapes in all

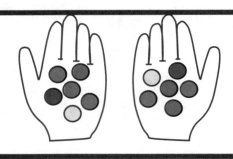

marbles in one hand
marbles in the other hand
marbles in all

people at the table
more people coming in
people in all

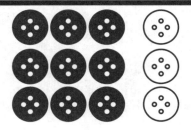

black buttons
white buttons
buttons in all

Problem Solving

Directions: Solve each problem.

Example:

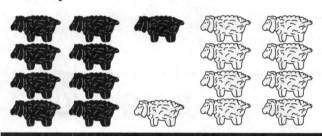

```
  9
+ 9
____
```
black sheep
white sheep
sheep in all

softballs
baseballs
balls in all

glasses of milkshakes
empty glasses
glasses in all

 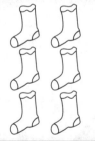  

white socks
gray socks
socks in all

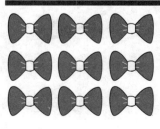 

bow ties
regular ties
ties in all

Name _____

Hop Along Numbers

Directions: Use the number line to count back.

Example: 8, __7__ , __6__

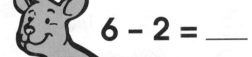

0 1 2 3 4 5 6 7 8 9 10

7 – 3 = ___

7,__,__,__

6 – 2 = ___

6,__,__

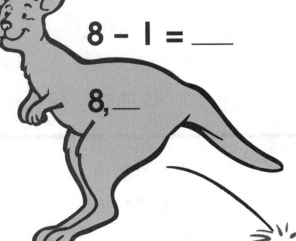

8 – 1 = ___

8,__

7 – 2 = ___

7,__,__

Bubbly Baths

Directions: Solve the subtraction sentences below. Write each answer on a rubber duck.

5 - 4

1 - 0

4 - 2

2 - 1

3 - 1

3 - 2

4 - 1

1 - 1

5 - 1

5 - 2

Name _____

Leaves Leaving the Limb

Directions: Subtract to find the difference. Use the code to color the leaves. Code: **0** = green   **1** = red   **2** = yellow   **3** = brown

$$1 - 0$$

$$5 - 2$$

$$3 - 3$$

$$2 - 1$$

$$3 - 1$$

$$2 - 2$$

$$4 - 2$$

$$5 - 3$$

$$3 - 0$$

$$5 - 4$$

$$1 - 1$$

$$2 - 1$$

How many of each color?

 _____    _____    _____    _____

Name _____

Secrets of Subtraction

Directions: Solve the subtraction problems. Use the code to find the secret message.

Code:

7	5	2	6	4	3
K	T	Y	E	W	A

PLEASE, DON'T EVER

8 -3	10 - 7	9 -2	10 - 4
___	___	___	___

9 -6	6 - 2	7 -4	8 -6
___	___	___	___

MY MATH!

Name _____

Subtraction Makes Al Tired

Directions: Write a different problem for each answer.

Example:

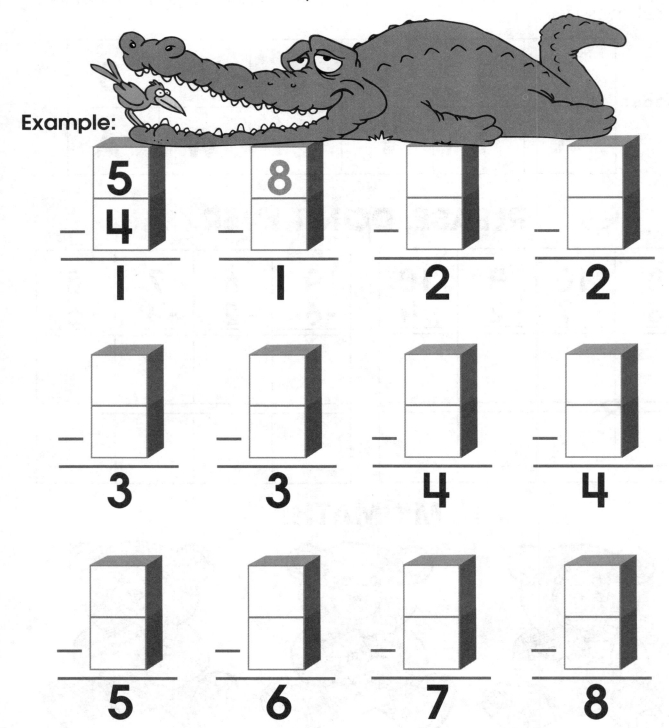

Name _____

Differences in Boxes

Directions: Color the two numbers in each box that show the given difference.

Difference of 1

6	4
3	8

3	1
5	6

4	0
1	7

Difference of 1

3	7
1	8

2	3
5	7

6	3
9	7

Difference of 2

3	0
7	1

3	8
6	9

7	1
4	6

Difference of 2

3	4
8	2

7	4
10	5

10	8
5	4

Difference of 0

2	1
4	2

7	3
8	3

5	6
5	4

Looping Differences

Directions: Circle the two numbers next to each other that make the given difference. Find as many as you can in each row.

Difference of 1

| 2 3 0 (8 7) 2 9 10 6 5 1 4 4 3 |

Difference of 1

| 8 4 5 3 7 1 2 4 9 8 0 1 7 6 |

Difference of 2

| 5 4 2 3 1 0 3 5 8 9 3 6 8 5 |

Difference of 2

| 7 5 10 8 1 4 6 3 2 6 7 9 2 0 |

Difference of 3

| 1 6 3 2 8 4 7 6 10 0 3 9 5 2 |

Hidden Differences of 2

Directions: Circle the pairs that have a difference of **2**.

85

Hidden Differences of 3

Directions: Circle the pairs that have a difference of **3**.

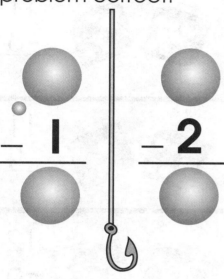
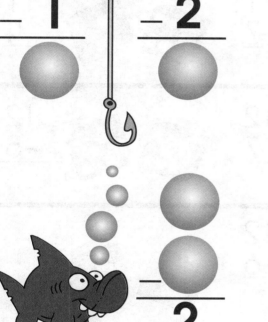

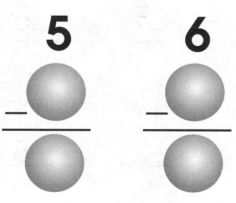

Gone Fishing

Directions: Complete the subtraction sentences to make each problem correct.

$-\ 1$ $-\ 2$ $-\ 3$ $-\ 4$ $-\ 5$

2 4 0 3

5 6 7 8 9

$-$ $-$ $-$ $-$ $-$

Subtraction Facts Through 12

Directions: Subtract.

11 −9		11 −2	11 −8		11 −3

11
−9   11
−2   11
−8   11
−3

11
−6      11
−5   11
−7   11
−4

12
−8   12
−4   12
−7   12
−5

12
−9       12
−3   12
−6

Directions: Subtract.

11 −3 8	11 −6 5	12 −3 8	11 −8 3	12 −7 5	12 −9 3
11 −7 4	12 −4 8	12 −5 7	12 −6 6	11 −2 9	12 −8 4

Name _____

Subtraction Facts Through 4

Directions: Subtract.
Examples:

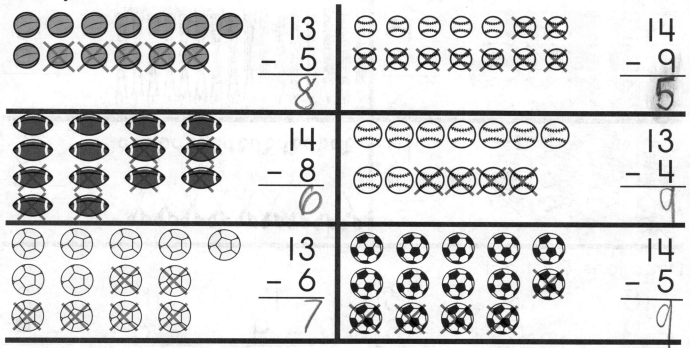

$$
\begin{array}{r} 13 \\ -\ 5 \\ \hline 8 \end{array}
\qquad
\begin{array}{r} 14 \\ -\ 9 \\ \hline 5 \end{array}
$$

$$
\begin{array}{r} 14 \\ -\ 8 \\ \hline 6 \end{array}
\qquad
\begin{array}{r} 13 \\ -\ 4 \\ \hline 9 \end{array}
$$

$$
\begin{array}{r} 13 \\ -\ 6 \\ \hline 7 \end{array}
\qquad
\begin{array}{r} 14 \\ -\ 5 \\ \hline 9 \end{array}
$$

Directions: Subtract.

$$
\begin{array}{r} 12 \\ -\ 7 \\ \hline 5 \end{array}
\quad
\begin{array}{r} 10 \\ -\ 2 \\ \hline 8 \end{array}
\quad
\begin{array}{r} 13 \\ -\ 4 \\ \hline 9 \end{array}
\quad
\begin{array}{r} 14 \\ -\ 9 \\ \hline 5 \end{array}
\quad
\begin{array}{r} 11 \\ -\ 8 \\ \hline 3 \end{array}
\quad
\begin{array}{r} 14 \\ -\ 5 \\ \hline 9 \end{array}
$$

$$
\begin{array}{r} 14 \\ -\ 6 \\ \hline 8 \end{array}
\quad
\begin{array}{r} 12 \\ -\ 8 \\ \hline 4 \end{array}
\quad
\begin{array}{r} 13 \\ -\ 5 \\ \hline 8 \end{array}
\quad
\begin{array}{r} 10 \\ -\ 6 \\ \hline 4 \end{array}
\quad
\begin{array}{r} 13 \\ -\ 6 \\ \hline 7 \end{array}
\quad
\begin{array}{r} 13 \\ -\ 7 \\ \hline 6 \end{array}
$$

$$
\begin{array}{r} 11 \\ -\ 6 \\ \hline 5 \end{array}
\quad
\begin{array}{r} 13 \\ -\ 9 \\ \hline 4 \end{array}
\quad
\begin{array}{r} 14 \\ -\ 8 \\ \hline 6 \end{array}
\quad
\begin{array}{r} 12 \\ -\ 3 \\ \hline 9 \end{array}
\quad
\begin{array}{r} 14 \\ -\ 7 \\ \hline 7 \end{array}
\quad
\begin{array}{r} 13 \\ -\ 8 \\ \hline 5 \end{array}
$$

Subtraction Facts Through 18

Directions: Subtract.
Example:

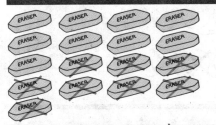

15
− 7
8

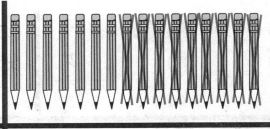

16
− 9
7

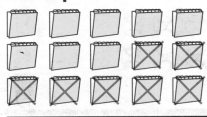

17
− 8
9

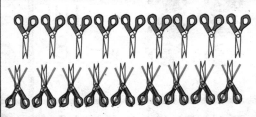

18
− 9
9

Directions: Subtract.

18	13	16	17	14	13
− 9	− 5	− 8	− 9	− 6	− 9

17	15	14	13	16	12
− 8	− 9	− 5	− 6	− 7	− 4

14	15	16	12	15	13
− 7	− 8	− 9	− 7	− 7	− 4

15	14	12	13	14	11
− 6	− 8	− 3	− 9	− 9	− 3

"Grrreat" Picture

Directions: Subtract. Write the answer in the space. Then, color the spaces according to the answers.

1 = white	2 = purple	3 = black	4 = green	5 = yellow
6 = blue	7 = pink	8 = gray	9 = orange	10 = red

Name _____

Crayon Count

Directions: Count the crayons. Write the number on the blank. Circle the problems that equal the answer.

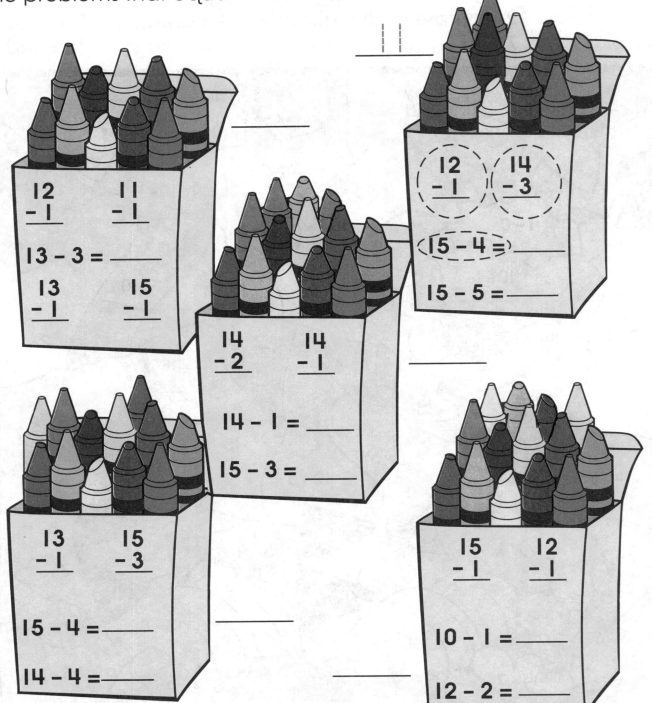

$$12 \atop -1 \qquad 11 \atop -1$$

$$13 - 3 = \rule{1cm}{0.15mm}$$

$$13 \atop -1 \qquad 15 \atop -1$$

_____

$$12 \atop -1 \qquad 14 \atop -3$$

$$15 - 4 = \rule{1cm}{0.15mm}$$

$$15 - 5 = \rule{1cm}{0.15mm}$$

$$14 \atop -2 \qquad 14 \atop -1$$

$$14 - 1 = \rule{1cm}{0.15mm}$$

$$15 - 3 = \rule{1cm}{0.15mm}$$

$$13 \atop -1 \qquad 15 \atop -3$$

$$15 - 4 = \rule{1cm}{0.15mm}$$

$$14 - 4 = \rule{1cm}{0.15mm}$$

$$15 \atop -1 \qquad 12 \atop -1$$

$$10 - 1 = \rule{1cm}{0.15mm}$$

$$12 - 2 = \rule{1cm}{0.15mm}$$

Connect the Facts

Directions: Solve the subtraction problems below.

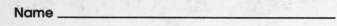

$$\begin{array}{r} 14 \\ -7 \\ \hline \end{array}$$

$$\begin{array}{r} 17 \\ -9 \\ \hline \end{array}$$

$$\begin{array}{r} 16 \\ -9 \\ \hline \end{array}$$

$$\begin{array}{r} 12 \\ -6 \\ \hline \end{array}$$

$$\begin{array}{r} 14 \\ -8 \\ \hline \end{array}$$

$$\begin{array}{r} 15 \\ -8 \\ \hline \end{array}$$

$$\begin{array}{r} 16 \\ -8 \\ \hline \end{array}$$

$$\begin{array}{r} 13 \\ -2 \\ \hline \end{array}$$

$$\begin{array}{r} 13 \\ -8 \\ \hline \end{array}$$

$$\begin{array}{r} 15 \\ -8 \\ \hline \end{array}$$

$$\begin{array}{r} 16 \\ -8 \\ \hline \end{array}$$

$$\begin{array}{r} 14 \\ -9 \\ \hline \end{array}$$

$$\begin{array}{r} 12 \\ -4 \\ \hline \end{array}$$

$$\begin{array}{r} 13 \\ -9 \\ \hline \end{array}$$

$$\begin{array}{r} 16 \\ -7 \\ \hline \end{array}$$

$$\begin{array}{r} 13 \\ -7 \\ \hline \end{array}$$

$$\begin{array}{r} 18 \\ -9 \\ \hline \end{array}$$

$$\begin{array}{r} 14 \\ -9 \\ \hline \end{array}$$

$$\begin{array}{r} 13 \\ -3 \\ \hline \end{array}$$

$$\begin{array}{r} 15 \\ -9 \\ \hline \end{array}$$

Swamp Stories

Directions: Read the story. Subtract to find the difference. Write the number in the box.

4 alligators were in the water. I got out. How many alligators were left in the water?

$$\begin{array}{r} 4 \\ -\ 1 \\ \hline \end{array}$$

6 frogs were sitting on lily pads. 2 hopped away. How many frogs were left on the lily pads?

$$\begin{array}{r} 6 \\ -\ 2 \\ \hline \end{array}$$

5 ducks were in the water. 3 flew away. How many ducks were left in the water?

$$\begin{array}{r} 5 \\ -\ 3 \\ \hline \end{array}$$

More Animal Stories

Directions: Subtract to find the difference. Cut out the subtraction sentences and glue them in the correct boxes. Write the difference in each small box.

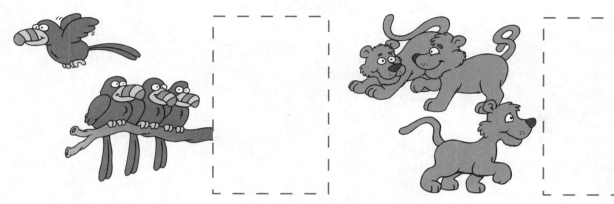

How many toucans were left?   How many lion cubs were left?

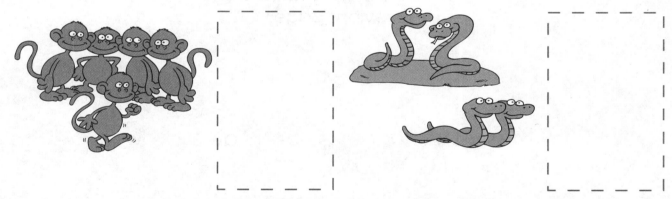

How many monkeys were left?   How many snakes were left?

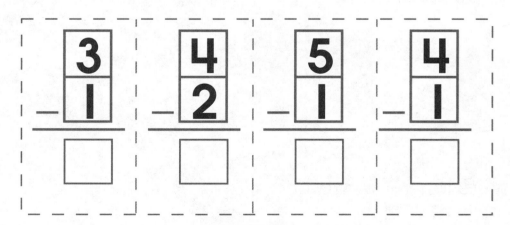

$$\begin{array}{r} 3 \\ -\ 1 \\ \hline \end{array}$$ $$\begin{array}{r} 4 \\ -\ 2 \\ \hline \end{array}$$ $$\begin{array}{r} 5 \\ -\ 1 \\ \hline \end{array}$$ $$\begin{array}{r} 4 \\ -\ 1 \\ \hline \end{array}$$

This page was left intentionally blank for cutting activity on previous page.

Facts Through 5

Directions: Add or subtract.

Examples:

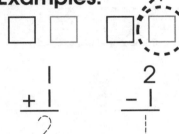
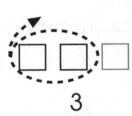

$$
\begin{array}{r} 1 \\ +1 \\ \hline 2 \end{array}
\qquad
\begin{array}{r} 2 \\ -1 \\ \hline \end{array}
\qquad
\begin{array}{r} 2 \\ +1 \\ \hline \end{array}
\qquad
\begin{array}{r} 1 \\ +2 \\ \hline \end{array}
\qquad
\begin{array}{r} 3 \\ -1 \\ \hline \end{array}
\qquad
\begin{array}{r} 3 \\ -2 \\ \hline \end{array}
$$

$\begin{array}{r} 3 \\ +1 \\ \hline \end{array} \qquad \begin{array}{r} 1 \\ +3 \\ \hline \end{array}$	$\begin{array}{r} 2 \\ +2 \\ \hline \end{array}$	$\begin{array}{r} 4 \\ +0 \\ \hline \end{array} \qquad \begin{array}{r} 0 \\ +4 \\ \hline \end{array}$
$\begin{array}{r} 4 \\ -1 \\ \hline \end{array} \qquad \begin{array}{r} 4 \\ -3 \\ \hline \end{array}$	$\begin{array}{r} 4 \\ -2 \\ \hline \end{array}$	$\begin{array}{r} 4 \\ -0 \\ \hline \end{array} \qquad \begin{array}{r} 4 \\ -4 \\ \hline \end{array}$
$\begin{array}{r} 3 \\ +2 \\ \hline \end{array} \qquad \begin{array}{r} 2 \\ +3 \\ \hline \end{array}$	$\begin{array}{r} 4 \\ +1 \\ \hline \end{array} \qquad \begin{array}{r} 1 \\ +4 \\ \hline \end{array}$	$\begin{array}{r} 5 \\ +0 \\ \hline \end{array} \qquad \begin{array}{r} 0 \\ +5 \\ \hline \end{array}$
$\begin{array}{r} 5 \\ -2 \\ \hline \end{array} \qquad \begin{array}{r} 5 \\ -3 \\ \hline \end{array}$	$\begin{array}{r} 5 \\ -1 \\ \hline \end{array} \qquad \begin{array}{r} 5 \\ -4 \\ \hline \end{array}$	$\begin{array}{r} 5 \\ -0 \\ \hline \end{array} \qquad \begin{array}{r} 5 \\ -5 \\ \hline \end{array}$

Facts for 6 and 7

Directions: Add or subtract.

Examples:

$$
\begin{array}{r} 5 \\ +\ 1 \\ \hline 6 \end{array}
\qquad
\begin{array}{r} 1 \\ +\ 5 \\ \hline \end{array}
\qquad
\begin{array}{r} 6 \\ -\ 1 \\ \hline 5 \end{array}
\qquad
\begin{array}{r} 6 \\ -\ 5 \\ \hline \end{array}
$$

$$
\begin{array}{r} 3 \\ +\ 3 \\ \hline \end{array}
\qquad
\begin{array}{r} 6 \\ -\ 3 \\ \hline \end{array}
\qquad
\begin{array}{r} 4 \\ +\ 2 \\ \hline \end{array}
\qquad
\begin{array}{r} 2 \\ +\ 4 \\ \hline \end{array}
\qquad
\begin{array}{r} 6 \\ -\ 2 \\ \hline \end{array}
\qquad
\begin{array}{r} 6 \\ -\ 4 \\ \hline \end{array}
$$

$$
\begin{array}{r} 4 \\ +\ 3 \\ \hline \end{array}
\qquad
\begin{array}{r} 3 \\ +\ 4 \\ \hline \end{array}
\qquad
\begin{array}{r} 5 \\ +\ 2 \\ \hline \end{array}
\qquad
\begin{array}{r} 2 \\ +\ 5 \\ \hline \end{array}
\qquad
\begin{array}{r} 6 \\ +\ 1 \\ \hline \end{array}
\qquad
\begin{array}{r} 1 \\ +\ 6 \\ \hline \end{array}
$$

$$
\begin{array}{r} 7 \\ -\ 3 \\ \hline \end{array}
\qquad
\begin{array}{r} 7 \\ -\ 4 \\ \hline \end{array}
\qquad
\begin{array}{r} 7 \\ -\ 2 \\ \hline \end{array}
\qquad
\begin{array}{r} 7 \\ -\ 5 \\ \hline \end{array}
\qquad
\begin{array}{r} 7 \\ -\ 1 \\ \hline \end{array}
\qquad
\begin{array}{r} 7 \\ -\ 6 \\ \hline \end{array}
$$

$$
\begin{array}{r} 3 \\ +\ 3 \\ \hline \end{array}
\qquad
\begin{array}{r} 5 \\ +\ 2 \\ \hline \end{array}
\qquad
\begin{array}{r} 6 \\ +\ 0 \\ \hline \end{array}
\qquad
\begin{array}{r} 7 \\ -\ 7 \\ \hline \end{array}
\qquad
\begin{array}{r} 7 \\ -\ 4 \\ \hline \end{array}
\qquad
\begin{array}{r} 6 \\ -\ 2 \\ \hline \end{array}
$$

Name _____

Facts for 8

Directions: Add or subtract.

Examples:

$$\begin{array}{r} 5 \\ +\ 3 \\ \hline 8 \end{array}$$
$$\begin{array}{r} 3 \\ +\ 5 \\ \hline \end{array}$$
$$\begin{array}{r} 8 \\ -\ 3 \\ \hline 5 \end{array}$$
$$\begin{array}{r} 8 \\ -\ 5 \\ \hline \end{array}$$

$$\begin{array}{r} 4 \\ +\ 4 \\ \hline \end{array}$$
$$\begin{array}{r} 6 \\ +\ 2 \\ \hline \end{array}$$
$$\begin{array}{r} 2 \\ +\ 6 \\ \hline \end{array}$$
$$\begin{array}{r} 7 \\ +\ 1 \\ \hline \end{array}$$
$$\begin{array}{r} 1 \\ +\ 7 \\ \hline \end{array}$$

$$\begin{array}{r} 8 \\ -\ 4 \\ \hline \end{array}$$
$$\begin{array}{r} 8 \\ -\ 2 \\ \hline \end{array}$$
$$\begin{array}{r} 8 \\ -\ 6 \\ \hline \end{array}$$
$$\begin{array}{r} 8 \\ -\ 1 \\ \hline \end{array}$$
$$\begin{array}{r} 8 \\ -\ 7 \\ \hline \end{array}$$

$$\begin{array}{r} 2 \\ +\ 6 \\ \hline \end{array}$$
$$\begin{array}{r} 4 \\ +\ 3 \\ \hline \end{array}$$
$$\begin{array}{r} 5 \\ +\ 1 \\ \hline \end{array}$$
$$\begin{array}{r} 3 \\ +\ 5 \\ \hline \end{array}$$
$$\begin{array}{r} 7 \\ +\ 1 \\ \hline \end{array}$$
$$\begin{array}{r} 0 \\ +\ 8 \\ \hline \end{array}$$

$$\begin{array}{r} 8 \\ -\ 1 \\ \hline \end{array}$$
$$\begin{array}{r} 7 \\ -\ 6 \\ \hline \end{array}$$
$$\begin{array}{r} 8 \\ -\ 5 \\ \hline \end{array}$$
$$\begin{array}{r} 6 \\ -\ 3 \\ \hline \end{array}$$
$$\begin{array}{r} 8 \\ -\ 0 \\ \hline \end{array}$$
$$\begin{array}{r} 8 \\ -\ 2 \\ \hline \end{array}$$

Name _____

Facts for 9

Directions: Add or subtract.

Examples:

  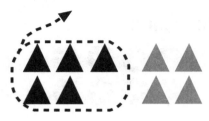

$$\begin{array}{r} 5 \\ +4 \\ \hline 9 \end{array}$$
$$\begin{array}{r} 4 \\ +5 \\ \hline \end{array}$$
$$\begin{array}{r} 9 \\ -4 \\ \hline 5 \end{array}$$
$$\begin{array}{r} 9 \\ -5 \\ \hline \end{array}$$

$$\begin{array}{r} 6 \\ +3 \\ \hline \end{array}$$
$$\begin{array}{r} 3 \\ +6 \\ \hline \end{array}$$
$$\begin{array}{r} 7 \\ +2 \\ \hline \end{array}$$
$$\begin{array}{r} 2 \\ +7 \\ \hline \end{array}$$
$$\begin{array}{r} 8 \\ +1 \\ \hline \end{array}$$
$$\begin{array}{r} 1 \\ +8 \\ \hline \end{array}$$

$$\begin{array}{r} 9 \\ -3 \\ \hline \end{array}$$
$$\begin{array}{r} 9 \\ -6 \\ \hline \end{array}$$
$$\begin{array}{r} 9 \\ -2 \\ \hline \end{array}$$
$$\begin{array}{r} 9 \\ -7 \\ \hline \end{array}$$
$$\begin{array}{r} 9 \\ -1 \\ \hline \end{array}$$
$$\begin{array}{r} 9 \\ -8 \\ \hline \end{array}$$

$$\begin{array}{r} 5 \\ +4 \\ \hline \end{array}$$
$$\begin{array}{r} 2 \\ +7 \\ \hline \end{array}$$
$$\begin{array}{r} 6 \\ +1 \\ \hline \end{array}$$
$$\begin{array}{r} 9 \\ +0 \\ \hline \end{array}$$
$$\begin{array}{r} 1 \\ +8 \\ \hline \end{array}$$
$$\begin{array}{r} 4 \\ +4 \\ \hline \end{array}$$

$$\begin{array}{r} 9 \\ -5 \\ \hline \end{array}$$
$$\begin{array}{r} 7 \\ -3 \\ \hline \end{array}$$
$$\begin{array}{r} 9 \\ -8 \\ \hline \end{array}$$
$$\begin{array}{r} 9 \\ -3 \\ \hline \end{array}$$
$$\begin{array}{r} 9 \\ -9 \\ \hline \end{array}$$
$$\begin{array}{r} 9 \\ -0 \\ \hline \end{array}$$

Addition and Subtraction Review

    Total Math Grade 2

Facts for 10

Directions: Add or subtract.

Examples:

$$\begin{array}{r} 5 \\ +5 \\ \hline 10 \end{array}$$

$$\begin{array}{r} 10 \\ -5 \\ \hline 5 \end{array}$$

$$\begin{array}{r} 6 \\ +4 \\ \hline \end{array}$$

$$\begin{array}{r} 4 \\ +6 \\ \hline \end{array}$$

$$\begin{array}{r} 10 \\ -4 \\ \hline \end{array}$$

$$\begin{array}{r} 10 \\ -6 \\ \hline \end{array}$$

$$\begin{array}{r} 7 \\ +3 \\ \hline \end{array}$$

$$\begin{array}{r} 3 \\ +7 \\ \hline \end{array}$$

$$\begin{array}{r} 10 \\ -3 \\ \hline \end{array}$$

$$\begin{array}{r} 10 \\ -7 \\ \hline \end{array}$$

$$\begin{array}{r} 8 \\ +2 \\ \hline \end{array}$$

$$\begin{array}{r} 2 \\ +8 \\ \hline \end{array}$$

$$\begin{array}{r} 10 \\ -2 \\ \hline \end{array}$$

$$\begin{array}{r} 10 \\ -8 \\ \hline \end{array}$$

$$\begin{array}{r} 9 \\ +1 \\ \hline \end{array}$$

$$\begin{array}{r} 1 \\ +9 \\ \hline \end{array}$$

$$\begin{array}{r} 10 \\ -1 \\ \hline \end{array}$$

$$\begin{array}{r} 10 \\ -9 \\ \hline \end{array}$$

$$\begin{array}{r} 4 \\ +6 \\ \hline \end{array}$$

$$\begin{array}{r} 5 \\ +5 \\ \hline \end{array}$$

$$\begin{array}{r} 9 \\ +1 \\ \hline \end{array}$$

$$\begin{array}{r} 10 \\ -8 \\ \hline \end{array}$$

$$\begin{array}{r} 10 \\ -3 \\ \hline \end{array}$$

$$\begin{array}{r} 10 \\ -0 \\ \hline \end{array}$$

Facts Through 10

Directions: Add.

Example:

5 + 4 9	4 + 3	1 + 2	5 + 3	4 + 6	4 + 4
0 + 6	4 + 1	8 + 1	9 + 1	8 + 2	2 + 2
2 + 7	5 + 2	1 + 6	5 + 5	4 + 5	6 + 2

Directions: Subtract.

Example:

10 − 6 4	8 − 2	5 − 3	7 − 6	4 − 3	10 − 5
9 − 3	10 − 2	7 − 2	8 − 6	10 − 9	8 − 8
10 − 4	9 − 6	9 − 8	8 − 1	10 − 7	7 − 4

Problem Solving

Directions: Solve each problem.

Example:

$$\begin{array}{r} 4 \\ +\ 3 \\ \hline 7 \end{array}$$

leaves on the ground

leaves falling

leaves in all

$$\begin{array}{r} \\ -\ \underline{\quad} \\ \end{array}$$

balls in all

balls falling

balls not falling

$$+\ \underline{\quad}$$

fish by a rock

more fish coming

fish in all

$$-\ \underline{\quad}$$

pencils in all

pencils taken

pencils not taken

$$+\ \underline{\quad}$$

puppies on a rug

more puppies coming

puppies in all

Checkup

Directions: Add.

2 + 4	7 + 3	4 + 5	6 + 2	2 + 3	0 + 4
4 + 3	1 + 5	2 + 8	3 + 3	6 + 4	2 + 1
3 + 1	7 + 0	8 + 1	5 + 2	3 + 6	5 + 5

Directions: Subtract.

3 − 3	5 − 2	10 − 6	9 − 2	7 − 3	10 − 5
9 − 1	8 − 7	1 − 0	6 − 4	8 − 5	10 − 8
9 − 6	4 − 3	6 − 3	7 − 5	10 − 9	8 − 4

Name _____

Addition and Subtraction Fun

Directions: Solve the number problem under each picture. Write **+** or **−** to show if you should add or subtract.

Example:

How many s in all?

4 ┼ **5 =** _____

How many s in all?

7 **5 =** _____

Example:

How many s are left?

12 ---- **3 =** _____

How many ☆s are left?

15 **8 =** _____

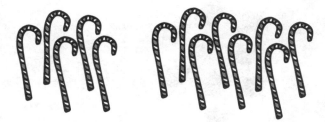 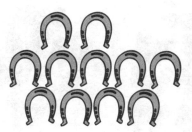

How many s in all?

5 **8 =** _____

How many s are left?

11 **4 =** _____

Addition and Subtraction

Directions: Solve the number problem under each picture. Write **+** or **–** to show if you should add or subtract.

Example:

How many s in all?

7 + 5 = __12__

How many s in all?

8 __ 3 = _____

Example:

How many s are left?

9 – 4 = __5__

How many s are left?

14 __ 1 = _____

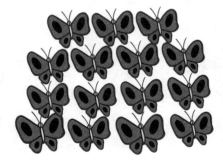

How many s in all?

15 __ 6 = _____

How many s are left?

9 __ 5 =

Hopping Around

Directions: Write the number sentence on the line below each number line.

Example:

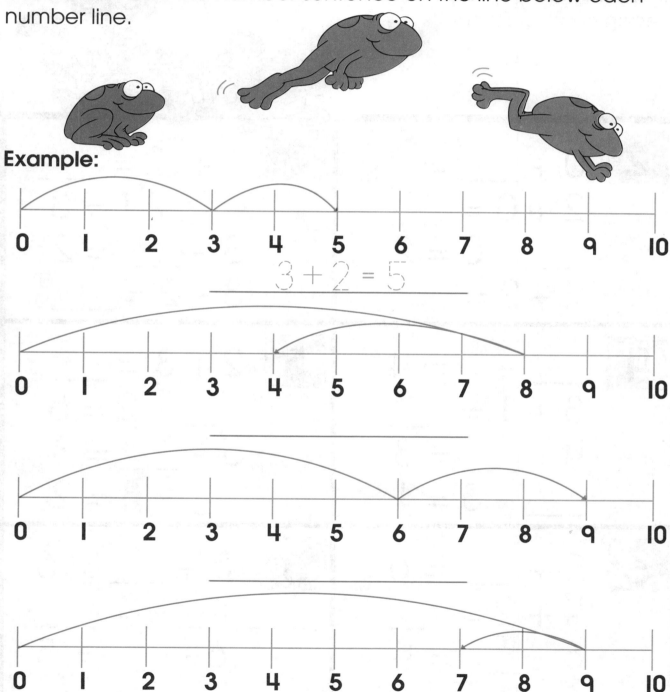

$3 + 2 = 5$

111

Name _____

Big Families

Directions: Complete each number sentence in each number family.

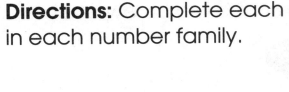

2	**3**
$0 + \underline{\hphantom{0}} = 2$	$1 + 2 = \underline{\hphantom{0}}$
$2 + 0 = \underline{\hphantom{0}}$	$\underline{\hphantom{0}} + 1 = 3$
$\underline{\hphantom{0}} - 0 = 2$	$3 - \underline{\hphantom{0}} = 2$
$2 - 2 = \underline{\hphantom{0}}$	$3 - 2 = \underline{\hphantom{0}}$
4	**5**
$\underline{\hphantom{0}} + 3 = 4$	$2 + 3 = \underline{\hphantom{0}}$
$3 + 1 = \underline{\hphantom{0}}$	$\underline{\hphantom{0}} + 2 = 5$
$4 - \underline{\hphantom{0}} = 3$	$5 - \underline{\hphantom{0}} = 3$
$\underline{\hphantom{0}} - 3 = 1$	$\underline{\hphantom{0}} - 3 = 2$
6	**6**
$2 + \underline{\hphantom{0}} = 6$	$5 + \underline{\hphantom{0}} = 6$
$4 + 2 = \underline{\hphantom{0}}$	$\underline{\hphantom{0}} + \underline{\hphantom{0}} = \underline{\hphantom{0}}$
$6 - \underline{\hphantom{0}} = 4$	$6 - \underline{\hphantom{0}} = 5$
$6 - 4 = \underline{\hphantom{0}}$	$\underline{\hphantom{0}} - 5 = \underline{\hphantom{0}}$

Sums and Differences

Directions: Color two numbers in each box to show the given sum or difference.

Sum of 8

3	7
1	4

3	6
7	2

6	5
4	4

3	8
1	5

Difference of 1

6	3
1	5

5	9
10	7

8	5
3	2

5	2
4	0

Sum of 9

0	5
6	4

4	3
6	2

8	3
1	2

5	5
7	2

Difference of 2

6	9
1	4

4	10
7	5

5	8
1	10

0	2
7	3

Name _____

Help the Hippo

Directions: Use the numbers in each thought bubble to write the number family.

Example:

Bigger Families

Directions: Complete each number sentence in the families.

7
___ + 4 = 7
4 + 3 = ___
___ – 3 = 4
7 – ___ = 3

8
3 + ___ = 8
5 + 3 = ___
8 – ___ = 5
___ – 5 = 3

9
4 + 5 = ___
___ + 4 = 9
9 – ___ = 5
___ – 5 = 4

10
___ + 6 = 10
6 + 4 = ___
10 – 4 = ___
___ – ___ = ___

11
3 + ___ = ___
___ + ___ = ___
11 – ___ = 8
___ – ___ = ___

12
5 + ___ = 12
___ + ___ = ___
12 – ___ = ___
___ + ___ = ___

Place Value: Ones, Tens

The **place value** of a digit or numeral is shown by where it is in the number. For example, in the number **23, 2** has the place value of **tens**, and **3** is **ones**.

Directions: Add the tens and ones and write your answers in the blanks.

Example:

$$3 \text{ tens} \qquad + \qquad 3 \text{ ones} \quad = \quad \underline{33}$$

	tens ones			**tens ones**
7 tens + 5 ones	= _____		4 tens + 0 ones	= _____
2 tens + 3 ones	= _____		8 tens + 1 one	= _____
5 tens + 2 ones	= _____		1 ten + 1 one	= _____
5 tens + 4 ones	= _____		6 tens + 3 ones	= _____
9 tens + 5 ones	= _____			

Directions: Draw a line to the correct number.

6 tens + 7 ones	73
4 tens + 2 ones	67
8 tens + 0 ones	51
7 tens + 3 ones	80
5 tens + 1 one	42

Finding Place Value: Ones and Tens

Directions: Write the numbers for the tens and ones. Then add.

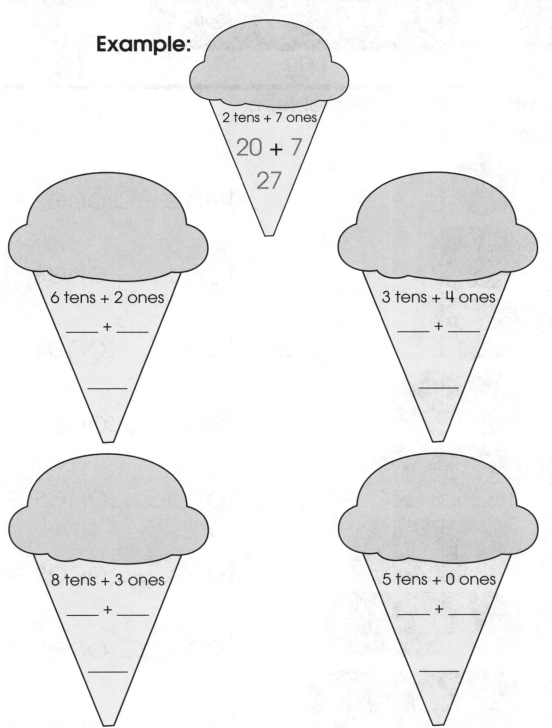

Example:

2 tens + 7 ones

20 + 7

27

6 tens + 2 ones

___ + ___

___

3 tens + 4 ones

___ + ___

___

8 tens + 3 ones

___ + ___

___

5 tens + 0 ones

___ + ___

___

Numbers 11 Through 18

1¢   **10¢**   **10¢**

Directions: Complete the problems.

Example:

      _1_ ten _1_ one = _11_

    ___ ten ___ ones = ___

    ___ ten ___ ones = ___

    ___ ten ___ ones = ___

    ___ ten ___ ones = ___

    ___ ten ___ ones = ___

    ___ ten ___ ones = ___

    ___ ten ___ ones = ___

Numbers 19 Through 39

Directions: Complete the problems.

Example:

_____2_____ tens = _____20_____

_____ tens _____ ones = _____

_____ tens _____ ones = _____

_____ tens _____ ones = _____

_____ tens = _____

_____ tens _____ ones = _____

_____ tens _____ ones = _____

_____ tens _____ ones = _____

Numbers 40 Through 99

Directions: Complete the problems.

Example:

_____4_____ tens = _____40_____

_____ tens _____ ones = _____

_____ tens _____ ones = _____

_____ tens _____ ones = _____

_____ tens = _____

_____ tens _____ ones = _____

_____ tens _____ ones = _____

_____ tens _____ ones = _____

Numbers 40 Through 99

Directions: Complete the problems.

Example:

__4__ tens __5__ ones = __45__   _____ tens _____ ones = _____

_____ tens = _____   _____ tens _____ ones = _____

_____ tens _____ ones = _____   _____ tens _____ ones = _____

_____ tens = _____   _____ tens _____ ones = _____

Numbers Through 99

Directions: Complete the problems.

Example:

4 tens   6 ones = $\underline{46}$ 2 tens   1 one   = _____

1 ten   2 ones = _____   5 tens   7 ones = _____

3 tens   7 ones = _____   1 ten   9 ones = _____

2 tens   4 ones = _____   8 tens   8 ones = _____

9 tens   = _____   6 tens   7 ones = _____

6 tens   = _____   7 tens   2 ones = _____

5 tens   3 ones = _____   9 tens   5 ones = _____

7 tens   8 ones = _____   4 tens   1 one   = _____

1 ten   1 one   = _____   3 tens   4 ones = _____

8 tens   4 ones = _____   6 tens   6 ones = _____

3 tens   5 ones = _____   8 tens   9 ones = _____

4 tens   9 ones = _____   2 tens   = _____

9 tens   6 ones = _____   5 tens   = _____

Hundreds, Tens, and Ones

Directions: Count the groups of crayons. Write the number of hundreds, tens, and ones.

Example:

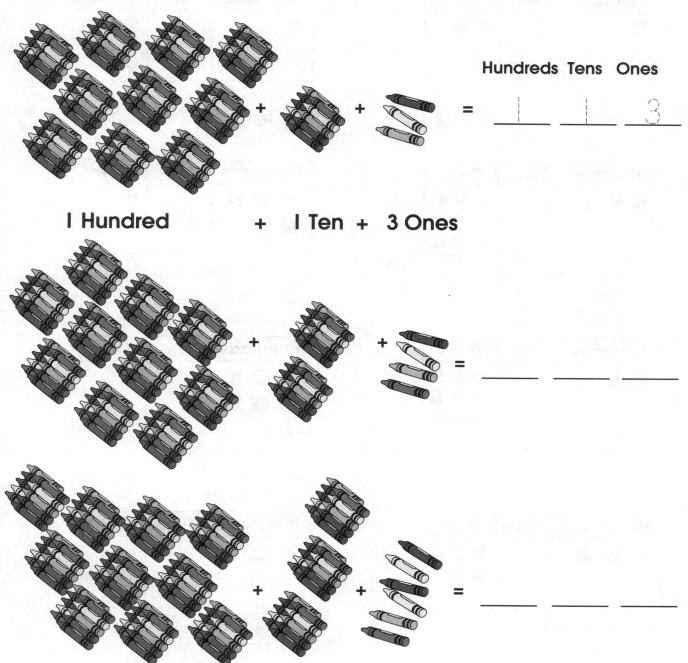

	Hundreds	Tens	Ones
=	1	1	3

1 Hundred   +   **1 Ten** + **3 Ones**

Name _____

What Big Numbers!

Directions: Write each number.

Example:

Hundreds	Tens	Ones
■	|||	●●

_1_ hundreds
_3_ tens
_2_ ones = __132__

Hundreds	Tens	Ones
■■■	|||	●●● ●●● ●●●

___ hundreds
___ tens
___ ones = _____

Hundreds	Tens	Ones
■■		●●● ●●● ●●●

___ hundreds
___ tens
___ ones = _____

Hundreds	Tens	Ones
■■■	||||	●●● ●●

___ hundreds
___ tens
___ ones = _____

Hundreds	Tens	Ones
■	||||	●●● ●●● ●

___ hundreds
___ tens
___ ones = _____

Hundreds	Tens	Ones
■■■ ■■			●

___ hundreds
___ tens
___ ones = _____

Hundreds	Tens	Ones
■■■ ■■■	|||||		●●●

___ hundreds
___ tens
___ ones = _____

Hundreds	Tens	Ones
■■	||||| |||	●●● ●●● ●

___ hundreds
___ tens
___ ones = _____

Name _____

Count 'Em Up!

Directions: Look at the example. Then, write the missing numbers in the blanks.

Example:

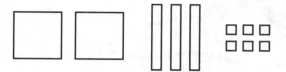

2 hundreds + 3 tens + 6 ones =

hundreds	tens	ones
2	3	6

= _236_

	hundreds	tens	ones	
3 hundreds + 4 tens + 8 ones =	3	4	8	= _____
___ hundreds + ___ ten + ___ ones =	2	1	7	= _____
___ hundreds + ___ tens + ___ ones =	6	3	5	= _____
___ hundreds + ___ tens + ___ ones =	4	7	9	= _____
___ hundreds + ___ tens + ___ ones =	2	9	4	= _____
___ hundreds + ___ tens + ___ ones =	4	2	0	= _____
3 hundreds + 1 ten + 3 ones = ____		____	____	= _____
3 hundreds + ___ tens + 7 ones = ____	5	____	= _____
6 hundreds + 2 tens + ___ ones = ____		____	8	= _____

Up, Up, and Away

Directions: Use the code to color the balloons. If the answer has:

7 hundreds, color it **red**.
6 hundreds, color it **green**.
5 hundreds, color it orange.
8 tens, color it yellow.
3 ones, color it **brown**.

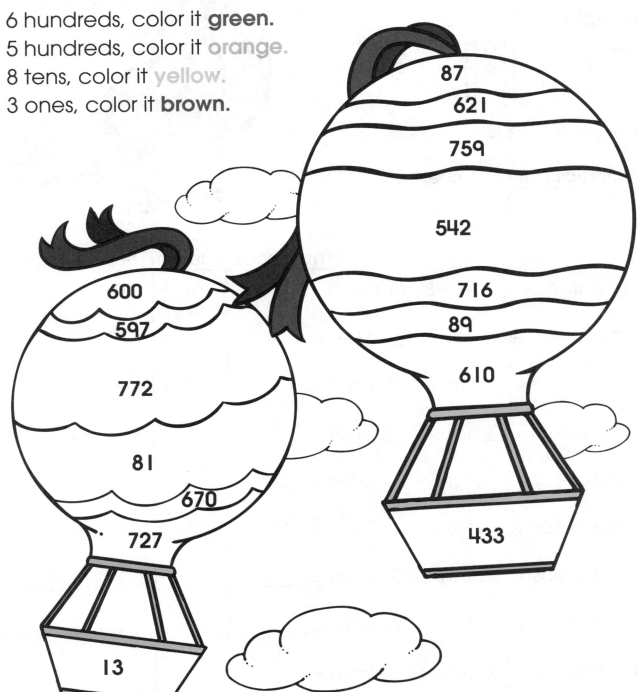

87
621
759
542
716
89
610
433

600
597
772
81
670
727
13

Place Value: Thousands

Directions: Study the example. Write the missing numbers.

Example:

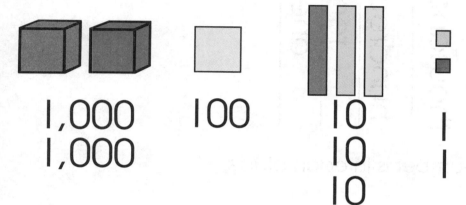

2 thousands + 1 hundred + __3__ tens + 2 ones = __2,132__

5,286 = ____ thousands + ____ hundreds + ____ tens + ____ ones

1,831 = ____ thousand + ____ hundreds + ____ tens + ____ one

8,972 = ____ thousands + ____ hundreds + ____ tens + ____ ones

4,528 = ____ thousands + ____ hundreds + ____ tens + ____ ones

3,177 = ____ thousands + ____ hundred + ____ tens + ____ ones

Directions: Draw a line to the number that has:

8 hundreds	7,103
5 ones	2,862
9 tens	5,996
7 thousands	1,485

Place Value: Thousands

6 , 4 3 1

thousands | hundreds | tens | ones

Directions: Tell which number is in each place.

 Thousands place:

2,456   4,621   3,456

_____   _____   _____

 Tens place:

4,286   1,234   5,678

_____   _____   _____

Hundreds place:

6,321   3,210   7,871

_____   _____   _____

 Ones place:

5,432   6,531   9,980

_____   _____   _____

Place Value: Thousands

Directions: Use the code to color the fan.

If the answer has:

9 thousands, color it pink.

6 thousands, color it **green**.

5 hundreds, color it orange.

8 tens, color it **red**.

3 ones, color it **blue**.

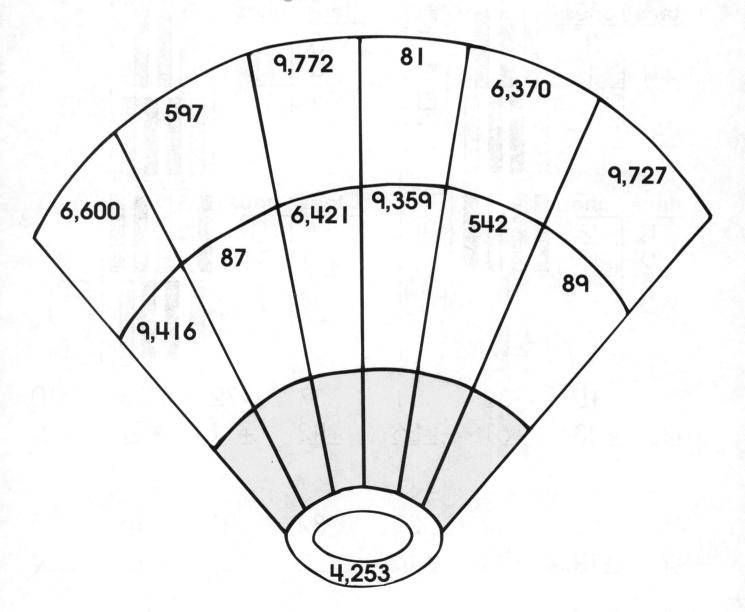

129

2-Digit Addition

Directions: Study the example. Follow the steps to add.

Example: 33
            +41

Step 1: Add the ones.

tens	ones
3	3
+4	1
	4

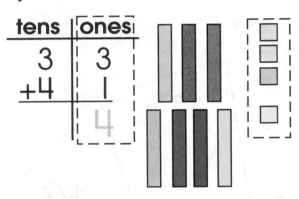

Step 2: Add the tens.

tens	ones
3	3
+4	1
7	4

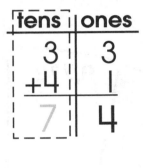

tens	ones
4	2
+2	4
6	6

tens	ones
5	0
+4	7
9	7

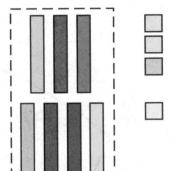

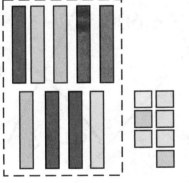

24	15	38	11	37	72	33	10
+62	+23	+61	+26	+42	+11	+51	+30

25	62	32	25	82	91	16	55
+42	+14	+44	+13	+ 6	+ 5	+71	+ 3

2-Digit Addition

Directions: Add the total points scored in each game. Remember to add **ones** first and **tens** second.

Example:

HOME **22**
VISITOR **17**

Total ___**39**___

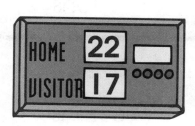

HOME **28**
VISITOR **30**

Total _____

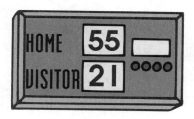

HOME **55**
VISITOR **21**

Total _____

HOME **14**
VISITOR **33**

Total _____

HOME **24**
VISITOR **13**

Total _____

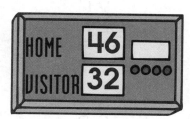

HOME **46**
VISITOR **32**

Total _____

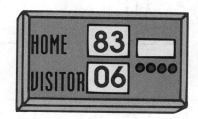

HOME **83**
VISITOR **06**

Total _____

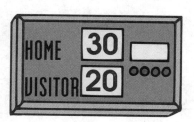

HOME **30**
VISITOR **20**

Total _____

HOME **17**
VISITOR **42**

Total _____

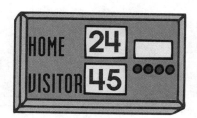

HOME **24**
VISITOR **45**

Total _____

Adding Tens

```
  3 tens        30            6 tens        60
+ 4 tens      + 40          + 2 tens      + 20
  7 tens        70            8 tens        80
```

Directions: Add.

```
  2 tens        20            6 tens        60
+ 4 tens      + 40          + 2 tens      + 20
    tens                         tens
```

```
  20        1 0         40          30          50
+ 20      + 50        + 20        + 40        + 30
```

```
  30          60          20          70        1 0
+ 20        + 1 0       + 50        + 1 0      + 1 0
```

```
1 0          40          80          60          20
+ 20        + 40        + 1 0       + 30        + 60
```

```
  70          40          30          50          30
+ 20        + 1 0       + 1 0       + 40        + 30
```

Problem Solving

Directions: Solve each problem.

Example:

There are 20 men in the plane.

30 women get in the plane.

How many men and women are in the plane?

Jill buys 10 apples.

Carol buys 20 apples.

How many apples in all?

There are 30 ears of corn in one pile.

There are 50 ears of corn in another pile.

How many ears of corn in all?

Henry cut 40 pieces of wood.

Art cut 20 pieces of wood.

How many pieces of wood were cut?

Adolpho had 60 baseball cards.

Maria had 30 baseball cards.

How many baseball cards in all?

Picture This

Directions: Add the ones, then the tens in each problem. Then, write the sum in the blank.

Example:

   2 tens and 6 ones
+ 1 ten and 3 ones
_____

3 tens and **9** ones = **39**

   1 ten and 4 ones
+ 3 tens and 3 ones
_____

___ tens and ___ ones = ____

   2 tens and 5 ones
+ 2 tens and 3 ones
_____

___ tens and ___ ones = ____

   1 ten and 6 ones
+ 5 tens and 1 one
_____

___ tens and ___ ones = ____

   1 ten and 3 ones
+ 1 ten and 1 one
_____

___ tens and ___ ones = ____

   2 tens and 5 ones
+ 2 tens and 0 ones
_____

___ tens and ___ ones = ____

   1 ten and 5 ones
+ 2 tens and 4 ones
_____

___ tens and ___ ones = ____

   7 tens and 6 ones
+ 2 tens and 2 ones
_____

___ tens and ___ ones = ____

Digital Addition

Add the ones.

tens	ones
2	4
+3	2
	6

Then, add the tens.

tens	ones
2	4
+3	2
5	6

Directions: Solve the addition problems below.

tens	ones
1	7
+2	1

tens	ones
3	4
+5	2

tens	ones
	5
+6	2

tens	ones
	6
+5	2

tens	ones
2	0
+4	0

tens	ones
5	1
+	8

tens	ones
7	2
+1	7

tens	ones
4	7
+2	1

tens	ones
2	5
+6	2

tens	ones
4	2
+2	4

tens	ones
8	3
+1	4

tens	ones
3	2
+2	5

Circus Fun

Directions: Add to solve the problems. Add the ones first. Then, add the tens.

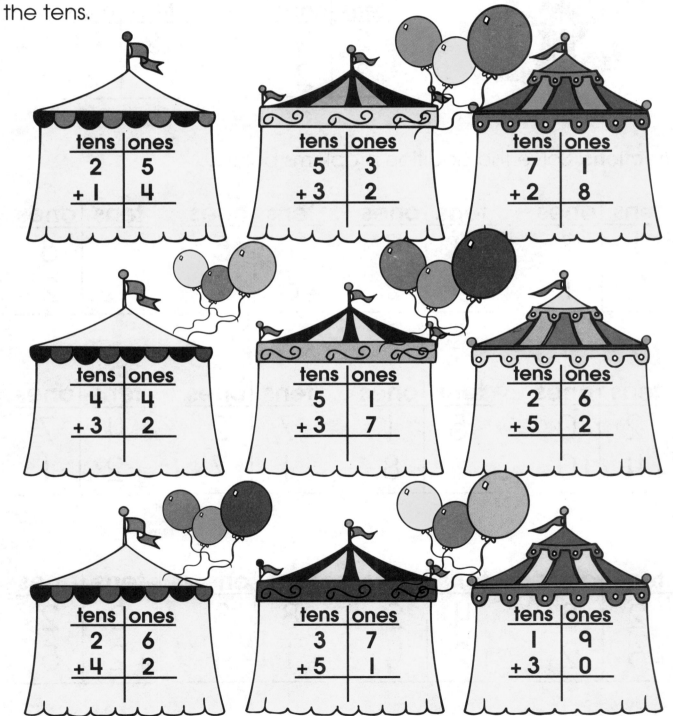

tens	ones
2	5
+1	4

tens	ones
5	3
+3	2

tens	ones
7	1
+2	8

tens	ones
4	4
+3	2

tens	ones
5	1
+3	7

tens	ones
2	6
+5	2

tens	ones
2	6
+4	2

tens	ones
3	7
+5	1

tens	ones
1	9
+3	0

Name _____

Scoreboard Sums

Directions: Add the total points scored in each game. Remember to add the ones first, then the tens.

Example:

Total __3 9__

HOME 28
VISITOR 30

Total _____

HOME 55
VISITOR 21

Total _____

HOME 14
VISITOR 33

Total _____

HOME 24
VISITOR 13

Total _____

HOME 46
VISITOR 32

Total _____

HOME 83
VISITOR 06

Total _____

HOME 30
VISITOR 20

Total _____

HOME 17
VISITOR 41

Total _____

HOME 24
VISITOR 45

Total _____

Name _____

Raccoon Roundup

Directions: Solve the addition problems. Write your answers inside the ropes.

$$\begin{array}{r} 26 \\ +\ 43 \\ \hline \end{array}$$

$$\begin{array}{r} 43 \\ +\ 31 \\ \hline \end{array}$$

$$\begin{array}{r} 34 \\ +\ 10 \\ \hline \end{array}$$

$$\begin{array}{r} 48 \\ +\ 20 \\ \hline \end{array}$$

$$\begin{array}{r} 57 \\ +\ 20 \\ \hline \end{array}$$

$$\begin{array}{r} 52 \\ +\ 34 \\ \hline \end{array}$$

$$\begin{array}{r} 43 \\ +\ 55 \\ \hline \end{array}$$

$$\begin{array}{r} 67 \\ +\ 22 \\ \hline \end{array}$$

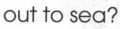
Anchors Away

Directions: Solve the addition problems. Use the code to find the answer to this riddle:

What did the pirate have to do before every trip out to sea?

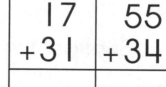

48	36	58	96	69	75	89	29
O	H	G	B	T	E	N	A

Example:

42 +16	34 +41	60 + 9
58		

G		

17 +31	55 +34

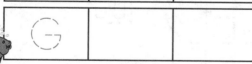

26 +43	14 +22	52 +23

83 +13	24 +24	5 +24	52 +17

			!

Two-Digit Subtraction

Directions: Look at the example.
Follow the steps to subtract.

Examples:

$$\begin{array}{r} 28 \\ -14 \\ \hline \end{array} \qquad \begin{array}{r} 24 \\ -12 \\ \hline \end{array}$$

Step 1: Subtract the ones.

tens	ones
2	8
-1	4
	4

Step 2: Subtract the tens.

tens	ones
2	8
-1	4
1	4

Step 1: Subtract the ones.

tens	ones
2	4
-1	2
	2

Step 2: Subtract the tens.

tens	ones
2	4
-1	2
1	2

$$\begin{array}{r} 24 \\ -12 \\ \hline \end{array} \qquad \begin{array}{r} 61 \\ -30 \\ \hline \end{array} \qquad \begin{array}{r} 77 \\ -44 \\ \hline \end{array} \qquad \begin{array}{r} 85 \\ -24 \\ \hline \end{array} \qquad \begin{array}{r} 57 \\ -23 \\ \hline \end{array} \qquad \begin{array}{r} 87 \\ -33 \\ \hline \end{array}$$

Subtracting Tens

Examples:

```
  6 tens          60                    8 tens          80
- 3 tens        - 3 0                 - 2 tens        - 2 0
  3 tens          3 0                    6 tens          60
```

Directions: Subtract.

```
  7 tens          70                    4 tens          40
- 5 tens        - 5 0                 - 2 tens        - 2 0
    tens                                  tens
```

```
   50             60             20             80             40
 - 3 0          - 2 0          - 1 0          - 4 0          - 4 0
```

```
   90             80             70             30             50
 - 5 0          - 2 0          - 3 0          - 2 0          - 4 0
```

```
   60             40             80             90             70
 - 3 0          - 1 0          - 3 0          - 2 0          - 5 0
```

```
   80             90             70             60             50
 - 7 0          - 8 0          - 4 0          - 4 0          - 2 0
```

Problem Solving

Directions: Solve each problem.

Example:

Mr. Cobb counts 70 🖊 s.

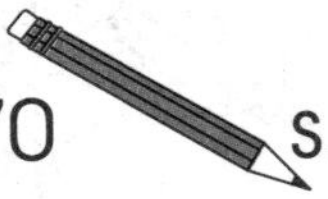

He sells 30 🖊 s.

How many 🖊 s are left?

$$\begin{array}{r} 70 \\ -30 \\ \hline 40 \end{array}$$

Keith has 20 🔨 s.

Leon has 10 🔨 s.

How many more 🔨 s does Keith have than Leon?

Tina plants 60 🌸 s.

Melody plants 30 🌸 s.

How many more 🌸 s did Tina plant than Melody?

Link has 80 ⚪ s.

Jessica has 50 ⚫ s.

How many more ⚪ s does Link have than Jessica?

Maranda hits 40 ⚾ s.

Harold hits 30 ⚾ s.

How many more ⚾ s does Maranda hit than Harold?

All Aboard

Directions: Count the tens and ones and write the numbers. Then, subtract to solve the problems.

	tens	ones
	4	2
−	2	1

	tens	ones
−		

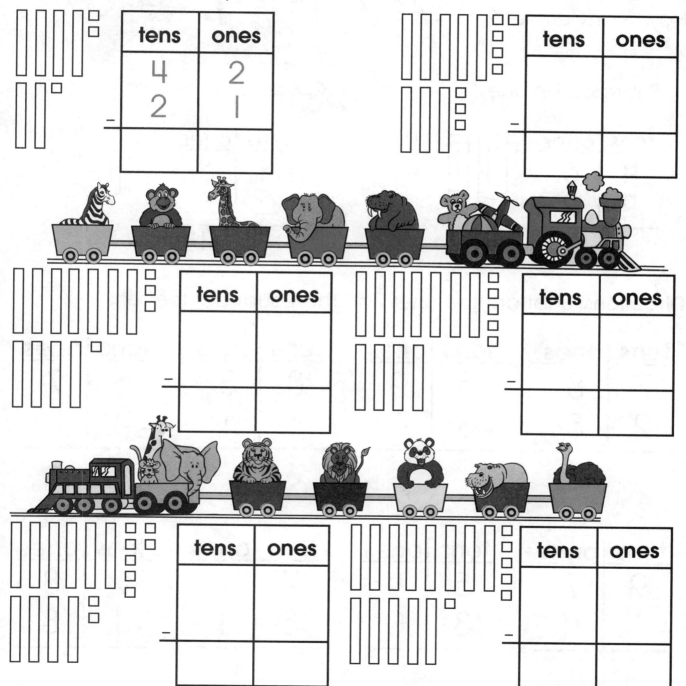

	tens	ones
−		

	tens	ones
−		

	tens	ones
−		

	tens	ones
−		

Cookie Mania

There are 46 cookies.
Bill eats 22 cookies.
How many are left?

$$\begin{array}{r} 46 \\ -\ 22 \\ \hline \end{array}$$

1. Subtract the ones.

tens	ones
4	6
- 2	2
	4

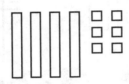

2. Subtract the tens.

tens	ones
4	6
- 2	2
2	4

Directions: Subtract the ones first. Then, subtract the tens.

tens	ones
7	8
- 2	5

tens	ones
5	9
- 3	6

tens	ones
8	3
- 6	1

tens	ones
6	7
- 4	3

tens	ones
9	7
- 1	4

tens	ones
5	4
- 3	0

tens	ones
4	2
- 3	1

tens	ones
2	8
- 1	8

Cookie Craze!

Directions: Subtract to solve the problems. Circle the answers. Color the cookies with answers greater than 30.

49
− 23
_____

16   (26)   25

67
− 41
_____

26   15   62

58
− 37
_____

81   11   21

75
− 50
_____

20   25   35

86
− 21
_____

67   86   65

64
− 52
_____

12   26   16

97
− 65
_____

31   33   32

77
− 43
_____

34   43   39

49
− 13
_____

56   36   37

Name _____

How's Your Pitch?

Directions: Solve the subtraction problems. Write each answer.

u
95
-14

n
68
-47

t
80
-20

r
79
-38

a
83
-52

h
84
-23

y
75
-31

i
99
-29

c
98
-36

o
84
-30

e
98
-16

g
74
-42

s
58
-38

p
82
-40

Use the answers and the letters on the baseballs to solve the code.

____ ____ ____ ____   ____ ____ ____ ____ ____   ____ ____
 44   54   81   41   42   70   60   62   61   70   20

____ ____ ____ ____ ____   ____ ____   ____ ____ ____ ____ ____ ____ !
 41   70   32   61   60   54   21   60   31   41   32   82   60

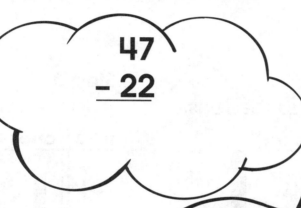

Prehistoric Problems

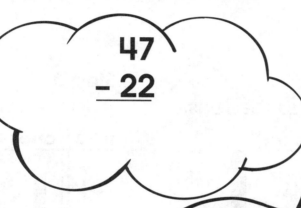

Directions: Solve the subtraction problems. Use the code to color the picture.

Code: 25 = blue   57 = green
           31 = yellow   14 = orange
           21 = brown   11 = red

47
− 22

52
− 21

25
− 11

62
− 31

77
− 20

51
− 40

69
− 12

98
− 41

55
− 34

2-Digit Addition: Regrouping

Addition is "putting together" or adding two or more numbers to find the sum. Regrouping is using **ten ones** to form **one ten**, **ten tens** to form **one 100**, **fifteen ones** to form **one ten** and **five ones,** and so on.

Directions: Study the examples. Follow the steps to add.

Example:
```
  14
+  8
```

Step 1:
Add the ones.

tens	ones
1	4
+	8
	12

Step 2:
Regroup the tens.

tens	ones
1	
1	4
+	8
	2

Step 3:
Add the tens.

tens	ones
1	
1	4
+	8
2	2

tens	ones
1	
1	6
+3	7
5	3

tens	ones
1	
3	8
+5	3
9	1

tens	ones
1	
2	4
+4	7
7	1

```
  28      32      54      19      44      25      29      79
+ 17    + 38    + 25    + 55    + 48    + 64    + 33    + 15
```

2-Digit Addition: Regrouping

Directions: Add the total points scored in the game. Remember to add the ones, regroup, and then add the tens.

Example:

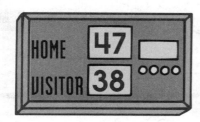

Total ___85___

Total _____

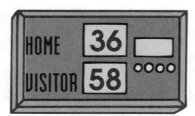

Total _____

Total _____

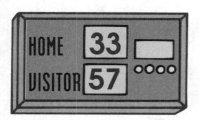

Total _____

Total _____

Total _____

Total _____

Total _____

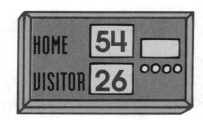

Total _____

2-Digit Addition

Directions: Add the ones.   Rename 15 as 10 + 5.   Add the tens.

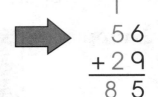

```
   56        6                          1               1
 +29       + 9                 56              56
           ___         ____  +29      ____  +29
          15 or 10 + 5 ____→   5              8 5
```

Directions: Add the ones.   Rename 12 as 10 + 2.   Add the tens.

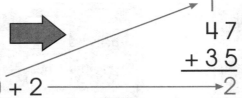 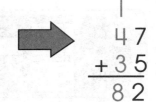

```
   47        7                          1               1
 +35       + 5                 47              47
           ___         ____  +35      ____  +35
          12 or 10 + 2 ____→   2              8 2
```

Directions: Add.

Examples:

```
   45        13        48        69        54
 +28       +19       +35       +18       +39
 ___       ___       ___       ___       ___
  73        32
```

```
   44        37        28        73        66
 +17       +18       +36       +18       +29
 ___       ___       ___       ___       ___
```

```
   52        38        64        29        75
 +39       +47       +18       +45       +17
 ___       ___       ___       ___       ___
```

2-Digit Addition

Directions: Add the ones.   Rename 11 as 10 + 1.   Add the tens.

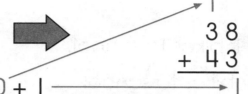
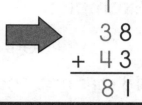

```
   3 8            8                          1              1
 + 4 3          + 3                        3 8            3 8
                ─────                     + 4 3          + 4 3
                11 or 10 + 1        1     ─────          ─────
                                                          8 1
```

Directions: Add.

Example:

```
   1 7        2 6        4 7        6 8        3 7
 + 3 4      + 4 7      + 3 5      + 2 4      + 2 8
 ─────
  5 1
```

```
   2 9        5 8        6 9        7 8        1 9
 + 4 8      + 2 7      + 1 7      + 1 3      + 4 4
```

```
   5 5        2 7        3 9        5 7        3 8
 + 2 8      + 3 5      + 5 2      + 2 7      + 3 6
```

```
   4 9        6 5        2 3        6 4        4 6
 + 4 3      + 1 8      + 1 8      + 1 8      + 3 9
```

```
   5 4        3 8        6 6        2 8        1 9
 + 2 7      + 4 4      + 2 6      + 3 4      + 5 6
```

Problem Solving

Directions: Solve each problem.

Example:

16 boys ride their bikes to school.

18 girls ride their bikes to school.

How many bikes are ridden to school?

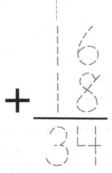

Dad reads 26 pages.

Mike reads 37 pages.

How many pages did Dad and Mike read?

Tiffany counts 46 stars.

Mike counts 39 stars.

How many stars did they count?

Mom has 29 golf balls.

Dad has 43 golf balls.

How many golf balls do they have?

Vicki ran in 26 races.

Kay ran in 14 races.

How many races did they run?

2-Digit Subtraction: Regrouping

Subtraction is "taking away" or subtracting one number from another to find the difference. Regrouping is using **one ten** to form **ten ones, one 100** to form **ten tens,** and so on.

Directions: Study the examples. Follow the steps to subtract.

Example:
$$\begin{array}{r} 37 \\ -19 \\ \hline \end{array}$$

Step 1:
Regroup.

tens	ones
2	17
3̷	7̷
-1	9

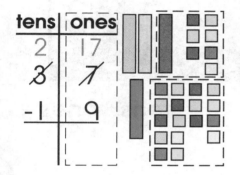

Step 2:
Subtract the ones.

tens	ones
2	17
3̷	7̷
-1	9
	8

Step 3:
Subtract the tens.

tens	ones
2	17
3̷	7̷
-1	9
1	8

tens	ones
0	12
1̷	2̷
-	9
	3

tens	ones
2	14
3̷	4̷
-1	6
1	8

tens	ones
3	15
4̷	5̷
-2	9
1	6

$$\begin{array}{r} 28 \\ -19 \\ \hline \end{array} \qquad \begin{array}{r} 46 \\ -18 \\ \hline \end{array} \qquad \begin{array}{r} 12 \\ -8 \\ \hline \end{array} \qquad \begin{array}{r} 30 \\ -12 \\ \hline \end{array} \qquad \begin{array}{r} 52 \\ -25 \\ \hline \end{array} \qquad \begin{array}{r} 47 \\ -35 \\ \hline \end{array} \qquad \begin{array}{r} 21 \\ -13 \\ \hline \end{array} \qquad \begin{array}{r} 45 \\ -25 \\ \hline \end{array}$$

2-Digit Subtraction: Regrouping

Directions: Study the steps for subtracting. Solve the problems using the steps.

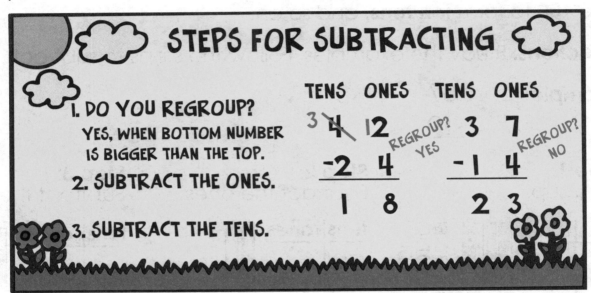

STEPS FOR SUBTRACTING

1. DO YOU REGROUP?
   YES, WHEN BOTTOM NUMBER IS BIGGER THAN THE TOP.
2. SUBTRACT THE ONES.
3. SUBTRACT THE TENS.

	TENS	ONES		TENS	ONES
	3 ̶4̶	12	REGROUP? YES	3	7	REGROUP? NO
	−2	4		−1	4
	1	8		2	3

tens	ones		tens	ones		tens	ones
4	7		6	4		5	3
− 2	8		− 3	4		− 3	9

56	83	43	75	91
− 27	− 47	− 39	− 53	− 18

73	35	67	26	68
− 66	− 14	− 58	− 7	− 45

Sea Shell Subtraction

Ellen found 32 shells on the beach. She gave 15 shells to Cindy. How many shells does Ellen have now?

Directions: Look at the problem below. Follow the steps to subtract.

Put the numbers on the tens and ones table.

tens	ones
3	2
−1	5

Subtract the ones. Ask: Do I need to regroup?

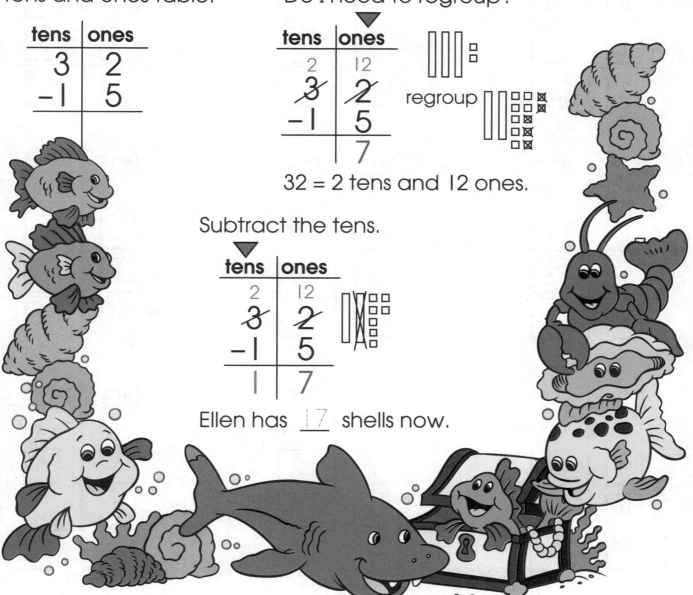

32 = 2 tens and 12 ones.

Subtract the tens.

Ellen has _17_ shells now.

Subtraction With Regrouping

Directions: Use manipulatives to find the difference.

Example:

1.
tens	ones
4	14
5̶	4̶
– 1	7
3	7

2.
tens	ones
3	3
– 1	5

3.
tens	ones
6	1
– 3	3

4.
tens	ones
2	7
– 1	6

5.
tens	ones
4	2
– 2	4

6.
tens	ones
5	2
– 2	6

7.
tens	ones
9	4
– 4	8

8.
tens	ones
7	7
– 3	4

9.
tens	ones
6	5
– 2	6

Subtraction With Regrouping

Directions: Subtract to find the difference. Regroup as needed.
Color the spaces with differences of:

10-19 = red   50-59 = brown   30-39 = green
40-49 = yellow   20-29 = blue   60-69 = orange

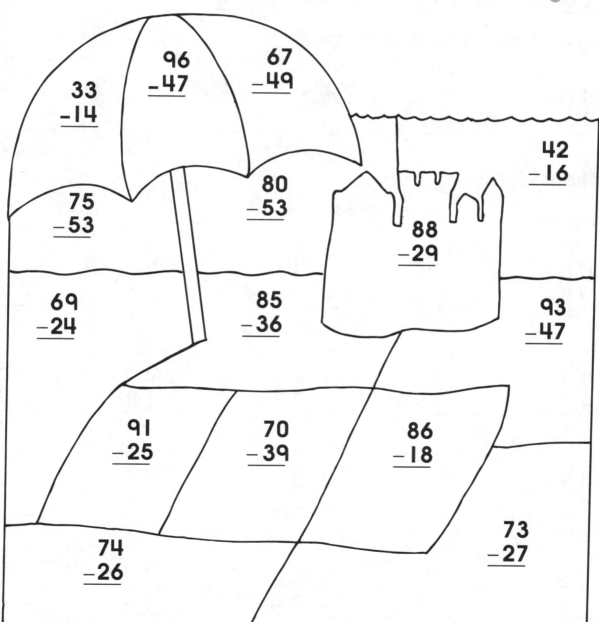

2-Digit Subtraction

Directions: Rename 53 as 4 tens and 13 ones.

```
         4 13
  5 3     5̶ 3̶
- 2 6   - 2 6
```

Subtract the ones.
```
  4 13
  5̶ 3̶
- 2 6
    7
```

Subtract the tens.
```
  4 13
  5̶ 3̶
- 2 6
  2 7
```

Rename 45 as 3 tens and 15 ones.

```
         3 15
  4 5     4̶ 5̶
- 1 8   - 1 8
```

```
  3 15
  4̶ 5̶
- 1 8
    7
```

```
  3 15
  4̶ 5̶
- 1 8
  2 7
```

Directions: Subtract.

Examples:

```
  5 13        6 14
  6̶ 3̶        7̶ 4̶        4 7        5 2        6 4
- 2 8       - 3 9     - 2 8      - 2 6      - 3 6
  3 5         3 5
```

```
  8 4        9 3        7 1        2 6        6 7
- 4 7      - 5 6      - 2 3      - 1 8      - 4 8
```

```
  4 4        5 3        8 2        9 4        5 5
- 2 8      - 3 7      - 4 6      - 6 6      - 3 9
```

```
  8 6        3 4        5 4        7 3        8 6
- 5 8      - 1 8      - 2 9      - 5 9      - 6 9
```

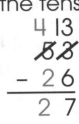

2-Digit Subtraction

Directions: Rename 73 as 6 tens and 13 ones.

```
        6 13
  7 3    7̶ 3̶
- 4 8  - 4 8
```

Subtract the ones.

```
  6 13
  7̶ 3̶
- 4 8
    5
```

Subtract the tens.

```
  6 13
  7̶ 3̶
- 4 8
  2 5
```

Directions: Subtract.

Example:

```
  5 13
  6̶ 3̶
- 4 8
  1 5
```

```
  8 3
- 4 5
```

```
  7 4
- 2 9
```

```
  9 4
- 4 8
```

```
  6 2
- 2 5
```

```
  4 5
- 2 7
```

```
  3 3
- 2 4
```

```
  2 4
-   8
```

```
  8 6
- 3 7
```

```
  7 2
- 4 8
```

```
  3 6
- 1 7
```

```
  2 6
- 1 8
```

```
  4 3
- 1 9
```

```
  6 3
- 4 8
```

```
  9 3
- 1 8
```

```
  8 2
- 2 6
```

```
  7 3
- 2 8
```

```
  9 5
- 6 9
```

```
  5 7
- 3 8
```

```
  4 1
- 2 5
```

```
  5 4
- 1 8
```

```
  6 1
- 3 4
```

```
  9 1
- 3 7
```

```
  8 1
- 4 4
```

```
  3 2
- 1 5
```

Problem Solving

Directions: Solve each problem.

Example:

Dad cooks 23 potatoes.

He uses 19 potatoes in the potato salad.

How many potatoes are left?

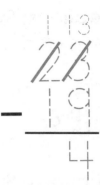

Susan draws 32 butterflies.

She colored 15 of them brown.

How many butterflies does she have left to color?

A book has 66 pages.

Pedro reads 39 pages.

How many pages are left to read?

Jerry picks up 34 sea shells.

He puts 15 of them in a box.

How many does he have left?

Beth buys 72 sheets of paper.

She uses 44 sheets for her school work.

How many sheets of paper are left?

Addition and Subtraction Review

Directions: Add.

4 + 9	8 + 6	9 + 8	7 + 6	5 + 7	6 + 5
9 + 6	5 + 8	7 + 4	9 + 9	8 + 7	7 + 9
30 + 40	20 + 30	45 + 23	52 + 23	60 + 25	83 + 15

Directions: Subtract.

16 − 7	15 − 9	13 − 4	12 − 7	11 − 9	17 − 8
18 − 9	17 − 9	16 − 8	15 − 8	4 − 7	16 − 9
40 − 30	60 − 10	85 − 23	73 − 41	96 − 43	54 − 44

Addition and Subtraction Review

Directions: Add.

4	9	5	6	7	9
+ 8	+ 2	+ 9	+ 6	+ 5	+ 4

8	7	3	7	6	6
+ 8	+ 6	+ 9	+ 7	+ 9	+ 5

40	50	75	66	47	34
+ 20	+ 30	+ 20	+ 31	+ 51	+ 23

Directions: Subtract.

17	15	12	13	14	16
- 9	- 6	- 3	- 7	- 6	- 8

15	14	13	15	12	11
- 7	- 9	- 6	- 7	- 9	- 8

30	50	65	87	75	66
- 10	- 30	- 30	- 34	- 23	- 43

Review: 2-Digit Addition

Directions: Add the ones.   Rename 12 as 10 + 2.   Add the tens.

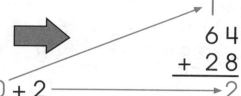

```
   6 4          4                        6 4            1
 + 2 8        + 8                      + 2 8          6 4
                      12 or 10 + 2 ──────→ 2        + 2 8
                                                     9 2
```

Directions: Add.

Example:

```
   2 8          3 4          2 5          4 6          5 4
 + 1 9        + 4 9        + 1 6        + 2 9        + 3 9
   4 7
```

```
   1 6          6 4          5 8          3 9          3 4
 + 3 9        + 2 8        + 2 4        + 1 7        + 1 9
```

```
   5 7          1 4          3 7          6 1          2 9
 + 3 9        + 4 8        + 3 9        + 1 9        + 4 4
```

```
   1 7          3 9          4 4          2 5          1 8
 + 3 5        + 1 4        + 3 7        + 4 9        + 1 8
```

```
   2 6          3 9          1 4          6 5          5 9
 + 4 8        + 2 7        + 2 7        + 2 5        + 1 8
```

Review: 2-Digit Addition

Directions: Add.

36 + 55	14 + 28	57 + 38	44 + 48	33 + 29
23 + 18	27 + 27	68 + 25	23 + 19	42 + 19
56 + 28	49 + 27	38 + 49	36 + 18	49 + 24
18 + 54	51 + 39	74 + 17	35 + 28	52 + 19
48 + 26	25 + 28	39 + 33	29 + 44	54 + 27

Problem Solving

Directions: Solve each problem.

Example:

Simon sees 36 birds flying.

Julie sees 28 birds flying.

How many birds do they see flying?

$$36 + 28 = 64$$

Brandon ran the race in 35 seconds.

Ryan ran the race in 28 seconds.

How many seconds did they run?

Tom has 63 nickels.

Connie has 29 nickels.

How many nickels do they have?

Pam sees 48 monkeys at the zoo.

Brenda sees 35 different monkeys.

How many monkeys did they see?

There are 29 cows in one pen.

There are 47 cows in the other pen.

How many cows in all?

Keep on Truckin'

Directions: Write each sum. Connect the sums of 83 to make a road for the truck.

$$\begin{array}{r} 17 \\ +66 \\ \hline \end{array} \qquad \begin{array}{r} 48 \\ +26 \\ \hline \end{array} \qquad \begin{array}{r} 42 \\ +19 \\ \hline \end{array}$$

$$\begin{array}{r} 28 \\ +38 \\ \hline \end{array} \quad \begin{array}{r} 64 \\ +19 \\ \hline \end{array} \quad \begin{array}{r} 26 \\ +57 \\ \hline \end{array} \quad \begin{array}{r} 58 \\ +25 \\ \hline \end{array} \quad \begin{array}{r} 17 \\ +75 \\ \hline \end{array} \quad \begin{array}{r} 65 \\ +29 \\ \hline \end{array}$$

$$\begin{array}{r} 37 \\ +39 \\ \hline \end{array} \quad \begin{array}{r} 48 \\ +35 \\ \hline \end{array} \quad \begin{array}{r} 58 \\ +37 \\ \hline \end{array} \quad \begin{array}{r} 65 \\ +16 \\ \hline \end{array} \quad \begin{array}{r} 38 \\ +25 \\ \hline \end{array} \quad \begin{array}{r} 39 \\ +59 \\ \hline \end{array}$$

$$\begin{array}{r} 59 \\ +27 \\ \hline \end{array} \quad \begin{array}{r} 55 \\ +28 \\ \hline \end{array} \quad \begin{array}{r} 39 \\ +44 \\ \hline \end{array}$$

Shoot for the Stars

Directions: Add the total points scored in the game. Remember to add the ones first and regroup. Then, add the tens.

Example:

HOME	53
VISITOR	27

Total ___80___

HOME	29
VISITOR	45

Total _____

HOME	57
VISITOR	39

Total _____

HOME	63
VISITOR	19

Total _____

HOME	66
VISITOR	28

Total _____

HOME	47
VISITOR	49

Total _____

HOME	36
VISITOR	45

Total _____

HOME	27
VISITOR	38

Total _____

HOME	54
VISITOR	39

Total _____

HOME	37
VISITOR	59

Total _____

Review: 2-Digit Subtraction

Directions: Rename 61 as 5 tens and 11 ones.

    6 1
  − 4 3

   5 11
   6̸1̸
  − 4 3

Subtract the ones.

   5 11
   6̸1̸
  − 4 3
     8

Subtract the tens.

   5 11
   6̸1̸
  − 4 3
   1 8

Directions: Subtract.

Example:

  3 17
  4̸7̸
 − 2 8
  1 9

7 3	8 4	9 5	6 4
− 4 8	− 6 6	− 1 8	− 2 9

5 6	3 1	2 5	3 3	4 6
− 3 8	− 1 5	− 1 7	− 1 9	− 2 9

9 3	8 2	7 2	4 5	6 1
− 6 4	− 5 5	− 1 4	− 2 8	− 2 3

5 1	6 2	3 7	5 0	8 3
− 4 4	− 4 8	− 1 9	− 3 2	− 4 7

9 2	8 2	7 6	4 7	7 4
− 7 3	− 7 5	− 3 8	− 2 9	− 3 9

Review: 2-Digit Subtraction

Directions: Subtract.

```
  85        93        72        63        43
- 16      - 48      - 35      - 27      - 38


  56        75        84        91        37
- 29      - 49      - 38      - 65      - 18


  21        35        42        72        81
- 14      - 18      - 29      - 47      - 54


  64        53        94        48        23
- 38      - 28      - 57      - 39      - 18


  74        83        62        54        32
- 58      - 36      - 26      - 28      - 17
```

Name _____

Go "Fore" It!

Directions: Add or subtract using regrouping.

tens	ones
2	15
3̶	5
-2	7
	8

35
+27

40
- 16

56
- 27

93
- 39

44
+28

42
-14

97
- 48

33
+18

73
- 24

56
- 17

68
- 49

49
+32

77
- 68

27
+19

Monster Math

Directions: Add or subtract using regrouping.

84		36
− 56		− 19

41		65
− 17		− 28

52		48
− 28	72	− 30
	− 19	

84	33	33
− 27	− 15	+ 18

57	64	25
− 39	+ 17	+ 35

Adding Hundreds

Examples:

```
  5 hundreds        5 0 0        4 hundreds        4 0 0
+ 3 hundreds      + 3 0 0      + 5 hundreds      + 5 0 0
  8 hundreds        8 0 0        9 hundreds        900
```

Directions: Add.

```
  3 hundreds        3 0 0        6 hundreds        6 0 0
+ 1 hundreds      + 1 0 0      + 2 hundreds      + 2 0 0
  4 hundreds        400          hundreds
```

```
  2 0 0            1 0 0            6 0 0            4 0 0
+ 2 0 0          + 7 0 0          + 3 0 0          + 5 0 0
```

```
  3 0 0            8 0 0            4 0 0            7 0 0
+ 4 0 0          + 1 0 0          + 4 0 0          + 2 0 0
```

```
  5 0 0            1 0 0            5 0 0            3 0 0
+ 1 0 0          + 6 0 0          + 2 0 0          + 2 0 0
```

```
  3 0 0            4 0 0            3 0 0            2 0 0
+ 3 0 0          + 2 0 0          + 5 0 0          + 1 0 0
```

Problem Solving

Directions: Solve each problem.

Example:

Ria packed 300 boxes.

Melvin packed 200 boxes.

How many boxes did Ria and Melvin pack?

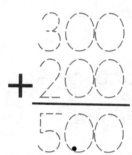

$$\begin{array}{r} 300 \\ + 200 \\ \hline 500 \end{array}$$

Santo typed 500 letters.

Hale typed 400 letters.

How many letters did they type?

Paula used 100 paper clips.

Milton used 600 paper clips.

How many paper clips did they use?

The grocery store sold 400 red apples.

The grocery store also sold 100 yellow apples.

How many apples did the grocery store sell in all?

Miles worked 200 days.

Julia worked 500 days.

How many days did they work?

3-Digit Addition

```
  2 4 5          2 4 5          2 4 5
+ 2 5 3   →    + 2 5 3   →    + 2 5 3
      8            9 8          4 9 8
```

Directions: Add.

Example:

```
  7 4 5                    6 2 3
+   2 3                  + 1 5 6
  7 6 8
```

— Add the ones.
— Add the tens.
— Add the hundreds.

— Add the ones.
— Add the tens.
— Add the hundreds.

```
  4 1 5        5 6 6        3 7 3        1 6 0
+ 3 4 2      +   3 3      + 2 2 1      + 3 3 4
```

```
  8 3 5        6 4 2        2 8 7        7 2 3
+   4 2      + 2 5 1      + 4 1 2      +   4 5
```

```
  1 3 3        4 5 4        3 1 4        6 5 4
+ 5 2 2      + 3 2 4      + 6 0 2      + 2 3 5
```

Problem Solving

Directions: Solve each problem.

Example:

Gene collected 342 rocks.

Lester collected 201 rocks.

How many rocks did they collect?

$$\begin{array}{r} 342 \\ +\ 201 \\ \hline 543 \end{array}$$

Tina jumped the rope 403 times.

Henry jumped the rope 426 times.

How many times did they jump?

There are 210 people wearing blue hats.

There are 432 people wearing red hats.

How many hats in all?

Asta used 135 paper plates.

Clyde used 143 paper plates.

How many paper plates did they use in all?

Aunt Mary had 536 dollars.

Uncle Lewis had 423 dollars.

How many dollars did they have in all?

Problem Solving

Directions: Solve each problem.

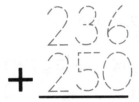

There are 236 boys in school.

There are 250 girls in school.

How many boys and girls are in school?

Mary saw 131 cars.

Marvin saw 268 trucks.

How many cars and trucks did they see in all?

Jack has 427 pennies.

Jill has 370 pennies.

How many pennies do they have in all?

There are 582 red apples.

There are 206 yellow apples.

How many apples are there in all?

Ann found 122 shells.

Pedro found 76 shells.

How many shells did they find?

Subtracting Hundreds

```
  8 hundreds      8 0 0        6 hundreds      6 0 0
- 3 hundreds    - 3 0 0      - 2 hundreds    - 2 0 0
  5 hundreds      5 0 0        4 hundreds      400
```

Directions: Subtract.

Example:

```
  9 hundreds      9 0 0        3 hundreds      3 0 0
- 7 hundreds    - 7 0 0      - 1 hundreds    - 1 0 0
  2 hundreds      200           hundreds
```

```
    7 0 0          5 0 0          9 0 0          8 0 0
  - 3 0 0        - 4 0 0        - 4 0 0        - 5 0 0
```

```
    6 0 0          3 0 0          5 0 0          4 0 0
  - 5 0 0        - 2 0 0        - 1 0 0        - 2 0 0
```

```
    9 0 0          8 0 0          6 0 0          5 0 0
  - 1 0 0        - 4 0 0        - 2 0 0        - 3 0 0
```

```
    4 0 0          7 0 0          8 0 0          9 0 0
  - 1 0 0        - 6 0 0        - 2 0 0        - 6 0 0
```

Problem Solving

Directions: Solve each problem.

Example:

There were 400 apples in a box.

Jesse took 100 apples from the box.

How many apples are still in the box?

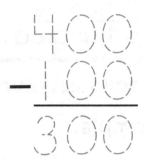

$$\begin{array}{r} 400 \\ -100 \\ \hline 300 \end{array}$$

Tommy bought 300 golf balls.

He gave Irene 200 golf balls.

How many golf balls does he have left?

The black horse ran 900 feet.

The brown horse ran 700 feet.

How many more feet did the black horse run?

The paint store has 800 gallons of paint.

It sells 300 gallons of paint.

How many gallons of paint are left?

There are 700 children.

There are 200 boys.

How many girls are there?

3-Digit Subtraction

Directions: Subtract the ones.

```
  7 4 6
- 4 2 4
      2
```

Subtract the tens.

```
  7 4 6
- 4 2 4
    2 2
```

Subtract the hundreds.

```
  7 4 6
- 4 2 4
  3 2 2
```

Directions: Add.

Example:

```
  8 7 9
-   4 6
  8 3 3
```

— Subtract the ones.
— Subtract the tens.
— Subtract the hundreds.

```
  5 8 6
- 1 4 2
```

— Subtract the ones.
— Subtract the tens.
— Subtract the hundreds.

```
  6 3 5
- 4 2 3
```

```
  4 7 8
- 2 4 1
```

```
  3 3 8
-   2 7
```

```
  9 5 7
- 7 3 4
```

```
  2 9 7
- 1 4 5
```

```
  8 4 6
- 3 2 5
```

```
  7 6 9
- 5 1 4
```

```
  6 5 3
- 1 4 2
```

```
  5 6 9
- 3 3 3
```

```
  3 6 5
- 2 1 3
```

```
  8 1 8
- 6 1 8
```

```
  9 3 6
- 4 2 4
```

Problem Solving

Directions: Solve each problem.

Example:

The grocery store buys 568 cans of beans.

It sells 345 cans of beans.

How many cans of beans are left?

$$\begin{array}{r} 568 \\ -345 \\ \hline 223 \end{array}$$

The cooler holds 732 gallons of milk.

It has 412 gallons of milk in it.

How many more gallons of milk
will it take to fill the cooler?

Ann does 635 push-ups.

Carl does 421 push-ups.

How many more push-ups does Ann do?

Kurt has 386 pennies.

Neal has 32 pennies.

How many more pennies does Kurt have?

It takes 874 nails to build a tree house.

Jillian has 532 nails.

How many more nails does she need?

Problem Solving

Directions: Solve each problem.

Example:

There were 787 bales of hay.

Glenda fed the cows 535 bales.

How many bales of hay are left?

$$
\begin{array}{r}
787 \\
-\ 535 \\
\hline
252
\end{array}
$$

There are 673 bolts in a box.

Maria took 341 bolts out of the box.

How many bolts are left in the box?

The secretary types 459 letters.

138 of the letters were mailed.

How many letters are left?

Mr. Jones had 569 dollars.

He spent 203 dollars.

How many dollars does he have left?

There are 342 riding horses in the rodeo.

There are 132 bucking horses in the rodeo.

How many more riding horses are there?

Review: Addition and Subtraction

Directions: Add.

```
   1 2 4          5 2 0          7 3 9          8 6 1
 + 3 2 3        + 4 0 7        + 1 5 0        +     6
```

Directions: Subtract.

```
   9 0 0          8 0 0          9 7 4          5 0 8
 - 6 0 0        - 2 0 0        - 5 6 4        -     7
```

```
   7 2 8          6 5 7          8 9 4          5 9 6
 - 3 2 6        -   4 5        - 4 6 4        - 3 5 2
```

Directions: Solve each problem.

There are 275 nails in a box.

123 nails are taken out of the box.

How many nails are still in the box?

_____

Gerald peeled 212 apples.

Anna peeled 84 apples.

How many apples did they peel in all?

Review: 3-Digit Addition

Directions: Add.

Examples:

```
   3 4 0          7 5 4          8 2 6          6 3 2
 + 2 2 5        +   3 2        +     3        + 3 2 2
   5 6 5          7 8 6
```

```
   1 9 8          4 5 6          5 4 1          2 7 3
 + 2 0 0        +   3 1        + 3 3 3        + 4 1 5
```

```
   9 0 0          8 4 7          7 2 1          4 0 2
 +   3 4        + 1 3 1        + 1 7 6        + 3 8 3
```

```
   1 5 6          6 4 4          2 1 5          3 7 2
 + 4 2 3        + 2 5 1        + 5 4 2        + 4 1 7
```

```
   5 1 8          7 8 3          6 8 4          7 1 0
 + 3 5 1        +     5        +   1 4        + 2 6 0
```

Review: 3-Digit Subtraction

Directions: Subtract.

Example:

```
  8 5 6        4 3 2        5 9 8        7 6 9
- 3 5 2      -   2 1      - 4 1 6      - 3 4 5
  5 0 4        4 1 1
```

```
  3 1 9        9 5 4        2 7 5        6 4 3
-     6      - 7 3 1      -     3      - 3 1 3
```

```
  7 7 5        8 3 4        9 4 2        4 7 8
- 2 6 1      -   1 2      - 1 1 1      - 3 2 4
```

```
  5 6 2        4 4 4        3 8 5        7 5 4
- 4 3 1      - 2 1 2      - 1 5 2      -     3
```

```
  8 6 8        9 4 3        6 8 9        5 7 7
- 2 3 4      - 8 4 3      - 4 1 7      -   3 7
```

Name _____

Multiplication

Multiplication is a short way to find the sum of adding the same number a certain amount of times. For example, 7 x 4 = 28 instead of 7 + 7 + 7 + 7 = 28.

Directions: Study the example. Solve the problems.

Example:
3 + 3 + 3 = 9
3 threes = 9
3 x 3 = 9

7 + 7 = ____
2 sevens = ____
2 x 7 = ____

4 + 4 + 4 + 4 = ____
4 fours = ____
4 x ____ = ____

5 + 5 = ____
2 fives = ____
2 x ____ = ____

2 + 2 + 2 + 2 = ____
4 twos = ____
4 x ____ = ____

6 + 6 = ____
2 sixes = ____
2 x ____ = ____

Multiplication

Multiplication is repeated addition.

Directions: Draw a picture for each problem.
Then, write the missing numbers.

Example:
Draw 2 groups of three apples.

$3 + 3 = 6$

or $2 \times 3 = 6$

Draw 3 groups of four hearts.

$4 + 4 + 4 =$ _____

or $3 \times$ _____ $=$ _____

Draw 2 groups of five boxes.

$5 +$ _____ $=$ _____

or $2 \times$ _____ $=$ _____

Draw 6 groups of two circles.

$2 +$ _____ $+$ _____ $+$ _____ $+$ _____ $+$ _____ $=$ _____

or $6 \times$ _____ $=$ _____

Draw 7 groups of three triangles.

$3 +$ _____ $+$ _____ $+$ _____ $+$ _____ $+$ _____ $+$ _____ $=$ _____

or _____ $\times$ _____ $=$ _____

Multiplication

Directions: Study the example. Draw the groups and write the total.

Example: 3x2
2+2+2   =   6

● ●   ● ●   ● ●

3x4

___ + ___ + ___ = _____

2x5

____ + ____ = _____

5x3

___ + ___ + ___ + ___ + ___ = _____

Name _____

Multiplication

Directions: Solve the problems.

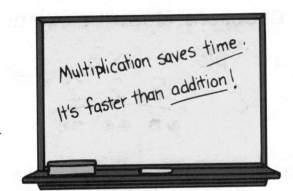

Multiplication saves time. It's faster than addition!

9 + 9 = ____   7 + 7 = ____

2 nines = ____   2 sevens = ____

2 x 9 = ____   2 x ____ = ____

4 + 4 + 4 + 4 = ____   8 + 8 + 8 + 8 + 8 = ____

____ fours = ____   ____ eights = ____

____ x 4 = ____   ____ x 8 = ____

5 + 5 + 5 = ____   9 + 9 = ____   6 + 6 + 6 = ____

____ fives = ____   ____ nines = ____   ____ sixes = ____

____ x 5 = ____   ____ x 9 = ____   ____ x 6 = ____

3 + 3 = ____   7 + 7 + 7 + 7 = ____   2 + 2 = ____

____ threes = ____   ____ sevens = ____   ____ twos = ____

____ x 3 = ____   ____ x 7 = ____   ____ x 2 = ____

Multiplication

Directions: Use the code to color the fish.

If the answer is:

 6, color it **red**.

 12, color it orange.

 16, color it **blue**.

27, color it **brown**.

 8, color it yellow.

 15, color it **green**.

 18, color it **purple**.

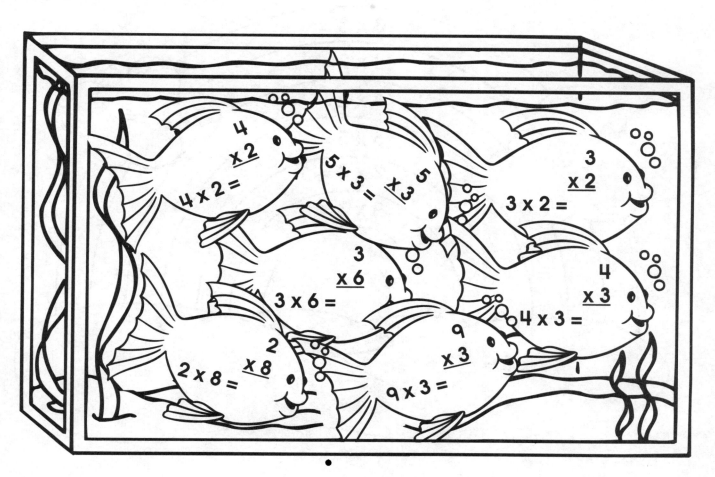

Name _____

Multiplication

Directions: Use the code to color the rainbow.

If the answer is:

6, color it **green**.   16, color it pink.   25, color it orange.

8, color it **purple**.   18, color it white.   27, color it **blue**.

9, color it **red**.   21, color it **brown**.

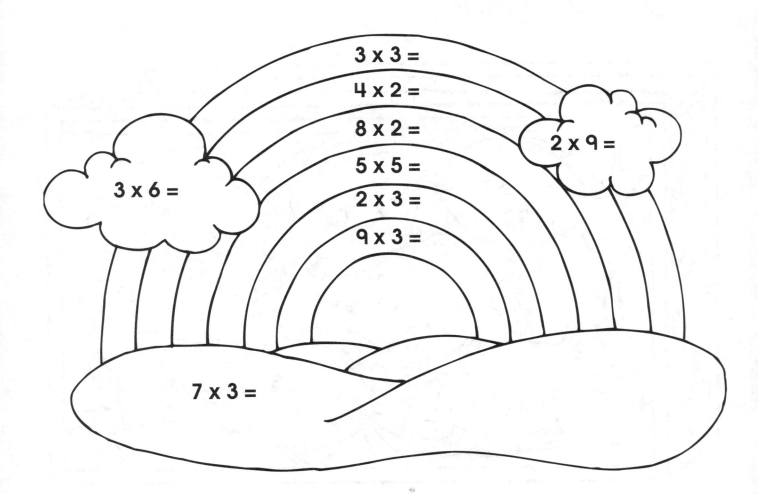

3 x 3 =

4 x 2 =

8 x 2 =

5 x 5 =

2 x 3 =

9 x 3 =

2 x 9 =

3 x 6 =

7 x 3 =

Problem Solving

Directions: Tell if you add, subtract, or multiply. Then, write the answers.
Hints: "In all" means to add. "Left" means to subtract. Groups with
the same number in each means to multiply.

Example:

There are 6 red birds and 7 blue birds.
How many birds in all?

____add____ ____13____ birds

The pet store had 25 goldfish, but 10 were sold.
How many goldfish are left?

_____ _____ goldfish

There are 5 cages of bunnies. There are two bunnies in each cage.
How many bunnies are there in the store?

_____ _____ bunnies

The store had 18 puppies this morning. It sold 7 puppies today.
How many puppies are left?

_____ _____ puppies

Problem Solving

Directions: Tell if you add, subtract, or multiply. Then, write the answers.

There were 12 frogs sitting
on a log by a pond, but
3 frogs hopped away.
How many frogs were left?

_____ _____ frogs

There are 9 flowers growing by the
pond. Each flower has 2 leaves.
How many leaves are there?

_____ _____ leaves

A tree had 7 squirrels playing in it. Then, 8 more came along.
How many squirrels are there in all?

_____ _____ squirrels

There were 27 birds living in the trees around the pond,
but 9 flew away.
How many birds are left?

_____ _____ birds

Name _____

Circle

A **circle** is a shape that is round. This is a circle:

Directions: Find the circles and draw squares around them.

Directions: Trace the word. Then, write the word.

circle

Square

A **square** is a shape with four corners and four sides of the same length. This is a square: ☐

Directions: Find the squares and draw circles around them.

Directions: Trace the word. Then, write the word.

_____

square

Rectangle

A **rectangle** is a shape with four corners and four sides. The sides opposite each other are the same length. This is a rectangle: ▭

Directions: Find the rectangles and draw circles around them.

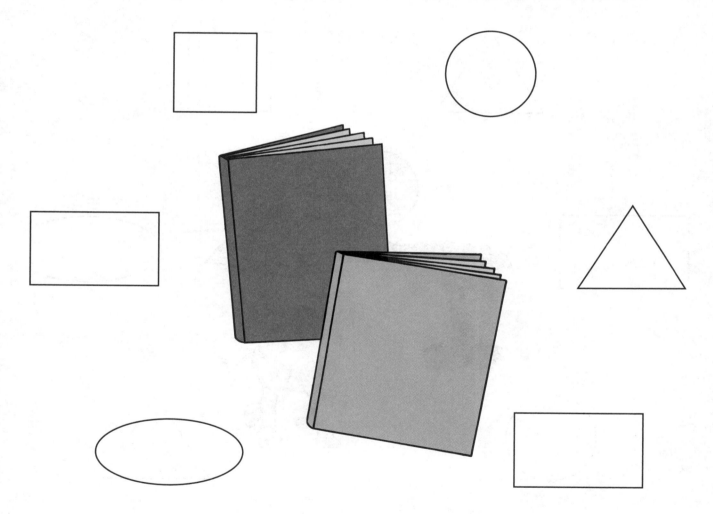

Directions: Trace the word. Then, write the word.

rectangle

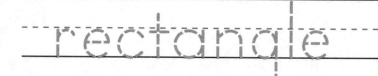

Triangle

A **triangle** is a shape with three corners and three sides.
This is a triangle: △

Directions: Find the triangles and draw circles around them.

Directions: Trace the word. Then, write the word.

triangle

Oval and Diamond

An **oval** is egg-shaped. This is an oval: ◯

A **diamond** is a shape with four sides of the same length. Its corners form points at the top, sides, and bottom. This is a diamond: ◇

Directions: Find the ovals. Color them **red.**
Find the diamonds. Color them **blue.**

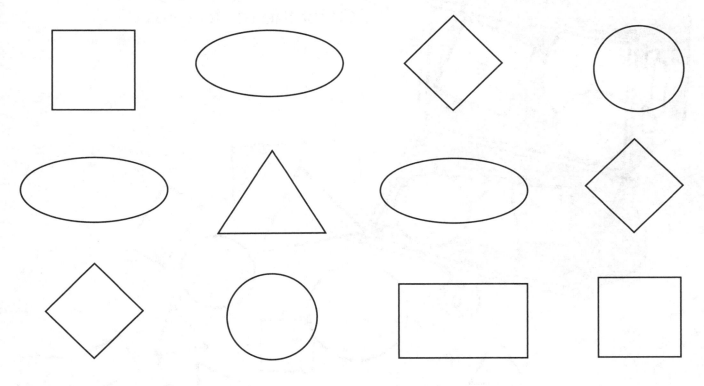

Directions: Trace the words. Then, write the words.

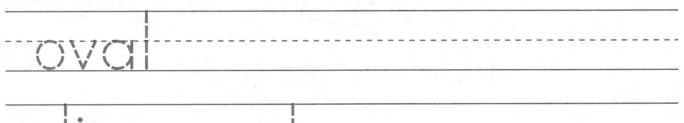

Geometry

Geometry is mathematics that has to do with lines and shapes.

Directions: Color the shapes.

Color the triangles **blue.**
Color the circles **red.**
Color the squares **green.**
Color the rectangles pink.

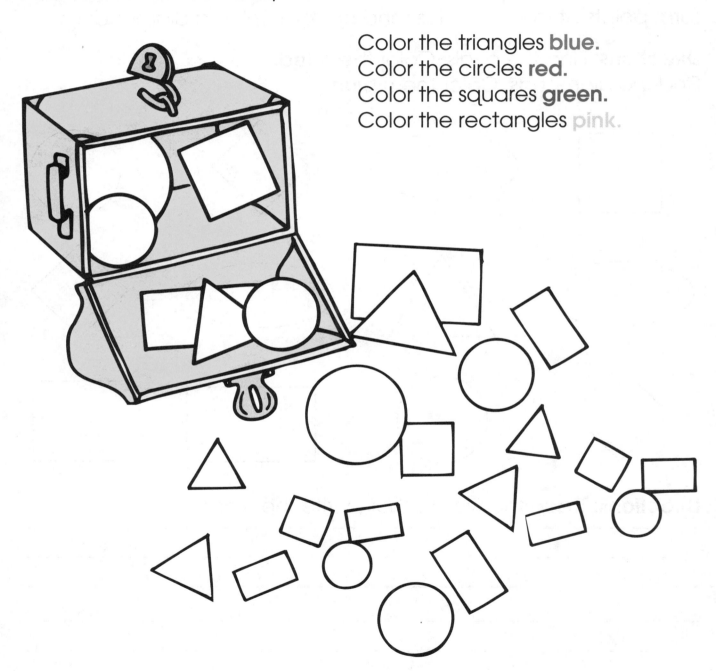

Geometry

Directions: Draw a line from the word to the shape.

Use a **red** line for circles.   Use a yellow line for rectangles.
Use a **blue** line for squares.   Use a **green** line for triangles.

Circle   **Square**   **Triangle**   **Rectangle**

Name _____

Shapes

Robbie the robot and his pal Roger are made of many different-shaped objects. Look at all the shapes on their bodies. Then, follow the directions below.

Directions: Use a **green** crayon to color all the circles on their bodies.

This is a circle: ◯ .

Use an **orange** crayon to color all the ovals on their bodies.

This is an oval: ⬭ .

Color the other shapes any way you like.

Shapes

Directions: Some shapes have sides. How many sides does each shape below have? Write the number of sides inside each shape.

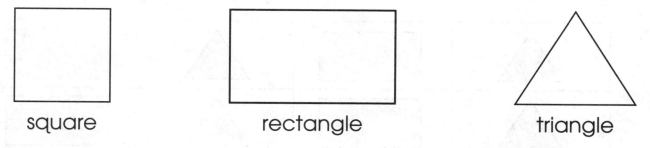

square   rectangle   triangle

Directions: Help Robbie get to his space car by tracing the path that has only squares, rectangles, and triangles.

Hint: You may want to draw an **X** on all the other shapes. This will help you see the path more clearly.

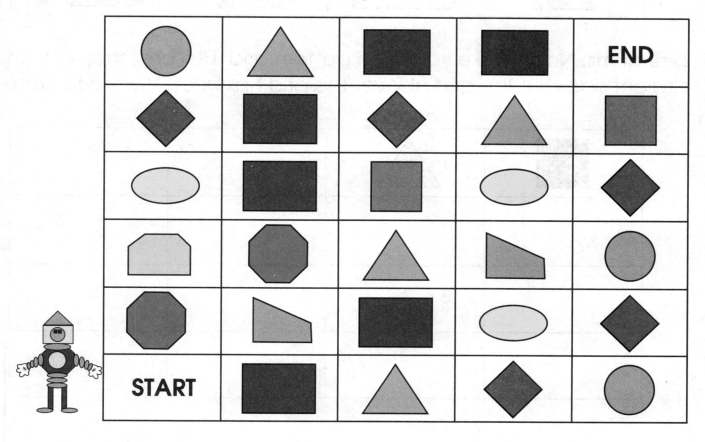

Name _____

Shapes

Directions: Look at the grid below. All the shapes have straight sides, like a square.

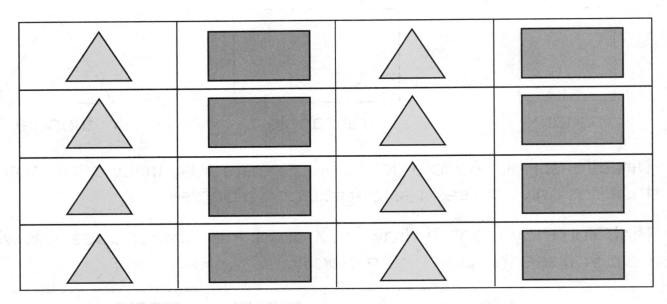

Directions: Now, make your own pattern grid. Use only shapes with straight sides like the grid above. The grid has been started for you.

Name _____

Measurement: Inches

Directions: Cut out the ruler. Measure each object to the nearest inch.

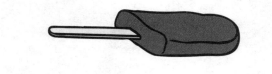

_____ inches

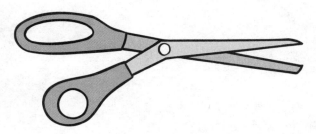

_____ inches

_____ inches

Directions: Measure objects around your house. Write the measurement to the nearest inch.

can of soup _____ inches

pen _____ inches

toothbrush _____ inches

paper clip _____ inches

small toy _____ inches

cut out

8 7 6 5 4 3 2 1

This page was left intentionally blank for cutting activity on previous page.

Measurement: Inches

Directions: Use the ruler from pg. 203 to measure the fish to the nearest inch.

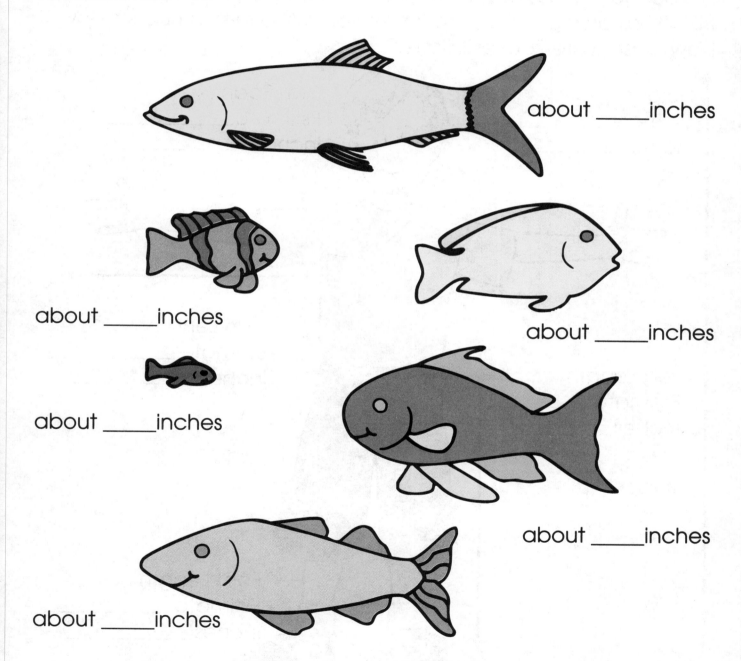

about _____ inches

about _____ inches

about _____ inches

about _____ inches

about _____ inches

about _____ inches

about _____ inches

How Big Are You?

Directions: How big are you? **Estimate,** or guess, how long some of your body parts are. Write your estimates below. Then, have a friend use an inch ruler to measure you. Write the numbers below. How close were your estimates?

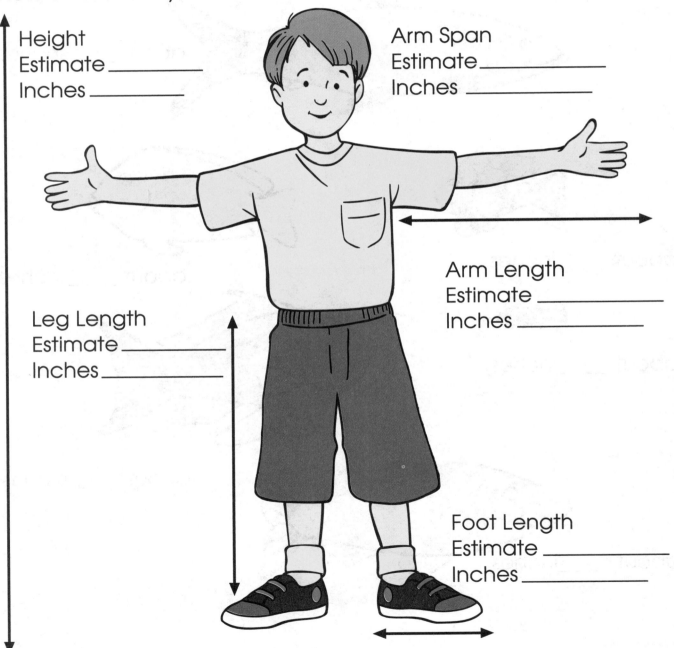

Height
Estimate _____
Inches _____

Arm Span
Estimate _____
Inches _____

Arm Length
Estimate _____
Inches _____

Leg Length
Estimate _____
Inches _____

Foot Length
Estimate _____
Inches _____

Measurement: Inches

An **inch** is a unit of length in the standard measurement system.

Directions: Use the ruler on pg. 203 to measure each object to the nearest inch.

Example: The paper clip is about 1 inch long.

I inch

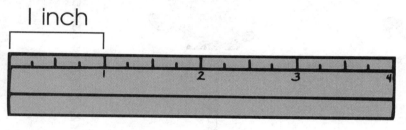

about __I__ inches

about _____ inches

about _____ inches

about _____ inches

about _____ inches

about _____ inches

about _____ inches

Name _____

Measuring Monkeys

Directions: Use the inch ruler on pg. 203 to measure the length of each rope. Write the answer in each blank.

Measurement: Centimeters

A **centimeter** is a unit of length in the metric system. There are 2.54 centimeters in an inch.

Directions: Use a centimeter ruler to measure the crayons to the nearest centimeter.

Example: The first crayon is about 7 centimeters long.

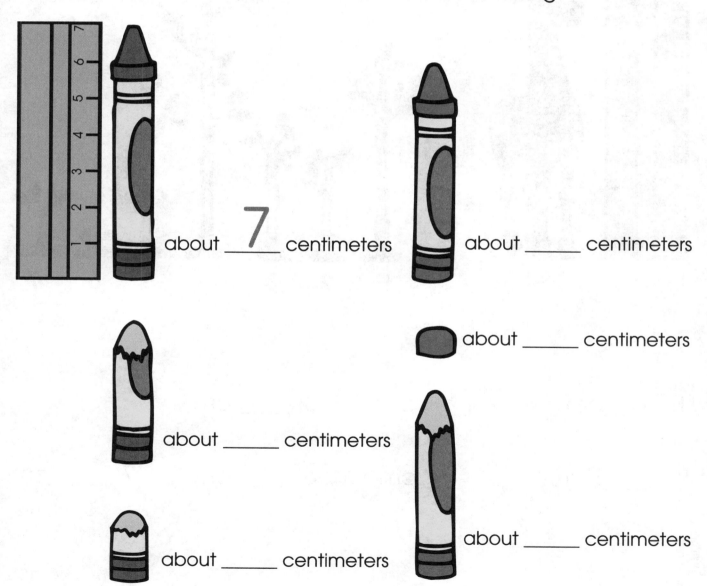

about __7__ centimeters

about _____ centimeters

about _____ centimeters

about _____ centimeters

about _____ centimeters

about _____ centimeters

Measurement: Centimeters

Directions: The giraffe is about 8 centimeters high. How many centimeters (cm) high are the trees? Write your answers in the blanks.

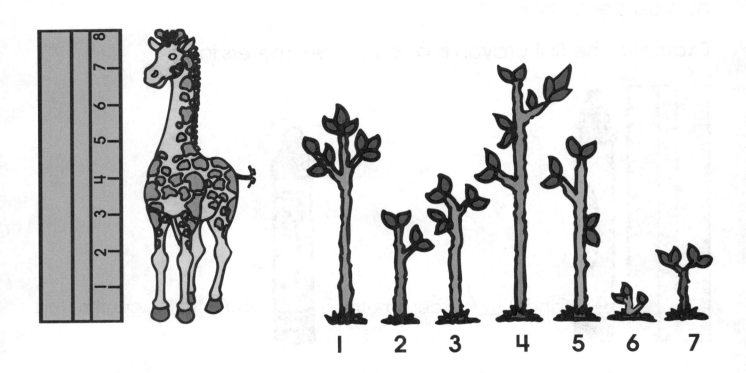

1. _____ cm   2. _____ cm   3. _____ cm

4. _____ cm   5. _____ cm   6. _____ cm   7. _____ cm

Name _____

Measuring in Centimeters

Directions: Use a centimeter ruler to find the height or the length of the objects below. Write the answer in each blank.

Example:

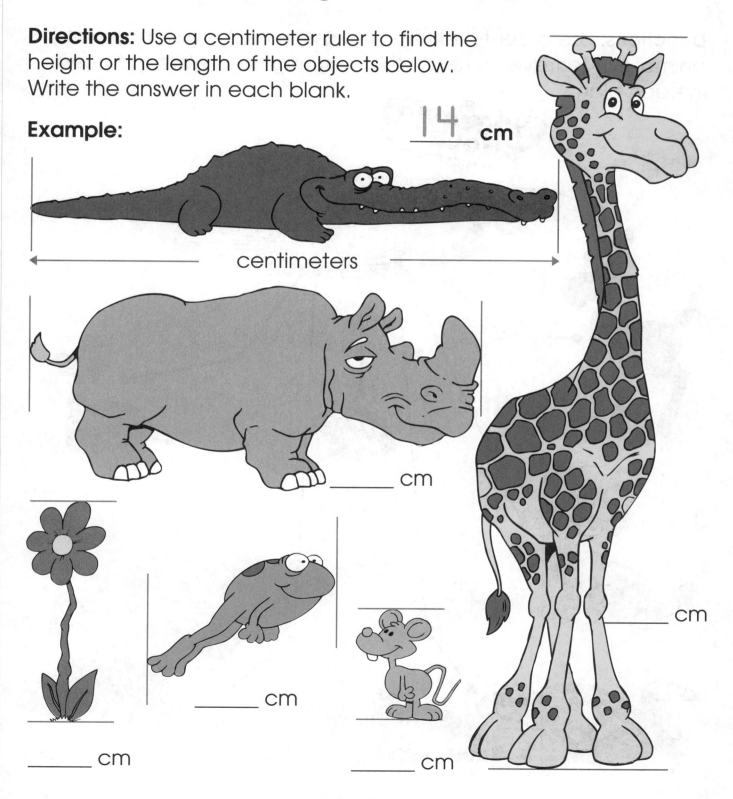

14 cm

centimeters

_____ cm

_____ cm

_____ cm

_____ cm

_____ cm

Trip to the Watering Hole

Directions: Use a centimeter ruler to measure the distance each animal has to travel to reach the watering hole. Write the answer in each blank.

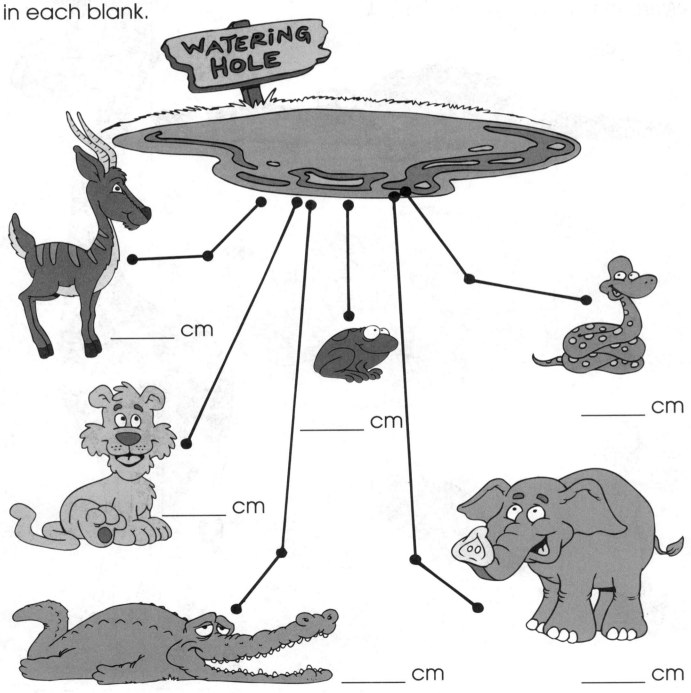

_____ cm

_____ cm

_____ cm

_____ cm

_____ cm

_____ cm

_____ cm

Centimeter Sharpening

Directions: Use a centimeter ruler to measure each pencil. Subtract to find how many centimeters were lost when sharpening each pencil.

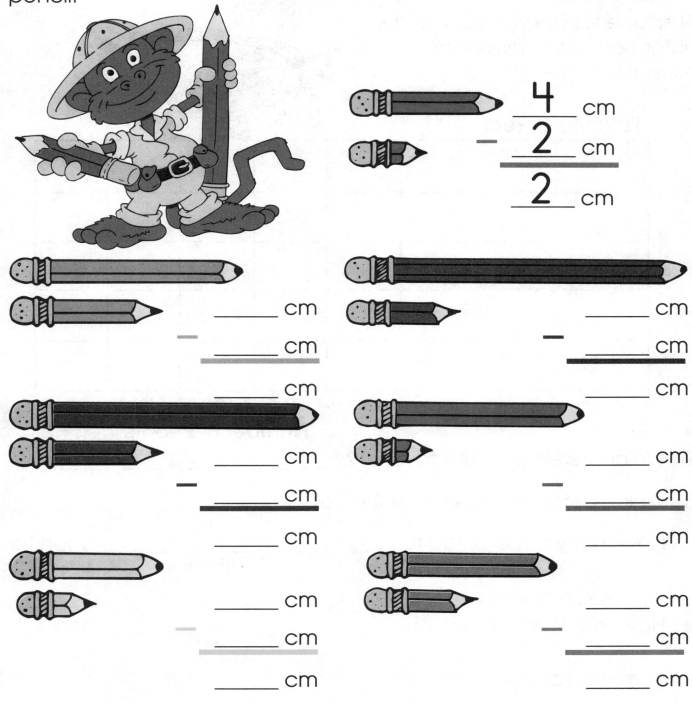

$$\begin{array}{r} \underline{4} \ \text{cm} \\ - \ \underline{2} \ \text{cm} \\ \hline \underline{2} \ \text{cm} \end{array}$$

_____ cm

_____ cm

_____ cm

_____ cm

_____ cm

_____ cm

_____ cm

_____ cm

_____ cm

_____ cm

_____ cm

_____ cm

_____ cm

_____ cm

_____ cm

_____ cm

_____ cm

Name _____

Good Morning

Directions: Make your own bar graph. List 5 kinds of cereal on the graph below. Ask 5 people to vote for one cereal. Record the votes on the graph by coloring in 1 space for each vote. Use the information to answer the questions.

Favorite Cereal

Cereals					
	1	2	3	4	5

Number of People

1. Which cereal was the favorite? _____

2. Which cereal had the fewest votes? _____

3. How many more voted for _____ than for
   (name of cereal)
   _____ ? _____
   (name of cereal)

4. How many people chose _____ and
   (name of cereal)
   _____ altogether? _____
   (name of cereal)

Jungle Weather

Directions: The pictures show the weather for one month. Count the number of sunny, cloudy, and rainy days.

Directions: Complete the pictograph using the tallies above.

Weather for 1 Month

Number of Days

What a Meal!

Directions: Use the pictograph to complete each sentence below.

= 2 worms

Grace Goldfish	
Willie Walleye	
Calvin Catfish	
Benny Bluegill	
Beth Bass	
Patty Perch	

1. _____ got the fewest worms.

2. _____ got the most worms.

3. _____ and _____ got the same number of worms.

4. Benny and Patty together caught the same number of worms as _____ .

5. Write the number of worms that each fish ate.

_____   _____   _____   _____   _____   _____
Grace   **Willie**   **Calvin**   **Benny**   **Beth**   **Patty**

"Play Ball"

Directions: Eight baseball teams have just completed their season. Each team played eight games. Use this pictograph to answer the questions below.

 = 1 win

Washington Wiggle Worms	⚾⚾⚾⚾⚾⚾⚾
Jersey Jaguars	⚾⚾⚾⚾⚾⚾⚾⚾
Pittsburgh Pandas	⚾⚾⚾⚾⚾⚾
Tampa Toucans	⚾⚾⚾
Kansas City Centipedes	⚾⚾⚾⚾
Lansing Lightning Bugs	⚾
Houston Hornets	⚾⚾
Memphis Monkeys	⚾

1. How many games did the Memphis Monkeys lose? _____

2. Which teams tied for last place?

_____ and _____

3. Which team won the most games? _____

4. How many more games did the Washington Wiggle Worms win than the Tampa Toucans? _____

5. Which four teams' total number of games won equal the Jersey Jaguars' number of games won? _____

_____

Graphs

A **graph** is a drawing that shows information about numbers.

Directions: Count the apples in each row. Color the boxes to show how many apples have bites taken out of them.

Example:

1	2	3	4	5	6	7	8

Graphs

Directions: Count the banana peels in each column. Color the boxes to show how many bananas have been eaten by the monkeys.

Example:

219

Name _____

Graphs

Directions: Count the fish. Color the bowls to make a graph that shows the number of fish.

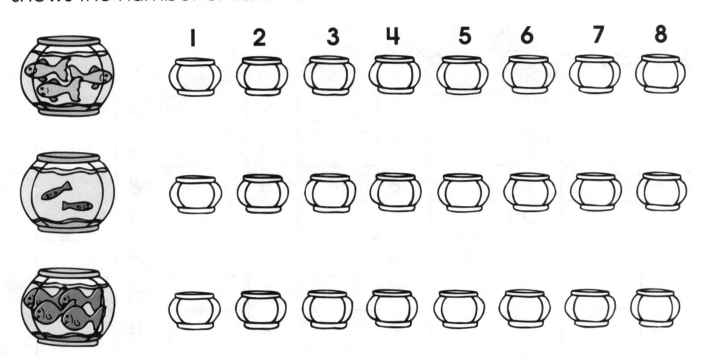

Directions: Use your fishbowl graphs to find the answers to the following questions. Draw a line to the correct bowl.

The most fish

The fewest fish

Graphing   **220**   **Total Math Grade 2**

Treasure Quest

Directions: Read the directions. Draw the pictures where they belong on the grid. Start at 0 and go . . .

over 2, up 5. Draw a

over 9, up 3. Draw a

over 8, up 6. Draw a

over 5, up 2. Draw a

over 1, up 7. Draw a

over 7, up 1. Draw a

over 6, up 4. Draw a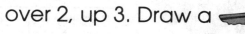

over 2, up 3. Draw a

over 3, up 1. Draw a

over 4, up 6. Draw a

8										
7										
6										
5										
4										
3										
2										
1										
0	**1**	**2**	**3**	**4**	**5**	**6**	**7**	**8**	**9**	**10**

Let's Get Things in Order!

Directions: Help Mrs. Brown pick flowers in her garden. The flowers she wants are listed in the chart. Use the descriptions to color the flowers in her garden.

↓	→	Color it:
1st row	6th flower	red
2nd row	4th flower	blue
3rd row	1st flower	yellow
4th row	9th flower	pink
5th row	10th flower	orange
6th row	2nd flower	green
7th row	5th flower	black
8th row	7th flower	grey
9th row	8th flower	purple
10th row	3rd flower	brown

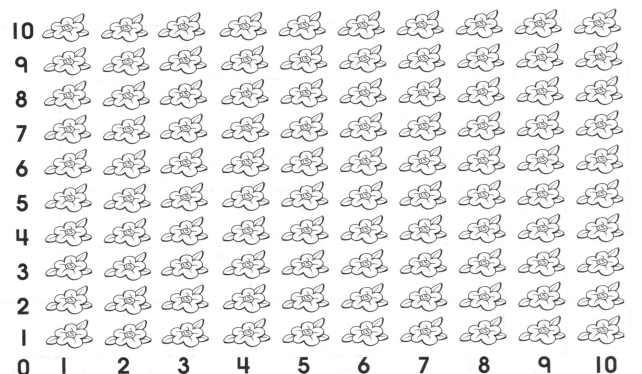

Name _____

Whole and Half

A **fraction** is a number that names part of a whole, such as $\frac{1}{2}$.

Directions: Color half of each thing.

Example: whole apple   half an apple

Name _____

One Third

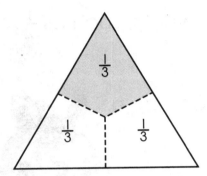

 part is blue.

The parts are the same size.

 of the inside is blue.

Directions: Complete the fraction statements.

Example:

_____ part is blue.

_____ parts are the same size.

_____ of the inside is blue.

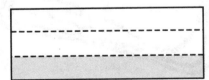

_____ part is blue.

_____ parts are the same size.

_____ of the inside is blue.

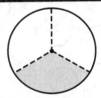

_____ part is blue.

_____ parts are the same size.

_____ of the inside is blue.

_____ part is blue.

_____ parts are the same size.

_____ of the inside is blue.

_____ of the inside is blue.

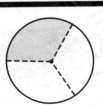

_____ of the inside is blue.

Name _____

One Fourth

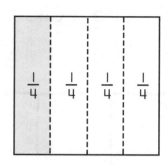

1 part is blue.

The $\frac{1}{4}$ parts are the same size.

$\frac{1}{4}$ of the inside is blue.

Directions: Complete the fraction statements.

Example:

_____ part is blue.

_____ parts are the same size.

_____ of the inside is blue.

_____ part is blue.

_____ parts are the same size.

_____ of the inside is blue.

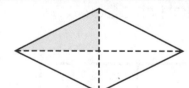

_____ part is blue.

_____ parts are the same size.

_____ of the inside is blue.

_____ part is blue.

_____ parts are the same size.

_____ of the inside is blue.

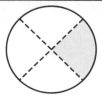

_____ of the inside is blue.

_____ of the inside is blue.

Thirds and Fourths

Directions: Each shape has **3** equal parts. Color one section, or $\frac{1}{3}$, of each shape.

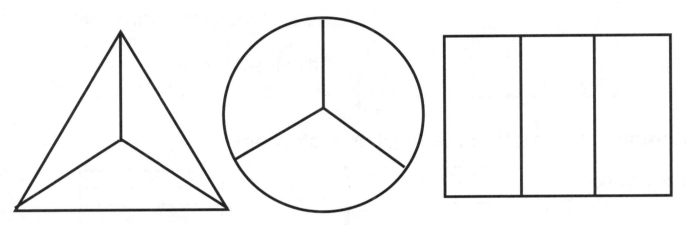

Directions: Each shape has **4** equal parts. Color one section, or $\frac{1}{4}$, of each shape.

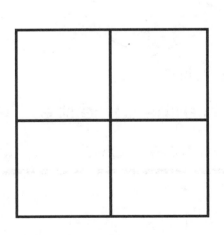
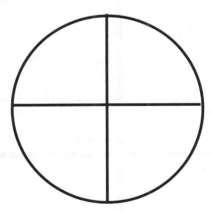
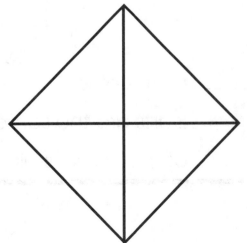

Fractions: Half, Third, Fourth

Directions: Color the correct fraction of each shape.

Examples:

shaded part   1
equal parts   2
$\frac{1}{2}$ (one-half)

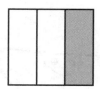

shaded part   1
equal parts   3
$\frac{1}{3}$ (one-third)

shaded part   1
equal parts   4
$\frac{1}{4}$ (one-fourth)

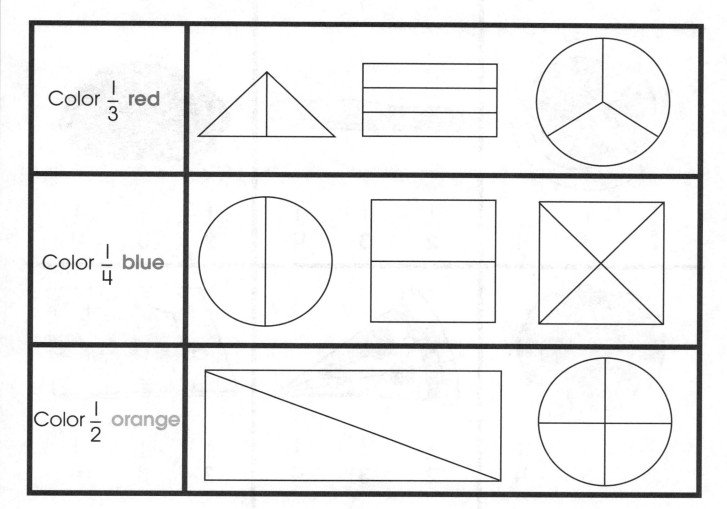

Color $\frac{1}{3}$ **red**

Color $\frac{1}{4}$ **blue**

Color $\frac{1}{2}$ **orange**

Fraction Food

Directions: Count the equal parts. Circle the fraction that names one of the parts.

$\dfrac{1}{2}$ $\dfrac{1}{3}$ $\dfrac{1}{4}$

$\dfrac{1}{2}$ $\dfrac{1}{3}$ $\dfrac{1}{4}$

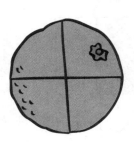

$\dfrac{1}{2}$ $\dfrac{1}{3}$ $\dfrac{1}{4}$

$\dfrac{1}{2}$ $\dfrac{1}{3}$ $\dfrac{1}{4}$

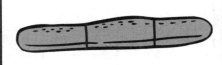

$\dfrac{1}{2}$ $\dfrac{1}{3}$ $\dfrac{1}{4}$

$\dfrac{1}{2}$ $\dfrac{1}{3}$ $\dfrac{1}{4}$

$\dfrac{1}{2}$ $\dfrac{1}{3}$ $\dfrac{1}{4}$

$\dfrac{1}{2}$ $\dfrac{1}{3}$ $\dfrac{1}{4}$

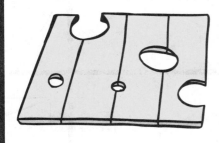

$\dfrac{1}{2}$ $\dfrac{1}{3}$ $\dfrac{1}{4}$

Shaded Shapes

Directions: Draw a line to match each fraction with its correct shape.

$\frac{1}{3}$ shaded

$\frac{2}{4}$ shaded

$\frac{1}{4}$ shaded

$\frac{1}{2}$ shaded

$\frac{3}{4}$ shaded

$\frac{2}{3}$ shaded

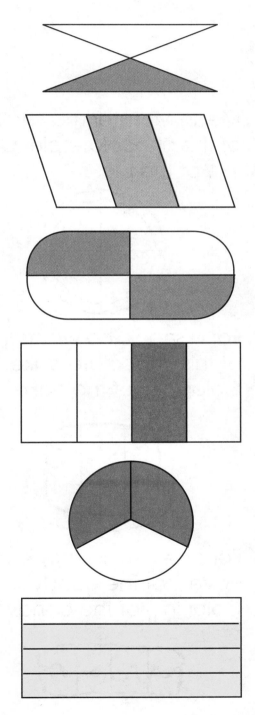

Name _____

Mean Monster's Diet

Directions: Help Mean Monster choose the right piece of food.

1. Mean Monster may have $\frac{1}{4}$ of this chocolate pie. Color in $\frac{1}{4}$ of the pie.

2. For a snack, he wants $\frac{1}{3}$ of this chocolate cake. Color in $\frac{1}{3}$ of the cake.

3. For an evening snack, he can have $\frac{1}{4}$ of the candy bar. Color in $\frac{1}{4}$ of the candy bar.

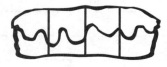

4. Mean Monster may eat $\frac{1}{3}$ of this pizza. Color in $\frac{1}{3}$ of the pizza.

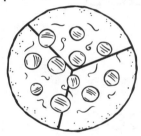

5. For lunch, Mean Monster gets $\frac{1}{2}$ of the sandwich. Color in $\frac{1}{2}$ of the sandwich.

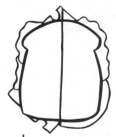

6. He ate $\frac{1}{2}$ of the apple for lunch. Color in $\frac{1}{2}$ of the apple.

Fractions: Half, Third, Fourth

Directions: Study the examples. Circle the fraction that shows the shaded part. Then, circle the fraction that shows the white part.

Examples:

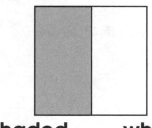

shaded   **white**

$\frac{1}{4}$ $\frac{1}{3}$ $\boxed{\frac{1}{2}}$ $\frac{1}{3}$ $\boxed{\frac{1}{2}}$ $\frac{1}{4}$

shaded   **white**

$\frac{1}{2}$ $\boxed{\frac{2}{3}}$ $\frac{3}{4}$ $\frac{2}{3}$ $\frac{1}{2}$ $\boxed{\frac{1}{3}}$

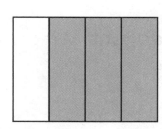

shaded   **white**

$\frac{1}{4}$ $\frac{1}{2}$ $\boxed{\frac{3}{4}}$ $\boxed{\frac{1}{4}}$ $\frac{2}{3}$ $\frac{1}{2}$

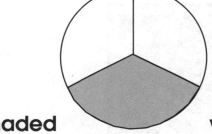

shaded   **white**

$\frac{1}{4}$ $\frac{1}{3}$ $\frac{1}{2}$ $\frac{2}{4}$ $\frac{2}{3}$ $\frac{2}{2}$

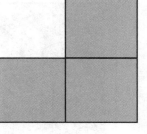

shaded   **white**

$\frac{3}{4}$ $\frac{1}{3}$ $\frac{3}{2}$ $\frac{1}{2}$ $\frac{1}{4}$ $\frac{1}{3}$

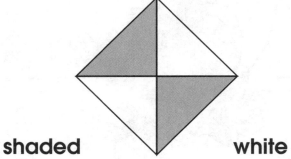

shaded   **white**

$\frac{2}{3}$ $\frac{2}{4}$ $\frac{2}{2}$ $\frac{1}{3}$ $\frac{2}{4}$ $\frac{2}{2}$

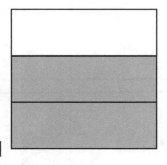

shaded   **white**

$\frac{1}{3}$ $\frac{2}{3}$ $\frac{2}{2}$ $\frac{1}{2}$ $\frac{1}{4}$ $\frac{1}{3}$

Fractions

One morning, Mrs. Murky asks her class:

"Which would you rather have, $\frac{1}{2}$ of a candy bar or $\frac{2}{4}$ of a candy bar?"

Directions: Which would you rather have? Explain your answer.

_____

_____

Fractions

Directions: Rodney, Jed, and Ursula had a pizza party. They ordered 1 large fish-eye pizza and 1 large toadstool pizza. Draw lines through the pizzas to divide them equally into slices. Color the pizza slices in 3 colors, 1 for each monster, to show how many slices each monster gets.

How many slices will each monster get? _____

Clocks: Identifying Parts

Directions: A clock face has numbers. Trace the numbers on the clock.

Writing the Time

An hour is sixty minutes long. It takes an hour for the BIG HAND to go around the clock. When the BIG HAND is on 12, and the little hand points to a number, that is the hour!

Directions: The **BIG HAND** is on the **12**. Color it **red**. The **little hand** is on the **8**. Color it **blue**.

The **BIG HAND** is on _____ .

The **little hand** is on _____ .

It is _____ o'clock.

Writing the Time

Directions: Color the little hour hand **red**. Fill in the blanks.

The **BIG HAND** is on _____ .

The **little hand** is on _____ .

It is _____ o'clock.

The **BIG HAND** is on _____ .

The **little hand** is on _____ .

It is _____ o'clock.

The **BIG HAND** is on _____ .

The **little hand** is on _____ .

It is _____ o'clock.

The **BIG HAND** is on _____ .

The **little hand** is on _____ .

It is _____ o'clock.

Name _____

Practice

Directions: What is the time?

_____ o'clock

_____ o'clock

_____ o'clock

_____ o'clock

_____ o'clock

_____ o'clock

_____ o'clock

_____ o'clock

_____ o'clock

_____ o'clock

_____ o'clock

_____ o'clock

Matching Digital and Face Clocks

Long ago, there were only wind-up clocks. Today, we also have electric and battery clocks. We may soon have solar clocks!

Directions: Match the digital and face clocks that show the same time.

Writing Time on the Half-Hour

Directions: Write the times.

Half-hour later

_____

_____ minutes past

_____ o'clock

Half-hour later

_____

_____ minutes past

_____ o'clock

What is your dinner time?

Directions: Circle the time you eat.

Total Math Grade 2

239

Telling Time

Writing Time on the Half-Hour

Directions: What time is it?

half past _____

half past _____

half past _____

half past _____

half past _____

half past _____

Time to the Quarter-Hour: Introduction

Each **hour** has **60** minutes. An **hour** has
4 quarter-hours. A **quarter-hour** is
15 minutes.

This clock face shows
a quarter of an hour.

From the **12** to the
3 is **15 minutes**.

From the 12 to the 3 is 15 minutes.

___15___ minutes after ___8___ o'clock

is ___8:15___

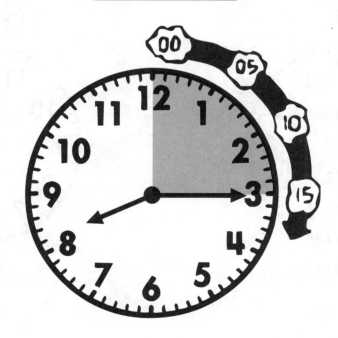

Writing Time on the Half-Hour

Directions: Draw the hands. Write the times.

5:15

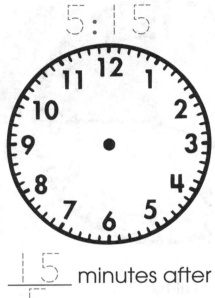

_15_ minutes after

_5_ o'clock

10:15

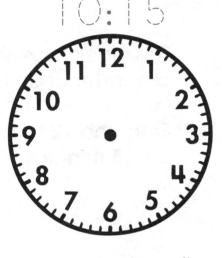

_____ minutes after

_____ o'clock

2:15

_____ minutes after

_____ o'clock

9:15

_____ minutes after

_____ o'clock

Time to the Minute Intervals: Introduction

Each **number** on the clock face stands for **5** minutes.

Directions: Count by **5s** beginning at the **12**.
Write the numbers here:

__00__ 05 10 15 20 25

It is __25__ minutes after __8__
o'clock. It is written 8:25.

Directions: Count by **5s.**

__00__ ___ ___ ___ ___ ___ ___ ___

It is _____ minutes after _____ o'clock.

_____ : _____

Drawing the Minute Hand

Directions: Draw the hands on these fish clocks.

7:45   8:05   11:15

3:20   5:55   1:50

12:10   10:25   4:40

Name _____

Counting Pennies

Directions: Count the pennies.
How many cents?

Example:

   = **4¢**

        = ▢

     = ▢

    = ▢

        = ▢

      = ▢

        = ▢

  = ▢

         = ▢

Total Math Grade 2   245   Money

Counting Pennies

Directions: Count the pennies in each triangle.

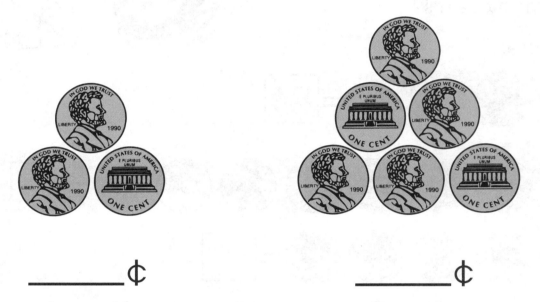

_____ ¢

_____ ¢

_____ ¢

Nickels: Introduction

Directions: Look at the two sides of a nickel. Color the nickels silver.

front   back

_____1_____ nickel = _____5_____ pennies

_____1_____ nickel = _____5_____ cents

_____1_____ nickel = _____5_____ ¢

Directions: Write the number of cents in a nickel.

5¢ = _____¢ + _____¢ + _____¢ + _____¢ + _____¢

Nickels: Counting by Fives

Directions: Count the nickels by 5s. Write the amount.

Example:

PICKLES 5¢ each

5 cents = 1 nickel

$$\boxed{15}\ ¢$$

$$\boxed{}\ ¢$$

Count __5__ , __10__ , __15__ .

$$\boxed{}\ ¢$$

Count ___ , ___ .

$$\boxed{}\ ¢$$

Count ___ , ___ , ___ ,
___ .

Count ___ , ___ , ___ , ___ ,
___ , ___ .

$$\boxed{}\ ¢$$

$$\boxed{}\ ¢$$

Count ___ , ___ , ___ ,
___ .

Count ___ , ___ , ___ ,
___ , ___ , ___ .

Dimes: Introduction

A dime is small, but quite strong. It can buy more than a penny or a nickel.

front   back

Directions: Each side of a dime is different. It has ridges on its edge. Color the dime **silver**.

Directions: Write the number of cents in a dime.

_____ dime   =   _____ pennies

_____ dime   =   _____ cents

_____ dime   =   _____ ¢

Dimes: Counting by Tens

Directions: Count by 10s. Write the number. Circle the group with more.

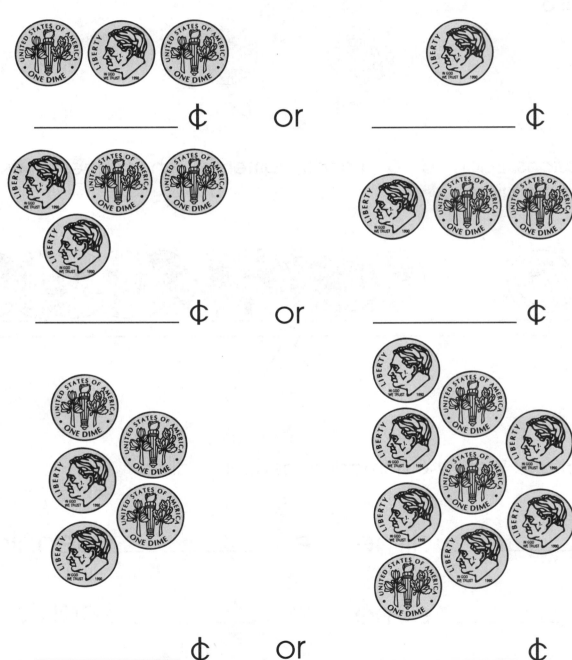

_____ ¢   or   _____ ¢

_____ ¢   or   _____ ¢

_____ ¢   or   _____ ¢

Name _____

Counting With Dimes, Nickels, and Pennies

Directions: Count the money. Start with the dime. Write the amount.

1.

_____ ¢

2.

_____ ¢

3. Circle the answer.
    Who has more money?

Quarters: Introduction

Our first president, George Washington, is on the front. The American eagle is on the back.

front   back

Directions: Write the number of cents in a quarter.

_____ quarter = _____ pennies

_____ quarter = _____ cents

_____ quarter = _____ ¢

Directions: Count these nickels by 5s. Is this another way to make 25¢?

yes   no

Counting With Quarters

These are some machines that use quarters.

Directions: Color each machine you have to put quarters into.
Circle the number of quarters you need.

I need _____ quarters to wash clothes.

I need _____ quarter(s) to make a phone call.

Counting With Quarters, Dimes, Nickels, and Pennies

Directions: Match the money with the amount.

35 ¢

36 ¢

40 ¢

27 ¢

15 ¢

21 ¢

8 ¢

Name _____

Counting With Quarters, Dimes, Nickels, and Pennies

Here are things to buy for your hair.

Directions: How many of each coin do you need?
Write 1, 2, 3, or 4.

	Quarters	Dimes	Nickels	Pennies

Subtracting for Change

Adam wanted to know how much change he would have left when he bought things. He made this picture to help him subtract.

4 dimes
− 1 dime
_____
3 dimes

40 ¢
− 10 ¢
_____
30 ¢

Directions: Cross out and subtract.

6 dimes
− 4 dimes
_____
  dimes

60 ¢
− 40 ¢
_____
   ¢

Problem-Solving With Money

Directions: Draw the coins you use. Write the number of coins on each blank.

1.

9¢

_____ dimes

_____ nickels

_____ pennies

2.

11¢

_____ dimes

_____ nickels

_____ pennies

3.

14¢

_____ dimes

_____ nickels

_____ pennies

4. Find another way to pay for the

14¢

_____ dimes

_____ nickels

_____ pennies

Problem-Solving With Money

Directions: Draw the coins you use. Write the number of coins on each blank.

1.

(35¢)

_____ quarters

_____ dimes

_____ nickels

_____ pennies

2.

(29¢)

_____ quarters

_____ dimes

_____ nickels

_____ pennies

3.

(43¢)

_____ quarters

_____ dimes

_____ nickels

_____ pennies

4. Find another way to pay for the

(43¢)

_____ quarters

_____ dimes

_____ nickels

_____ pennies

Name _____.

Making Exact Amounts of Money: Two Ways to Pay

Directions: Find two ways to pay. Show what coins you use.

27¢

1.

_____ quarters

_____ dimes

_____ nickels

_____ pennies

2.

_____ quarters

_____ dimes

_____ nickels

_____ pennies

32¢

3.

_____ quarters

_____ dimes

_____ nickels

_____ pennies

4.

_____ quarters

_____ dimes

_____ nickels

_____ pennies

Name _____

Making Exact Amounts of Money: Two Ways to Pay

Directions: Find two ways to pay. Show what coins you use.

50¢

1.

_____ quarters

_____ dimes

_____ nickels

_____ pennies

2.

_____ quarters

_____ dimes

_____ nickels

_____ pennies

65¢

3.

_____ quarters

_____ dimes

_____ nickels

_____ pennies

4.

_____ quarters

_____ dimes

_____ nickels

_____ pennies

Making Exact Amounts of Money: How Much More?

Directions: Count the coins. Find out how much more money you need to pay the exact amount.

How much money do you have? _____¢

How much more money do you need? _____¢

How much money do you have? _____¢

How much more money do you need? _____¢

Solve this puzzle.

How much more money does Monkey need?

_____¢

I have 1 quarter and 4 dimes. I need one more coin to pay for the banana-van.

Glossary

Addition: "Putting together," or adding, two or more numbers to find the sum. For example: 3 + 5 = 8.

Circle: A figure that is round.

Classifying: Putting similar things into groups or categories.

Comparing: Looking at two numbers to determine which is larger and which is smaller.

Counting: Naming or writing numbers in sequence.

Diamond: A figure with four sides of the same length.

Difference: The answer in a subtraction problem.

Digit: The symbols used to write numbers: 0, 1, 2, 3, 4, 5, 6, 7, 8, and 9.

Dime: A coin which is worth ten cents. It is written 10¢ or $.10.

Dollar: A bill which is worth one hundred cents. It is written $1.00.

Estimate: Determining an approximate number or amount before counting or measuring to find the actual number or amount.

Fact Family: A group of three numbers in which the two smaller numbers are the addends.

Fractions: Equal parts of a whole designated by symbols like $\frac{1}{2}$ and $\frac{3}{4}$.

Geometry: The study of lines and shapes in mathematics.

Graph: A diagram that shows the relationship between two or more sets of objects with a series of lines, bars, or pictures.

Measurement: The process of determining size, quantity, or amount.

Multiplication: A short way to find the sum of adding the same number a certain number of times.

Nickel: A coin which is worth five cents. It is written 5¢ or $.05.

Ordinal Numbers: Numbers that show place or order in a series, such as first, second, third, etc.

Oval: A figure that is egg-shaped.

Pattern: A repeated arrangement of numbers, shapes, or pictures.

Penny: A coin which is worth one cent. It is written 1¢ or $.01.

Place Value: Where a digit or numeral is in the number.
In the number **23**, **2** has the place value of **tens** and **3** is **ones.**

Quarter: A coin which is worth twenty-five cents. It is written 25¢ or $.25.

Rectangle: A figure with four corners and four sides. The sides opposite each other are the same length.

Sequencing: Putting numbers in the correct order.

Sorting: To organize or arrange objects in groups by similar properties.

Square: A figure with four corners and four sides of the same length.

Subtraction: "Taking away," or subtracting, one number from another.

Sum: The answer in an addition problem.

Telling Time: The ability to look at a clock and read or write the time in minutes before or after the hour.

Triangle: A figure with three corners and three sides.

Page 4

Dapper Dog's Campout

Directions: Dapper Dog is going on a camping trip. Draw an **X** on the word in each row that does not belong.

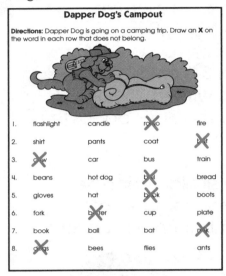

1.	flashlight	candle	~~radio~~	fire
2.	shirt	pants	coat	~~hat~~
3.	~~cow~~	car	bus	train
4.	beans	hot dog	~~ball~~	bread
5.	gloves	hat	~~book~~	boots
6.	fork	~~butter~~	cup	plate
7.	book	ball	bat	~~ink~~
8.	~~dogs~~	bees	flies	ants

Page 5

Classification Fun

Directions: Write each word in the correct row at the bottom of the page.

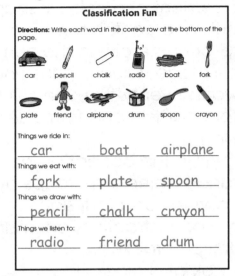

car   pencil   chalk   radio   boat   fork
plate   friend   airplane   drum   spoon   crayon

Things we ride in:
car   boat   airplane

Things we eat with:
fork   plate   spoon

Things we draw with:
pencil   chalk   crayon

Things we listen to:
radio   friend   drum

Page 6

Where Does It Belong?

Directions: Read the words in the fish tank. Write each word in its correct place.

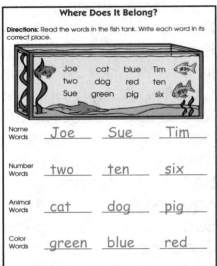

Joe   cat   blue   Tim
two   dog   red   ten
Sue   green   pig   six

Name Words	Joe	Sue	Tim
Number Words	two	ten	six
Animal Words	cat	dog	pig
Color Words	green	blue	red

Page 7

Classifying

Directions: The words in each list form a group. Choose the word from the box that describes each group and write it on the line.

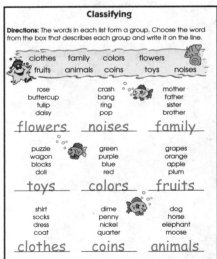

clothes   family   colors   flowers
fruits   animals   coins   toys   noises

rose	crash	mother
buttercup	bang	father
tulip	ring	sister
daisy	pop	brother
flowers	noises	family

puzzle	green	grapes
wagon	purple	orange
blocks	blue	apple
doll	red	plum
toys	colors	fruits

shirt	dime	dog
socks	penny	horse
dress	nickel	elephant
coat	quarter	moose
clothes	coins	animals

Page 8

Classifying: A Rainy Day

Directions: Read the story. Then, circle the objects Jonathan needs to stay dry.

It is raining. Jonathan wants to play outdoors. What should he wear to stay dry? What should he carry to stay dry?

Page 9

Classifying: Outdoor/Indoor Games

Classifying is putting things that are alike into groups.

Directions: Read about games. Draw an **X** on the games you can play indoors. Circle the objects used for outdoor games.

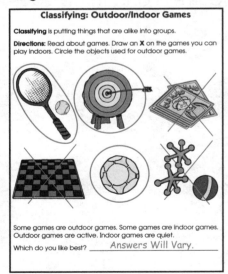

Some games are outdoor games. Some games are indoor games. Outdoor games are active. Indoor games are quiet.

Which do you like best? _____Answers Will Vary._____

Page 10

Classifying: Art Tools

Directions: Read about art tools. Then, color only the art tools.

Andrea uses different art tools to help her design her masterpieces. To cut, she needs scissors. To draw, she needs a pencil. To color, she needs crayons. To paint, she needs a brush.

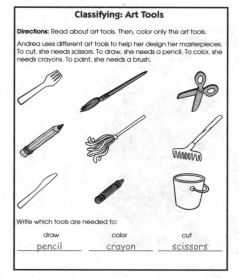

Write which tools are needed to:

draw	color	cut
pencil	crayon	scissors

Page 11

Classifying: Foods

Darcy likes fruit and things made from fruit. She also likes bread.

Directions: Circle the things on the menu that Darcy will eat.

MENU

- (apple pie)   corn
- peas   (rolls)
- beans   (banana bread)
- (oranges)   (grape drink)
- chicken

Page 12

Classifying: Animal Habitats

Directions: Read the story. Then, write each animal's name under **WATER** or **LAND** to tell where it lives.

Animals live in different habitats. A **habitat** is the place of an animal's natural home. Many animals live on land and others live in water. Most animals that live in water breathe with gills. Animals that live on land breathe with lungs.

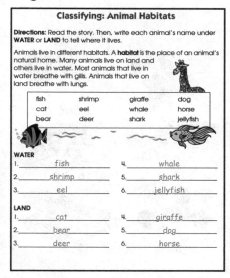

fish	shrimp	giraffe	dog
cat	eel	whale	horse
bear	deer	shark	jellyfish

WATER
1. fish
2. shrimp
3. eel
4. whale
5. shark
6. jellyfish

LAND
1. cat
2. bear
3. deer
4. giraffe
5. dog
6. horse

Page 13

Dot-to-Dot Fun

Directions: Connect the dots. Color the creature.

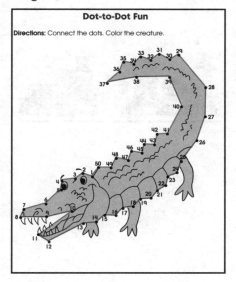

Page 14

Happy Hikers

Directions: Trace a path through the maze by counting from 1 to 10 in the correct order. Color the picture.

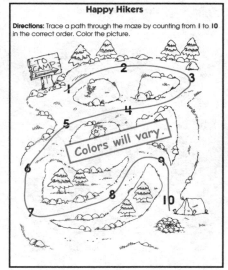

Colors will vary.

Page 15

Rainbow-Colored Numbers

Directions: Color the spaces: 1 = red, 2 = blue, 3 = yellow, 4 = green, and 5 = orange

Page 16

Food Favorites

Directions: Count the pictures in each group. Circle the number. Color the pictures.

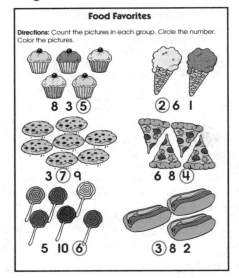

8 3 (5)   (2) 6 1

3 (7) 9   6 8 (4)

5 10 (6)   (3) 8 2

Page 17

Zany Zoo

Directions: Count and color each group of animals. Cut out the numbers and glue them in the correct boxes.

1
2
3
4
5

Colors will vary.

Page 19

Clown Capers

Directions: Count the number of each thing in the picture. Write the number on the line.

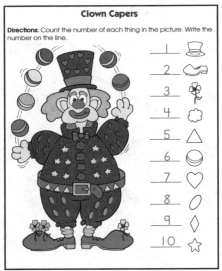

1 🎩
2 👞
3 ☘
4 ☁
5 △
6 ⬭
7 ♡
8 ⬭
9 ◇
10 ☆

Page 20

Take an Animal Count!

Directions: Count each group of zoo animals. Draw a line from the number to the correct number word. The first one shows you what to do.

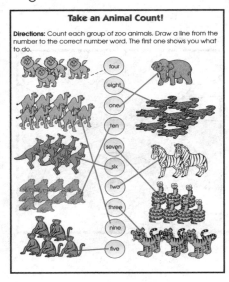

four
eight
one
ten
seven
six
two
three
nine
five

Page 21

Sheepish Shepherd

Directions: Count the sheep on the hill. Then, write that number on each tree.

Page 22

Number Words

Directions: Number the buildings from one to six.

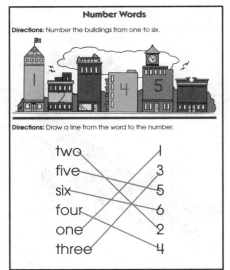

Directions: Draw a line from the word to the number.

two   1
five   3
six   5
four   6
one   2
three   4

Page 23

Number Words

Directions: Number the buildings from five to ten.

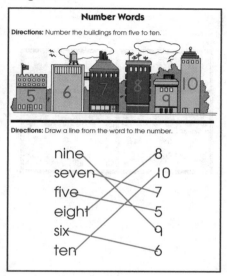

Directions: Draw a line from the word to the number.

nine — 6
seven — 7
five — 5
eight — 8
six — 9
ten — 10

Page 24

Number Words

Directions: Write each number beside the correct picture. Then, write it again.

| one | two | three | four | five | six | seven | eight | nine | ten |

Example:

six — six
three — three
two — two
nine — nine
four — four
seven — seven
five — five
one — one
eight — eight

Page 25

Sequencing Numbers

Sequencing is putting numbers in the correct order.

Directions: Write the missing numbers.

Example: 4, _5_, 6

3, _4_, 5   7, _8_, 9   8, _9_, 10
6, _7_, 8   _2_, 3, 4   _4_, 5, 6
5, 6, _7_   _5_, 6, 7   _2_, 3, 4
_8_, 9, 10   _6_, 7, 8   2, _3_, 4
2, 3, _4_   1, 2, _3_   7, 8, _9_
2, _3_, 4   _6_, 7, 8   4, _5_, 6
6, 7, _8_   2, 3, _4_   1, _2_, 3
7, 8, _9_   _2_, 3, 4   _8_, 9, 10

Page 26

Counting

Directions: Write the numbers that are:

next in order	one less	one greater
22, 23, _24_, _25_	_15_, 16	6, _7_
674, _675_, _676_	_246_, 247	125, _126_
227, _228_, _229_	_549_, 550	499, _500_
199, _200_, _201_	_332_, 333	750, _751_
329, _330_, _331_	_861_, 862	933, _934_

Directions: Write the missing numbers.

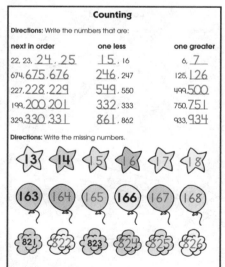

13 14 15 16 17 18

163 164 165 166 167 168

821 822 823 824 825 826

Page 27

Too Much for Mo

Directions: Count the number of each vegetable in the picture. Write the number in the correct box.

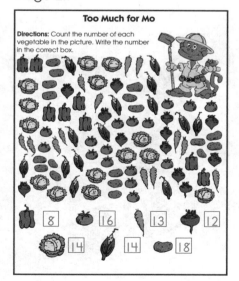

8   16   13   12
14   14   18

Page 28

Mystery Animal

Directions: Connect the dots from 1 to 75. Color the animal.

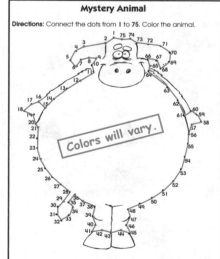

Colors will vary.

Page 29

Note the Count

Directions: Count the number of notes on each page of music. Write the number on the line below it. In each box, circle the greater number of notes.

8 6   4 7

10 9   8 9

Directions: Color the note in each box that is greater.

49 25   19 41

32 54   38 29   35 46   37 43

Page 30

Plump Piglets

Directions: Read the clues to find out how many ears of corn each pig ate. Write the number on the line below each pig.

I ate the number that comes before 26.
Patsy 25

I ate the number that comes between 87 and 89.
Horace 88

I ate the number that comes after 92.
Pinky 93

I ate the number that comes before 57.
Hilda 56

I ate the number that comes between 39 and 41.
Porky 40

Who ate the most? Pinky Who ate the least? Patsy

Page 31

Teddy Bears in a Row

Directions: Cut out the bears at the bottom of the page. Glue them where they belong in number order.

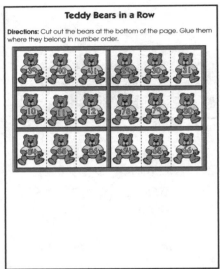

39 40 41   29 30 31
10 11 12   78 79 80
84 85 86   64 65 66

Page 33

Counting by Twos

Directions: Count by 2s to draw the path to the store.

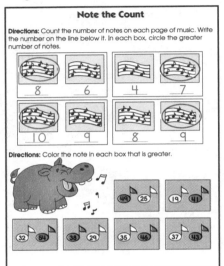

Page 34

Two for the Pool

Directions: Count by 2s. Write the numbers to 30 in the water drops. Begin at the top of the slide and go down.

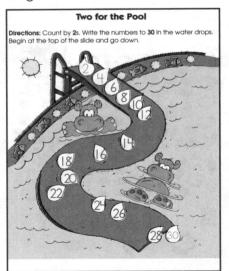

Page 35

Cookie Clues

Directions: Find out what holds something good! Count by 5s to connect the dots. Color the picture.

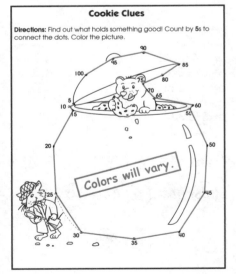

Colors will vary.

Page 36

Counting by Fives

Directions: Count by 5s to draw the path to the playground.

Page 37

I'm Counting on You

Directions: Count by 2s. Trace and write the numbers below.

2 4 6 8 10 12 14 16 18 20

Directions: Count by 5s. Trace and write the numbers below.

5 10 15 20 25 30 35 40 45 50

Directions: Count by 2s.
Connect the dots.
Color the picture.

Directions: Count by 5s.
Connect the dots.
Color the picture.

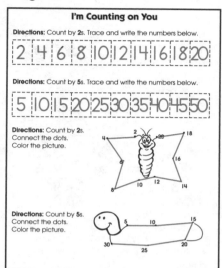

Page 38

Desert Trek

Directions: Count by 10s. Color each canteen with a 10 to lead the camel to the watering hole.

Page 39

Caterpillar Count

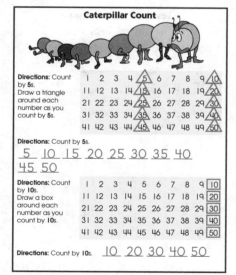

Directions: Count by 5s. Draw a triangle around each number as you count by 5s.

1	2	3	4	5	6	7	8	9	10
11	12	13	14	15	16	17	18	19	20
21	22	23	24	25	26	27	28	29	30
31	32	33	34	35	36	37	38	39	40
41	42	43	44	45	46	47	48	49	50

Directions: Count by 5s.

5 10 15 20 25 30 35 40
45 50

Directions: Count by 10s. Draw a box around each number as you count by 10s.

1	2	3	4	5	6	7	8	9	10
11	12	13	14	15	16	17	18	19	20
21	22	23	24	25	26	27	28	29	30
31	32	33	34	35	36	37	38	39	40
41	42	43	44	45	46	47	48	49	50

Directions: Count by 10s. 10 20 30 40 50

Page 40

Counting by Twos, Fives, and Tens

Directions: Write the missing numbers.

Count by 2s.

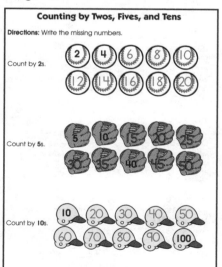

Count by 5s.

Count by 10s.

Page 41

Critter Count

Directions: Count by 2s, 5s, and 10s to find the "critter count."

Each worm = 2. Count by 2s to find the total.

= 10

= 16

Each turtle = 5. Count by 5s to find the total.

= 20

= 35

Each ladybug = 10. Count by 10s to find the total.

= 50

= 60

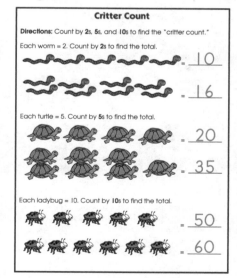

Page 43

Largest and Smallest

Directions: In each shape, circle the smallest number. Draw a square around the largest number.

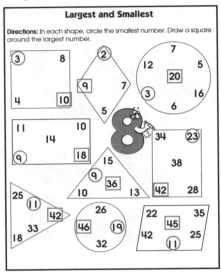

Page 44

Fishing for Answers

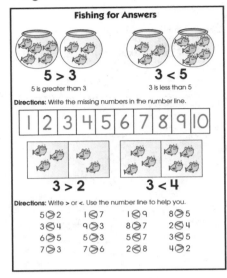

5 > 3

5 is greater than 3

3 < 5

3 is less than 5

Directions: Write the missing numbers in the number line.

| 1 | 2 | 3 | 4 | 5 | 6 | 7 | 8 | 9 | 10 |

3 > 2   3 < 4

Directions: Write > or <. Use the number line to help you.

5 > 2	1 < 7	1 < 9	8 > 5
3 < 4	9 > 3	8 > 7	2 < 4
6 > 5	5 > 3	5 < 7	3 < 5
7 > 3	7 > 6	2 < 8	4 > 2

Page 45

"Mouth" Math

Directions: Write < or > in each circle. Make sure the "mouth" is open toward the greater number!

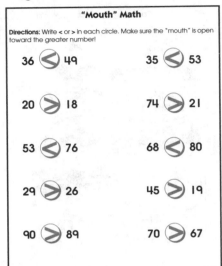

36 < 49   35 < 53

20 > 18   74 > 21

53 < 76   68 < 80

29 > 26   45 > 19

90 > 89   70 > 67

Page 46

Who Has the Most?

Directions: Circle the correct answer.

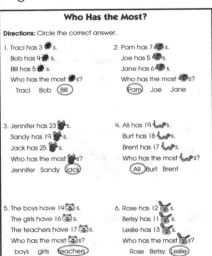

1. Traci has 3 🐞s.
   Bob has 4 🐞s.
   Bill has 5 🐞s.
   Who has the most 🐞s?
   Traci   Bob   **Bill**

2. Pam has 7 🐝s.
   Joe has 5 🐝s.
   Jane has 6 🐝s.
   Who has the most 🐝s?
   Pam   Joe   Jane

3. Jennifer has 23 🐾s.
   Sandy has 19 🐾s.
   Jack has 25 🐾s.
   Who has the most 🐾s?
   Jennifer   Sandy   **Jack**

4. Ali has 19 🐛s.
   Burt has 18 🐛s.
   Brent has 17 🐛s.
   Who has the most 🐛s?
   Ali   Burt   Brent

5. The boys have 14 🐶s.
   The girls have 16 🐶s.
   The teachers have 17 🐶s.
   Who has the most 🐶s?
   boys   girls   **teachers**

6. Rose has 12 🐰s.
   Betsy has 11 🐰s.
   Leslie has 13 🐰s.
   Who has the most 🐰s?
   Rose   Betsy   **Leslie**

Page 47

Who Has the Fewest?

Directions: Circle the correct answer.

1. Pat had 4 ⚽s.
   Charles had 3 ⚽s.
   Andrea had 5 ⚽s.
   Who had the fewest number of ⚽s?
   Pat   **Charles**   Andrea

2. Jeff has 5 🏀s.
   John has 4 🏀s.
   Bill has 6 🏀s.
   Who has the fewest number of 🏀s?
   Jeff   **John**   Bill

3. Jane has 7 ⚫s.
   Susan has 9 ⚫s.
   Fred has 8 ⚫s.
   Who has the fewest number of ⚫s?
   Jane   Susan   Fred

4. Charles bought 12 ⚪s.
   Rose bought 6 ⚪s.
   Dawn bought 24 ⚪s.
   Who bought the fewest number of ⚪s?
   Charles   **Rose**   Dawn

5. John had 9 🏈s.
   Jack had 8 🏈s.
   Mark had 7 🏈s.
   Who had the fewest number of 🏈s?
   John   Jack   **Mark**

6. Edith bought 12 ⊗s.
   Michelle bought 16 ⊗s.
   Marty bought 13 ⊗s.
   Who bought the fewest number of ⊗s?
   Edith   Michelle   Marty

Page 48

Less Than, Greater Than

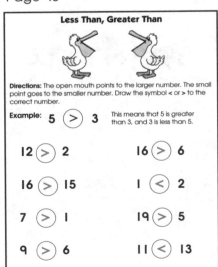

Directions: The open mouth points to the larger number. The small point goes to the smaller number. Draw the symbol < or > to the correct number.

Example: 5 > 3

This means that 5 is greater than 3, and 3 is less than 5.

12 > 2   16 > 6

16 > 15   1 < 2

7 > 1   19 > 5

9 > 6   11 < 13

Page 49

Have a Ball!

Directions: Color the second ball brown.

Color the sixth ball yellow.

Color the fourth ball orange.

Color the first ball **black**.

Color the fifth ball green.

Color the seventh ball purple.

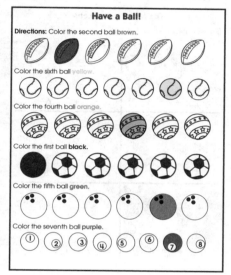

Page 50

Swimming in Style!

Directions: Color the swimsuits. The first person is wearing a yellow mask.

Color the fourth suit brown.
Color the second suit purple.
Color the first suit red.
Color the seventh suit pink.
Color the third suit blue.
Color the eighth suit green.
Color the fifth suit orange.
Color the sixth suit yellow.

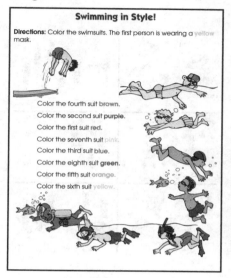

Page 51

Orderly Ordinals

Directions: Write each word on the correct line to put the words in order.

second	fifth	seventh	first	tenth
third	eighth	sixth	fourth	ninth

1. first
2. second
3. third
4. fourth
5. fifth
6. sixth
7. seventh
8. eighth
9. ninth
10. tenth

Directions: Which picture is circled in each row? Underline the word that tells the correct number.

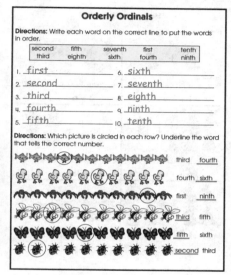

third   <u>fourth</u>

fourth   <u>sixth</u>

first   <u>ninth</u>

<u>third</u>   fifth

<u>fifth</u>   sixth

<u>second</u>   third

Page 52

Which Place in the Race?

Directions: Write the correct word to tell each runner's place in the race.

fifth
first
fourth
third
seventh
second
sixth

Page 53

Flags First

Directions:
Color the ninth flag red.
Write **O** on the second flag.
Color the eighth flag blue.
Write **D** on the first flag.
Color the sixth flag yellow.
Write **G** on the fourth flag.
Color the tenth flag purple.
Write **O** on the third flag.
Color the seventh flag green.
Color the fifth flag orange.
What word did you spell? _Good_

Page 54

How Many Robots in All?

Directions: Look at the pictures. Complete the addition sentences.

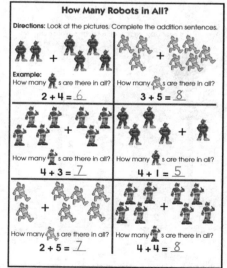

Example:
How many 🤖s are there in all?
2 + 4 = 6

How many 🤖s are there in all?
3 + 5 = 8

How many 🤖s are there in all?
4 + 3 = 7

How many 🤖s are there in all?
4 + 1 = 5

How many 🤖s are there in all?
2 + 5 = 7

How many 🤖s are there in all?
4 + 4 = 8

Total Math Grade 2

271

Answer Key

Page 55

How Many Rabbits?

Directions: Look at the pictures. Complete the addition sentences.

Example:

How many 🐰s are there in all?

$1 + 1 = 2$

How many 🐰s are there in all?

$3 + 6 = 9$

How many 🐰s are there in all?

$6 + 1 = 7$

How many 🐰s are there in all?

$3 + 4 = 7$

How many 🐰s are there in all?

$4 + 5 = 9$

How many 🐰s are there in all?

$2 + 3 = 5$

Page 56

Alien Problems

Directions: Look at the pictures. Complete the addition sentences.

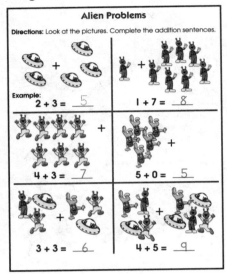

Example:

$2 + 3 = 5$

$1 + 7 = 8$

$4 + 3 = 7$

$5 + 0 = 5$

$3 + 3 = 6$

$4 + 5 = 9$

Page 57

The Missing Chickens

Directions: Draw the missing pictures. Complete the addition sentences.

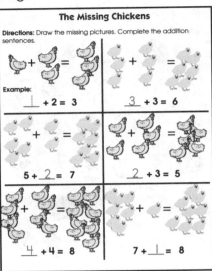

Example:

$1 + 2 = 3$

$3 + 3 = 6$

$5 + 2 = 7$

$2 + 3 = 5$

$4 + 4 = 8$

$7 + 1 = 8$

Page 58

Signs of Gain

Directions: Roll a die. Write the addend from the die in the top box. Add to find the sum. Roll again to make each sentence different.

Answers will vary.

Page 59

How Many in All?

Directions: Count the number in each group and write the number on the line. Then, add the groups together and write the sum.

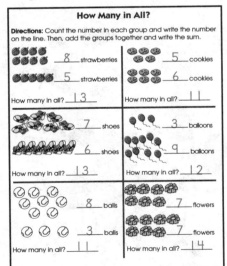

8 strawberries
5 strawberries
How many in all? 13

5 cookies
6 cookies
How many in all? 11

7 shoes
6 shoes
How many in all? 13

3 balloons
9 balloons
How many in all? 12

8 balls
3 balls
How many in all? 11

7 flowers
7 flowers
How many in all? 14

Page 60

Adding 1

Directions: Write a number in the top box of each problem. Complete the problem. Make each problem different.

Answers will vary.

Page 61

Counting Up

Directions: Count up to get the sum. Write the missing addend in each blank.

3 + _3_ = 6
4 + _1_ = 5
7 + _2_ = 9
2 + _2_ = 4
3 + _5_ = 8
5 + _0_ = 5
8 + _2_ = 10
7 + _1_ = 8
6 + _3_ = 9

8 + _1_ = 9
4 + _2_ = 6
6 + _0_ = 6
5 + _2_ = 7
4 + _3_ = 7
9 + _1_ = 10
5 + _3_ = 8
7 + _3_ = 10
6 + _2_ = 8

Page 62

Animal Addition

Directions: Add to find the sum. **Example:**

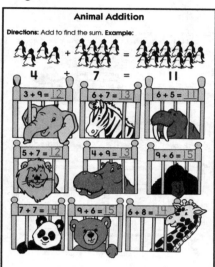

4 + 7 = 11

3 + 9 = 12
6 + 7 = 13
6 + 5 = 11
5 + 7 = 12
4 + 9 = 13
9 + 6 = 15
7 + 7 = 14
9 + 6 = 15
6 + 8 = 14

Page 63

It's All the Same

Directions: Count the objects and fill in the blanks. Then, switch the addends and write another addition sentence.

Example:

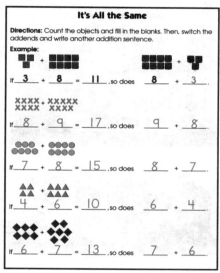

If _3_ + _8_ = _11_, so does _8_ + _3_.

If _8_ + _9_ = _17_, so does _9_ + _8_.

If _7_ + _8_ = _15_, so does _8_ + _7_.

If _4_ + _6_ = _10_, so does _6_ + _4_.

If _6_ + _7_ = _13_, so does _7_ + _6_.

Page 64

Add the Apples

Directions: Match the addition sentences with their sums.

3 + 2   10
6 + 8   14
5 + 5   5

8 + 2   15
9 + 6   4
2 + 2   10

1 + 2   11
6 + 7   3
5 + 6   13

6 + 6   12
6 + 3   9
3 + 4   7

6 + 2   8
1 + 1   13
1 + 5   2

7 + 2   15
6 + 9   13
12 + 1   13

10 + 1   14
9 + 5   13
7 + 1   11

Page 65

Target Practice

Directions: Add the numbers from the inside out. The first one has been done for you.

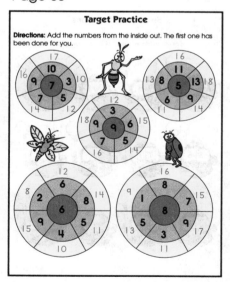

Page 66

Ride the Rapids

Directions: Write each problem on the life jacket with the correct answer.

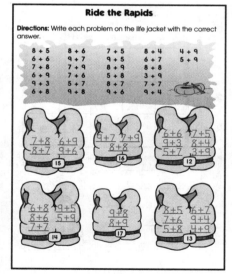

8 + 5   8 + 6   7 + 5   8 + 4   4 + 9
6 + 6   9 + 7   9 + 5   6 + 7   5 + 9
7 + 8   7 + 9   8 + 9   8 + 8
6 + 9   7 + 6   5 + 8   3 + 9
9 + 3   5 + 7   8 + 7   7 + 7
6 + 8   9 + 8   9 + 6   9 + 4

Page 67

Math-Minded Mermaids

Directions: Look at each number. Then, look in each seashell. Circle each pair of numbers that can be added together to equal that number.

Page 68

Ancient Adding

Directions: Roll a pair of dice. Write the addend from each die on the lines below. Add to find the sum. Roll again to make each sentence different.

Answers will vary.

Page 69

Lots of Number Partners

Directions: Connect as many pairs as you can to make each sum.

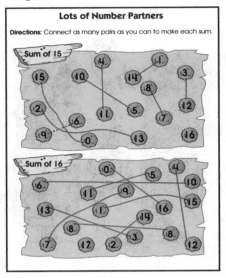

Page 70

Solve the Riddle

Directions: Add to find the sums. Connect the dots in order. Use the sums and letters from the boxes to answer the riddle.

Row 1	G 5 +3 = 8	A 6 +6 = 12	T 2 +2 = 4	W 7 +6 = 13	C 3 +2 = 5
Row 2	L 8 +8 = 16	R 7 +8 = 15	Y 5 +5 = 10	U 4 +3 = 7	E 9 +9 = 18
Row 3	N 2 +9 = 11	O 5 +4 = 9	P 9 +8 = 17	I 6 +8 = 14	E 1 +2 = 3

RIDDLE: What will you get when you cross an eel and a goat?

Y O U   W I L L
10 8 7   16 10 16

G E T   A N
8 18 4   6 11

E L E C T R I C
3 16 18 5 4 15 14 5

C A N
5 12 11

O P E N E R
9 17 18 11 18 15

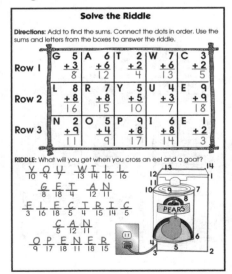

Page 71

Snorkeling Solutions

Directions: Add the numbers in each mask. Write the sums in the bubbles. Color the bubbles of the four largest sums.

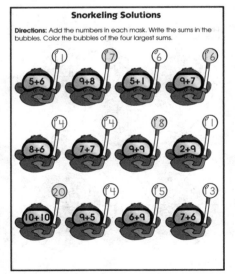

Page 72

Coloring by Number

Directions: Find each sum.
If the sum is **13**, color the space brown.
If the sum is **14**, color the space yellow.
If the sum is **16**, color the space red.
If the sum is **17**, color the space blue.

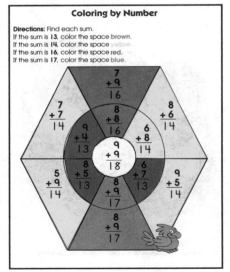

Page 73

Counting Up the Coins

Directions: Solve the problem on each bag. Write the answer on the coin below it. Color the odd sums yellow.

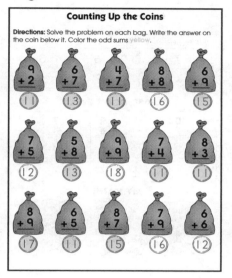

9 + 2 = 11	6 + 7 = 13	4 + 7 = 11	8 + 8 = 16	6 + 9 = 15
7 + 5 = 12	5 + 8 = 13	9 + 9 = 18	7 + 4 = 11	8 + 3 = 11
8 + 9 = 17	6 + 5 = 11	8 + 7 = 15	7 + 9 = 16	6 + 6 = 12

Page 74

Mys-sss-terious Music

Directions: Solve the problems. Color the spaces using the answers.

ANSWER COLOR KEY:

= 0 – 2
= 3 – 6
= 7 – 9
= 10 – 12
= 13 – 16
= 17 – 20

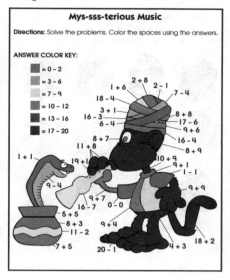

Page 75

Food Facts

Directions: Draw pictures to show what happens in each story. Solve the problem.

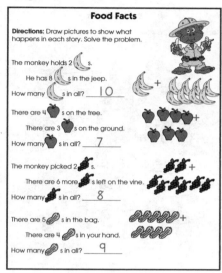

The monkey holds 2 🍌s.
He has 8 🍌s in the jeep.
How many 🍌s in all? __10__

There are 4 🍎s on the tree.
There are 3 🍎s on the ground.
How many 🍎s in all? __7__

The monkey picked 2 🍇s.
There are 6 more 🍇s left on the vine.
How many 🍇s in all? __8__

There are 5 🥜s in the bag.
There are 4 🥜s in your hand.
How many 🥜s in all? __9__

Page 76

Problem Solving

Directions: Solve each problem.

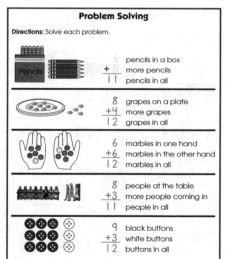

	6	pencils in a box
	+ 5	more pencils
	11	pencils in all

	8	grapes on a plate
	+4	more grapes
	12	grapes in all

	6	marbles in one hand
	+6	marbles in the other hand
	12	marbles in all

	8	people at the table
	+3	more people coming in
	11	people in all

	9	black buttons
	+3	white buttons
	12	buttons in all

Page 77

Problem Solving

Directions: Solve each problem.

Example:

	9	black sheep
	+ 9	white sheep
	18	sheep in all

	9	softballs
	+7	baseballs
	16	balls in all

	7	glasses of milkshakes
	+8	empty glasses
	15	glasses in all

	6	white socks
	+8	gray socks
	14	socks in all

	9	bow ties
	+8	regular ties
	17	ties in all

Page 78

Hop Along Numbers

Directions: Use the number line to count back.

Example: 8, __7__, __6__

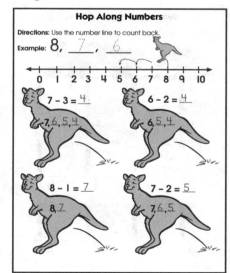

0 1 2 3 4 5 6 7 8 9 10

7 – 3 = 4
7, 6, 5, 4

6 – 2 = 4
6, 5, 4

8 – 1 = 7
8, 7

7 – 2 = 5
7, 6, 5

Page 79

Bubbly Baths

Directions: Solve the subtraction sentences below. Write each answer on a rubber duck.

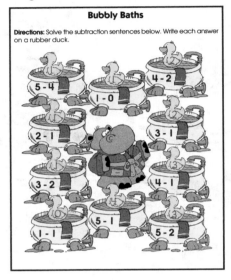

Page 80

Leaves Leaving the Limb

Directions: Subtract to find the difference. Use the code to color the leaves. Code: **0** = green **1** = red **2** = yellow **3** = brown

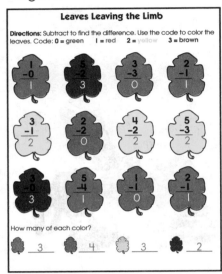

How many of each color?

🍀 3   🍀 4   🍀 3   🍀 2

Page 81

Secrets of Subtraction

Directions: Solve the subtraction problems. Use the code to find the secret message.

Code:	7	5	2	6	4	3
	K	T	Y	E	W	A

PLEASE, DON'T EVER

8 -3	10 -7	9 -2	10 -4		9 -6	6 -2	7 -4	8 -6
5	3	7	6		3	4	3	2
T	A	K	E		A	W	A	Y

MY MATH!

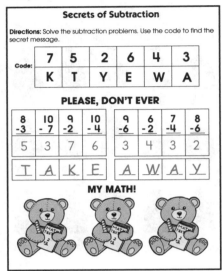

Page 82

Subtraction Makes Al Tired

Directions: Write a different problem for each answer.

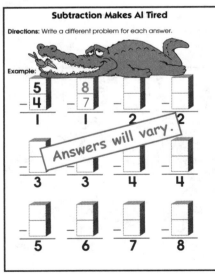

Example:

5 -4	8 -7		
1	1	2	2

Answers will vary.

3	3	4	4

5	6	7	8

Page 83

Differences in Boxes

Directions: Color the two numbers in each box that show the given difference.

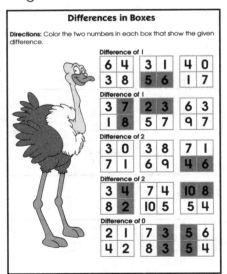

Difference of 1

6 4	3 1	4 0
3 8	5 6	1 7

Difference of 1

3 7	2 3	6 3
1 8	5 7	9 7

Difference of 2

3 0	3 8	7 1
7 1	6 9	4 6

Difference of 2

3 4	7 4	10 8
8 2	10 5	5 4

Difference of 0

2 1	7 3	5 6
4 2	8 3	5 4

Page 84

Looping Differences

Directions: Circle the two numbers next to each other that make the given difference. Find as many as you can in each row.

Difference of 1

(2 3) 0 (8 7) 2 (9 10) (6 5) 1 (4 3)

Difference of 1

8 (4 5) 3 7 (1 2) 4 (9 8) 0 (1 7) 6

Difference of 2

5 (4 2) (3 1) 0 (3 5) 8 9 3 (6 8) 5

Difference of 2

(7 5) (10 8) 1 (4 6) 3 2 6 (7 9) 2 0

Difference of 3

1 (6 3) 2 8 (4 7) 6 10 (0 3) 9 (5 2)

Page 85

Hidden Differences of 2

Directions: Circle the pairs that have a difference of 2.

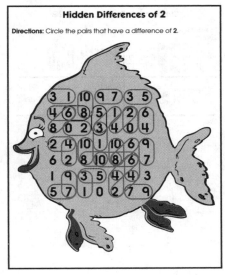

Page 86

Hidden Differences of 3

Directions: Circle the pairs that have a difference of 3.

Page 87

Hidden Differences

Directions: Find the shape with the correct difference. Copy the numbers that make that difference.

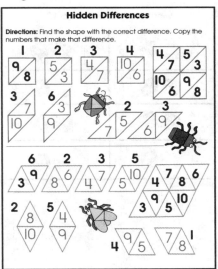

Page 88

Subtraction Fun

Directions: Subtract to find each difference.

10	7	9	8	10
−5	−2	−8	−4	−10
5	5	1	4	0

8	7	10	9	9
−3	−6	−3	−7	−1
5	1	7	2	8

9	6	10	8	10
−6	−3	−9	−5	−4
3	3	1	3	6

Page 89

A Nose for Subtraction

Directions: Cut out the elephant heads at the bottom of the page. Glue each head on the body with the correct answer.

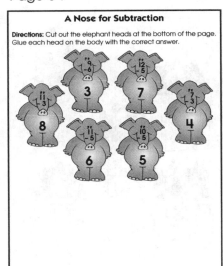

Page 91

Gone Fishing

Directions: Complete the subtraction sentences to make each problem correct.

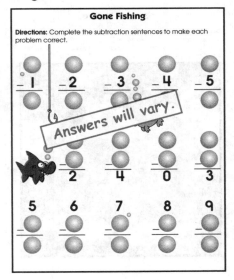

Answers will vary.

Page 92

Subtraction Facts Through 12

Directions: Subtract.

11−9=2	11−2=9	11−8=3	11−3=8
11−6=5	11−5=6	11−7=4	11−4=7
12−8=4	12−4=8	12−7=5	12−5=7
12−9=3	12−3=9	12−6=6	

Directions: Subtract.

11−3=8	11−6=5	12−3=9	11−8=3	12−7=5	12−9=3
11−7=4	12−4=8	12−5=7	12−6=6	11−2=9	12−8=4

Page 93

Subtraction Facts Through 14

Directions: Subtract.
Examples:

13−5=8	14−9=5
14−8=6	13−4=9
13−6=7	14−5=9

Directions: Subtract.

12−7=5	10−2=8	13−4=9	14−9=5	11−8=3	14−5=9
14−6=8	12−8=4	13−5=8	10−6=4	13−6=7	13−7=6
11−6=5	13−9=4	14−8=6	12−3=9	14−7=7	13−8=5

Page 94

Subtraction Facts Through 18

Directions: Subtract.
Example:

15−7=8	16−9=7
17−8=9	18−9=9

Directions: Subtract.

18−9=9	13−5=8	16−8=8	17−9=8	14−6=8	13−9=4
17−8=9	15−9=6	14−5=9	13−6=7	16−7=9	12−4=8
14−7=7	15−8=7	16−9=7	12−7=5	15−7=8	13−4=9
15−6=9	14−8=6	12−3=9	13−9=4	14−9=5	11−3=8

Page 95

"Grrreat" Picture

Directions: Subtract. Write the answer in the space. Then, color the spaces according to the answers.

1 = white	2 = purple	3 = black	4 = green	5 = yellow
6 = blue	7 = pink	8 = gray	9 = orange	10 = red

Page 96

Crayon Count

Directions: Count the crayons. Write the number on the blank. Circle the problems that equal the answer.

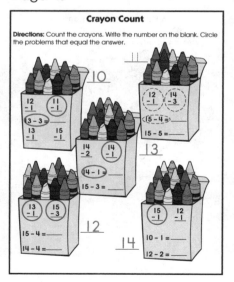

Page 97

Connect the Facts

Directions: Solve the subtraction problems below.

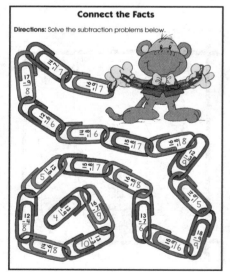

Page 98

Swamp Stories

Directions: Read the story. Subtract to find the difference. Write the number in the box.

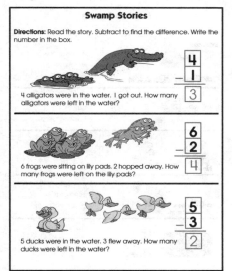

4 alligators were in the water. I got out. How many alligators were left in the water?

$$\begin{array}{r} 4 \\ -1 \\ \hline 3 \end{array}$$

6 frogs were sitting on lily pads. 2 hopped away. How many frogs were left on the lily pads?

$$\begin{array}{r} 6 \\ -2 \\ \hline 4 \end{array}$$

5 ducks were in the water. 3 flew away. How many ducks were left in the water?

$$\begin{array}{r} 5 \\ -3 \\ \hline 2 \end{array}$$

Page 99

More Animal Stories

Directions: Subtract to find the difference. Cut out the subtraction sentences and glue them in the correct boxes. Write the difference in each small box.

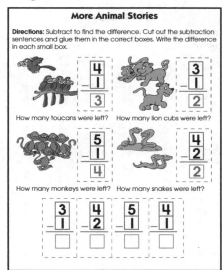

How many toucans were left?

$$\begin{array}{r} 4 \\ -1 \\ \hline 3 \end{array}$$

How many lion cubs were left?

$$\begin{array}{r} 3 \\ -1 \\ \hline 2 \end{array}$$

How many monkeys were left?

$$\begin{array}{r} 5 \\ -1 \\ \hline 4 \end{array}$$

How many snakes were left?

$$\begin{array}{r} 4 \\ -2 \\ \hline 2 \end{array}$$

$$\begin{array}{r} 3 \\ -1 \\ \hline \square \end{array} \quad \begin{array}{r} 4 \\ -2 \\ \hline \square \end{array} \quad \begin{array}{r} 5 \\ -1 \\ \hline \square \end{array} \quad \begin{array}{r} 4 \\ -1 \\ \hline \square \end{array}$$

Page 101

Facts Through 5

Directions: Add or subtract.

Examples:

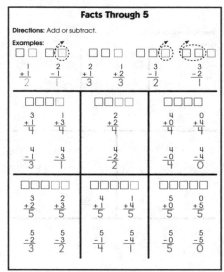

$$\begin{array}{r} 1 \\ +1 \\ \hline 2 \end{array} \quad \begin{array}{r} 2 \\ -1 \\ \hline 1 \end{array} \quad \begin{array}{r} 2 \\ +1 \\ \hline 3 \end{array} \quad \begin{array}{r} 1 \\ +2 \\ \hline 3 \end{array} \quad \begin{array}{r} 3 \\ -1 \\ \hline 2 \end{array} \quad \begin{array}{r} 3 \\ -2 \\ \hline 1 \end{array}$$

$$\begin{array}{r} 3 \\ +1 \\ \hline 4 \end{array} \quad \begin{array}{r} 1 \\ +3 \\ \hline 4 \end{array} \quad \begin{array}{r} 2 \\ +2 \\ \hline 4 \end{array} \quad \begin{array}{r} 4 \\ +0 \\ \hline 4 \end{array} \quad \begin{array}{r} 0 \\ +4 \\ \hline 4 \end{array}$$

$$\begin{array}{r} 4 \\ -1 \\ \hline 3 \end{array} \quad \begin{array}{r} 4 \\ -3 \\ \hline 1 \end{array} \quad \begin{array}{r} 4 \\ -2 \\ \hline 2 \end{array} \quad \begin{array}{r} 4 \\ -0 \\ \hline 4 \end{array} \quad \begin{array}{r} 4 \\ -4 \\ \hline 0 \end{array}$$

$$\begin{array}{r} 3 \\ +2 \\ \hline 5 \end{array} \quad \begin{array}{r} 2 \\ +3 \\ \hline 5 \end{array} \quad \begin{array}{r} 4 \\ +1 \\ \hline 5 \end{array} \quad \begin{array}{r} 1 \\ +4 \\ \hline 5 \end{array} \quad \begin{array}{r} 5 \\ +0 \\ \hline 5 \end{array} \quad \begin{array}{r} 0 \\ +5 \\ \hline 5 \end{array}$$

$$\begin{array}{r} 5 \\ -2 \\ \hline 3 \end{array} \quad \begin{array}{r} 5 \\ -3 \\ \hline 2 \end{array} \quad \begin{array}{r} 5 \\ -1 \\ \hline 4 \end{array} \quad \begin{array}{r} 5 \\ -4 \\ \hline 1 \end{array} \quad \begin{array}{r} 5 \\ -0 \\ \hline 5 \end{array} \quad \begin{array}{r} 5 \\ -5 \\ \hline 0 \end{array}$$

Page 102

Facts for 6 and 7

Directions: Add or subtract.

Examples:

$$\begin{array}{r} 5 \\ +1 \\ \hline 6 \end{array} \quad \begin{array}{r} 1 \\ +5 \\ \hline 6 \end{array} \quad \begin{array}{r} 6 \\ -1 \\ \hline 5 \end{array} \quad \begin{array}{r} 6 \\ -5 \\ \hline 1 \end{array}$$

$$\begin{array}{r} 3 \\ +3 \\ \hline 6 \end{array} \quad \begin{array}{r} 6 \\ -3 \\ \hline 3 \end{array} \quad \begin{array}{r} 4 \\ +2 \\ \hline 6 \end{array} \quad \begin{array}{r} 2 \\ +4 \\ \hline 6 \end{array} \quad \begin{array}{r} 6 \\ -2 \\ \hline 4 \end{array} \quad \begin{array}{r} 6 \\ -4 \\ \hline 2 \end{array}$$

$$\begin{array}{r} 4 \\ +3 \\ \hline 7 \end{array} \quad \begin{array}{r} 3 \\ +4 \\ \hline 7 \end{array} \quad \begin{array}{r} 5 \\ +2 \\ \hline 7 \end{array} \quad \begin{array}{r} 2 \\ +5 \\ \hline 7 \end{array} \quad \begin{array}{r} 6 \\ +1 \\ \hline 7 \end{array} \quad \begin{array}{r} 1 \\ +6 \\ \hline 7 \end{array}$$

$$\begin{array}{r} 7 \\ -3 \\ \hline 4 \end{array} \quad \begin{array}{r} 7 \\ -4 \\ \hline 3 \end{array} \quad \begin{array}{r} 7 \\ -2 \\ \hline 5 \end{array} \quad \begin{array}{r} 7 \\ -5 \\ \hline 2 \end{array} \quad \begin{array}{r} 7 \\ -1 \\ \hline 6 \end{array} \quad \begin{array}{r} 7 \\ -6 \\ \hline 1 \end{array}$$

$$\begin{array}{r} 3 \\ +3 \\ \hline 6 \end{array} \quad \begin{array}{r} 5 \\ +2 \\ \hline 7 \end{array} \quad \begin{array}{r} 6 \\ +0 \\ \hline 6 \end{array} \quad \begin{array}{r} 7 \\ -7 \\ \hline 0 \end{array} \quad \begin{array}{r} 7 \\ -4 \\ \hline 3 \end{array} \quad \begin{array}{r} 6 \\ -2 \\ \hline 4 \end{array}$$

Page 103

Facts for 8

Directions: Add or subtract.

Examples:

$$\begin{array}{r} 5 \\ +3 \\ \hline 8 \end{array} \quad \begin{array}{r} 3 \\ +5 \\ \hline 8 \end{array} \quad \begin{array}{r} 8 \\ -3 \\ \hline 5 \end{array} \quad \begin{array}{r} 8 \\ -5 \\ \hline 3 \end{array}$$

$$\begin{array}{r} 4 \\ +4 \\ \hline 8 \end{array} \quad \begin{array}{r} 6 \\ +2 \\ \hline 8 \end{array} \quad \begin{array}{r} 2 \\ +6 \\ \hline 8 \end{array} \quad \begin{array}{r} 7 \\ +1 \\ \hline 8 \end{array} \quad \begin{array}{r} 1 \\ +7 \\ \hline 8 \end{array}$$

$$\begin{array}{r} 8 \\ -4 \\ \hline 4 \end{array} \quad \begin{array}{r} 8 \\ -2 \\ \hline 6 \end{array} \quad \begin{array}{r} 8 \\ -6 \\ \hline 2 \end{array} \quad \begin{array}{r} 8 \\ -1 \\ \hline 7 \end{array} \quad \begin{array}{r} 8 \\ -7 \\ \hline 1 \end{array}$$

$$\begin{array}{r} 2 \\ +8 \\ \hline 8 \end{array} \quad \begin{array}{r} 4 \\ +3 \\ \hline 7 \end{array} \quad \begin{array}{r} 5 \\ +6 \\ \hline 8 \end{array} \quad \begin{array}{r} 3 \\ +5 \\ \hline 8 \end{array} \quad \begin{array}{r} 7 \\ +1 \\ \hline 8 \end{array} \quad \begin{array}{r} 0 \\ +8 \\ \hline 8 \end{array}$$

$$\begin{array}{r} 8 \\ -1 \\ \hline 7 \end{array} \quad \begin{array}{r} 7 \\ -6 \\ \hline 1 \end{array} \quad \begin{array}{r} 8 \\ -5 \\ \hline 3 \end{array} \quad \begin{array}{r} 6 \\ -3 \\ \hline 3 \end{array} \quad \begin{array}{r} 8 \\ -0 \\ \hline 8 \end{array} \quad \begin{array}{r} 8 \\ -2 \\ \hline 6 \end{array}$$

Page 104

Facts for 9

Directions: Add or subtract.

Examples:

$$\begin{array}{r} 5 \\ +4 \\ \hline 9 \end{array} \quad \begin{array}{r} 4 \\ +5 \\ \hline 9 \end{array} \quad \begin{array}{r} 9 \\ -4 \\ \hline 5 \end{array} \quad \begin{array}{r} 9 \\ -5 \\ \hline 4 \end{array}$$

$$\begin{array}{r} 6 \\ +3 \\ \hline 9 \end{array} \quad \begin{array}{r} 3 \\ +6 \\ \hline 9 \end{array} \quad \begin{array}{r} 7 \\ +2 \\ \hline 9 \end{array} \quad \begin{array}{r} 2 \\ +7 \\ \hline 9 \end{array} \quad \begin{array}{r} 8 \\ +1 \\ \hline 9 \end{array} \quad \begin{array}{r} 1 \\ +8 \\ \hline 9 \end{array}$$

$$\begin{array}{r} 9 \\ -3 \\ \hline 6 \end{array} \quad \begin{array}{r} 9 \\ -6 \\ \hline 3 \end{array} \quad \begin{array}{r} 9 \\ -2 \\ \hline 7 \end{array} \quad \begin{array}{r} 9 \\ -7 \\ \hline 2 \end{array} \quad \begin{array}{r} 9 \\ -1 \\ \hline 8 \end{array} \quad \begin{array}{r} 9 \\ -8 \\ \hline 1 \end{array}$$

$$\begin{array}{r} 5 \\ +4 \\ \hline 9 \end{array} \quad \begin{array}{r} 2 \\ +7 \\ \hline 9 \end{array} \quad \begin{array}{r} 6 \\ +1 \\ \hline 7 \end{array} \quad \begin{array}{r} 9 \\ +0 \\ \hline 9 \end{array} \quad \begin{array}{r} 1 \\ +8 \\ \hline 9 \end{array} \quad \begin{array}{r} 4 \\ +5 \\ \hline 9 \end{array}$$

$$\begin{array}{r} 9 \\ -5 \\ \hline 4 \end{array} \quad \begin{array}{r} 7 \\ -3 \\ \hline 4 \end{array} \quad \begin{array}{r} 9 \\ -8 \\ \hline 1 \end{array} \quad \begin{array}{r} 9 \\ -3 \\ \hline 6 \end{array} \quad \begin{array}{r} 9 \\ -9 \\ \hline 0 \end{array} \quad \begin{array}{r} 9 \\ -0 \\ \hline 9 \end{array}$$

Page 105

Facts for 10

Directions: Add or subtract.

Examples:

$$\begin{array}{r}5\\+5\\\hline 10\end{array}\quad\begin{array}{r}6\\+4\\\hline 10\end{array}\quad\begin{array}{r}4\\+6\\\hline 10\end{array}\quad\begin{array}{r}7\\+3\\\hline 10\end{array}\quad\begin{array}{r}3\\+7\\\hline 10\end{array}$$

$$\begin{array}{r}10\\-5\\\hline 5\end{array}\quad\begin{array}{r}10\\-4\\\hline 6\end{array}\quad\begin{array}{r}10\\-6\\\hline 4\end{array}\quad\begin{array}{r}10\\-3\\\hline 7\end{array}\quad\begin{array}{r}10\\-7\\\hline 3\end{array}$$

$$\begin{array}{r}8\\+2\\\hline 10\end{array}\quad\begin{array}{r}2\\+8\\\hline 10\end{array}\quad\begin{array}{r}9\\+1\\\hline 10\end{array}\quad\begin{array}{r}1\\+9\\\hline 10\end{array}$$

$$\begin{array}{r}10\\-2\\\hline 8\end{array}\quad\begin{array}{r}10\\-8\\\hline 2\end{array}\quad\begin{array}{r}10\\-1\\\hline 9\end{array}\quad\begin{array}{r}10\\-9\\\hline 1\end{array}$$

$$\begin{array}{r}4\\+6\\\hline 10\end{array}\quad\begin{array}{r}5\\+5\\\hline 10\end{array}\quad\begin{array}{r}9\\+1\\\hline 10\end{array}\quad\begin{array}{r}10\\-8\\\hline 2\end{array}\quad\begin{array}{r}10\\-3\\\hline 7\end{array}\quad\begin{array}{r}10\\-0\\\hline 10\end{array}$$

Page 106

Facts Through 10

Directions: Add.

Example:

$$\begin{array}{r}5\\+4\\\hline 9\end{array}\quad\begin{array}{r}4\\+3\\\hline 7\end{array}\quad\begin{array}{r}1\\+2\\\hline 3\end{array}\quad\begin{array}{r}5\\+3\\\hline 8\end{array}\quad\begin{array}{r}4\\+6\\\hline 10\end{array}\quad\begin{array}{r}4\\+4\\\hline 8\end{array}$$

$$\begin{array}{r}0\\+6\\\hline 6\end{array}\quad\begin{array}{r}4\\+1\\\hline 5\end{array}\quad\begin{array}{r}8\\+1\\\hline 9\end{array}\quad\begin{array}{r}9\\+1\\\hline 10\end{array}\quad\begin{array}{r}8\\+2\\\hline 10\end{array}\quad\begin{array}{r}2\\+2\\\hline 4\end{array}$$

$$\begin{array}{r}2\\+7\\\hline 9\end{array}\quad\begin{array}{r}5\\+2\\\hline 7\end{array}\quad\begin{array}{r}1\\+6\\\hline 7\end{array}\quad\begin{array}{r}5\\+5\\\hline 10\end{array}\quad\begin{array}{r}4\\+5\\\hline 9\end{array}\quad\begin{array}{r}6\\+2\\\hline 8\end{array}$$

Directions: Subtract.

Example:

$$\begin{array}{r}10\\-6\\\hline 4\end{array}\quad\begin{array}{r}8\\-2\\\hline 6\end{array}\quad\begin{array}{r}5\\-3\\\hline 2\end{array}\quad\begin{array}{r}7\\-6\\\hline 1\end{array}\quad\begin{array}{r}4\\-3\\\hline 1\end{array}\quad\begin{array}{r}10\\-5\\\hline 5\end{array}$$

$$\begin{array}{r}9\\-3\\\hline 6\end{array}\quad\begin{array}{r}10\\-2\\\hline 8\end{array}\quad\begin{array}{r}7\\-2\\\hline 5\end{array}\quad\begin{array}{r}8\\-6\\\hline 2\end{array}\quad\begin{array}{r}10\\-9\\\hline 1\end{array}\quad\begin{array}{r}8\\-8\\\hline 0\end{array}$$

$$\begin{array}{r}10\\-4\\\hline 6\end{array}\quad\begin{array}{r}9\\-6\\\hline 3\end{array}\quad\begin{array}{r}9\\-8\\\hline 1\end{array}\quad\begin{array}{r}8\\-1\\\hline 7\end{array}\quad\begin{array}{r}10\\-7\\\hline 3\end{array}\quad\begin{array}{r}7\\-4\\\hline 3\end{array}$$

Page 107

Problem Solving

Directions: Solve each problem.

Example:

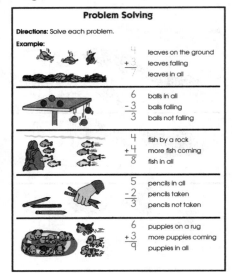

$$\begin{array}{r}4\\+3\\\hline 7\end{array}$$ leaves on the ground / leaves falling / leaves in all

$$\begin{array}{r}6\\-3\\\hline 3\end{array}$$ balls in all / balls falling / balls not falling

$$\begin{array}{r}4\\+4\\\hline 8\end{array}$$ fish by a rock / more fish coming / fish in all

$$\begin{array}{r}5\\-2\\\hline 3\end{array}$$ pencils in all / pencils taken / pencils not taken

$$\begin{array}{r}6\\+3\\\hline 9\end{array}$$ puppies on a rug / more puppies coming / puppies in all

Page 108

Checkup

Directions: Add.

$$\begin{array}{r}2\\+4\\\hline 6\end{array}\quad\begin{array}{r}7\\+3\\\hline 10\end{array}\quad\begin{array}{r}4\\+5\\\hline 9\end{array}\quad\begin{array}{r}6\\+2\\\hline 8\end{array}\quad\begin{array}{r}2\\+3\\\hline 5\end{array}\quad\begin{array}{r}0\\+4\\\hline 4\end{array}$$

$$\begin{array}{r}4\\+3\\\hline 7\end{array}\quad\begin{array}{r}1\\+5\\\hline 6\end{array}\quad\begin{array}{r}2\\+8\\\hline 10\end{array}\quad\begin{array}{r}3\\+3\\\hline 6\end{array}\quad\begin{array}{r}6\\+4\\\hline 10\end{array}\quad\begin{array}{r}2\\+1\\\hline 3\end{array}$$

$$\begin{array}{r}3\\+1\\\hline 4\end{array}\quad\begin{array}{r}7\\+0\\\hline 7\end{array}\quad\begin{array}{r}8\\+1\\\hline 9\end{array}\quad\begin{array}{r}5\\+2\\\hline 7\end{array}\quad\begin{array}{r}3\\+6\\\hline 9\end{array}\quad\begin{array}{r}5\\+5\\\hline 10\end{array}$$

Directions: Subtract.

$$\begin{array}{r}3\\-3\\\hline 0\end{array}\quad\begin{array}{r}5\\-2\\\hline 3\end{array}\quad\begin{array}{r}10\\-6\\\hline 4\end{array}\quad\begin{array}{r}9\\-2\\\hline 7\end{array}\quad\begin{array}{r}7\\-3\\\hline 4\end{array}\quad\begin{array}{r}10\\-5\\\hline 5\end{array}$$

$$\begin{array}{r}9\\-1\\\hline 8\end{array}\quad\begin{array}{r}8\\-7\\\hline 1\end{array}\quad\begin{array}{r}1\\-0\\\hline 1\end{array}\quad\begin{array}{r}6\\-4\\\hline 2\end{array}\quad\begin{array}{r}8\\-5\\\hline 3\end{array}\quad\begin{array}{r}10\\-8\\\hline 2\end{array}$$

$$\begin{array}{r}9\\-6\\\hline 3\end{array}\quad\begin{array}{r}4\\-3\\\hline 1\end{array}\quad\begin{array}{r}6\\-3\\\hline 3\end{array}\quad\begin{array}{r}7\\-5\\\hline 2\end{array}\quad\begin{array}{r}10\\-9\\\hline 1\end{array}\quad\begin{array}{r}8\\-4\\\hline 4\end{array}$$

Page 109

Addition and Subtraction Fun

Directions: Solve the number problem under each picture. Write + or – to show if you should add or subtract.

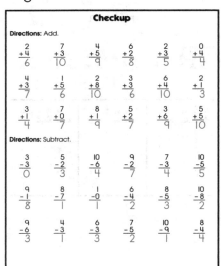

Example:
How many ⚾ s in all?
$4 + 5 = 9$

How many 🍫 s in all?
$7 + 5 = 12$

Example:
How many 🐛 s are left?
$12 - 3 = 9$

How many ⭐ s are left?
$15 - 8 = 7$

How many 🍬 s in all?
$5 + 8 = 13$

How many 🧲 s are left?
$11 - 4 = 7$

Page 110

Addition and Subtraction

Directions: Solve the number problem under each picture. Write + or – to show if you should add or subtract.

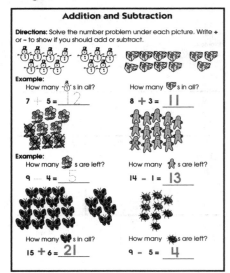

Example:
How many ⛄ s in all?
$7 + 5 = 12$

How many 🦌 s in all?
$8 + 3 = 11$

Example:
How many 🌸 s are left?
$9 - 4 = 5$

How many 🧍 s are left?
$14 - 1 = 13$

How many 🦋 s in all?
$15 + 6 = 21$

How many 🐞 s are left?
$9 - 5 = 4$

Page 111

Hopping Around

Directions: Write the number sentence on the line below each number line.

Example:

0 1 2 3 4 5 6 7 8 9 10
3 + 2 = 5

0 1 2 3 4 5 6 7 8 9 10
8 - 4 = 4

0 1 2 3 4 5 6 7 8 9 10
6 + 3 = 9

0 1 2 3 4 5 6 7 8 9 10
9 - 2 = 7

Page 112

Big Families

Directions: Complete each number sentence in each number family.

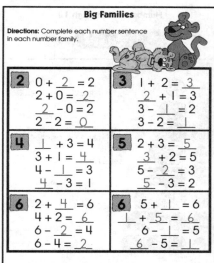

2
0 + _2_ = 2
2 + 0 = _2_
_2_ − 0 = 2
2 − 2 = _0_

3
1 + 2 = _3_
_2_ + 1 = 3
3 − _1_ = 2
3 − 2 = _1_

4
_1_ + 3 = 4
3 + 1 = _4_
4 − _1_ = 3
_4_ − 3 = 1

5
2 + 3 = _5_
_3_ + 2 = 5
5 − _2_ = 3
_5_ − 3 = 2

6
2 + _4_ = 6
4 + 2 = _6_
6 − _2_ = 4
6 − 4 = _2_

6
5 + _1_ = 6
_1_ + _5_ = _6_
6 − _1_ = 5
_6_ − 5 = _1_

Page 113

Sums and Differences

Directions: Color two numbers in each box to show the given sum or difference.

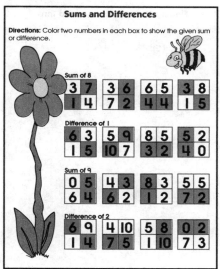

Sum of 8
| 3 7 | 3 6 | 6 5 | 3 8 |
| 1 4 | 7 2 | 4 4 | 1 5 |

Difference of 1
| 6 3 | 5 9 | 8 5 | 5 2 |
| 1 5 | 10 7 | 3 2 | 4 0 |

Sum of 9
| 0 5 | 4 3 | 8 3 | 5 5 |
| 6 4 | 6 2 | 1 2 | 7 2 |

Difference of 2
| 6 9 | 4 10 | 5 8 | 0 2 |
| 1 4 | 7 5 | 1 10 | 7 3 |

Page 114

Help the Hippo

Directions: Use the numbers in each thought bubble to write the number family.

Example:

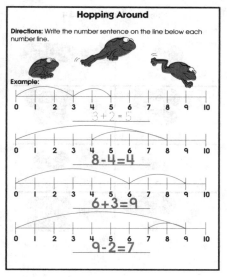

2 + 1 = 3
1 + 2 = 3
3 − 1 = 2
3 − 2 = 1
2, 1, 3

2 + 4 = 6
4 + 2 = 6
6 − 2 = 4
6 − 4 = 2
2, 4, 6

4 + 1 = 5
1 + 4 = 5
5 − 1 = 4
5 − 4 = 1
1, 4, 5

2 + 5 = 7
5 + 2 = 7
7 − 5 = 2
7 − 2 = 5
2, 5, 7

3 + 4 = 7
4 + 3 = 7
7 − 4 = 3
7 − 3 = 4
3, 4, 7

2 + 3 = 5
3 + 2 = 5
5 − 3 = 2
5 − 2 = 3
2, 3, 5

Page 115

Bigger Families

Directions: Complete each number sentence in the families.

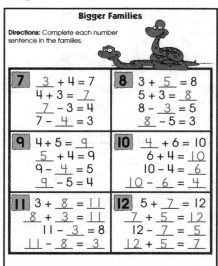

7
_3_ + 4 = 7
4 + 3 = _7_
_7_ − 3 = 4
7 − _4_ = 3

8
3 + _5_ = 8
5 + 3 = _8_
8 − _3_ = 5
_8_ − 5 = 3

9
4 + 5 = _9_
_5_ + 4 = 9
9 − _4_ = 5
_9_ − 5 = 4

10
_4_ + 6 = 10
6 + 4 = _10_
10 − 4 = _6_
10 − 6 = _4_

11
3 + _8_ = _11_
_8_ + _3_ = _11_
11 − _3_ = 8
_11_ − _8_ = _3_

12
5 + _7_ = 12
_7_ + _5_ = _12_
12 − _7_ = _5_
_12_ + _5_ = _7_

Page 116

Place Value: Ones, Tens

The **place value** of a digit or numeral is shown by where it is in the number. For example, in the number **23**, **2** has the place value of **tens**, and **3** is **ones**.

Directions: Add the tens and ones and write your answers in the blanks.

Example:

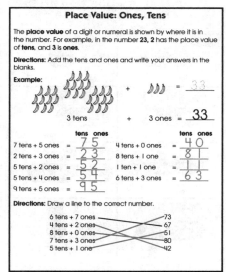

3 tens + 3 ones = _33_
3 tens + 3 ones = **33**

	tens ones
7 tens + 5 ones =	7 5
2 tens + 3 ones =	2 3
5 tens + 2 ones =	5 2
5 tens + 4 ones =	5 4
9 tens + 5 ones =	9 5

	tens ones
4 tens + 0 ones =	4 0
8 tens + 1 one =	8 1
1 ten + 1 one =	1 1
6 tens + 3 ones =	6 3

Directions: Draw a line to the correct number.

6 tens + 7 ones — 73
4 tens + 2 ones — 67
8 tens + 0 ones — 51
7 tens + 3 ones — 80
5 tens + 1 one — 42

Page 117

Finding Place Value: Ones and Tens

Directions: Write the numbers for the tens and ones. Then add.

Example:

2 tens + 7 ones
20 + 7
27

6 tens + 2 ones
60, 2
62

3 tens + 4 ones
30, 4
34

8 tens + 3 ones
80, 3
83

5 tens + 0 ones
50, 0
50

Page 118

Numbers 11 Through 18

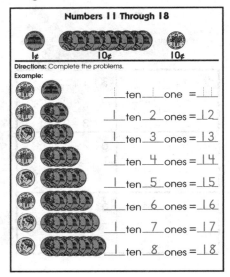

1¢   10¢   10¢

Directions: Complete the problems.

Example:

_1_ ten _1_ one = _11_

_1_ ten _2_ ones = _12_

_1_ ten _3_ ones = _13_

_1_ ten _4_ ones = _14_

_1_ ten _5_ ones = _15_

_1_ ten _6_ ones = _16_

_1_ ten _7_ ones = _17_

_1_ ten _8_ ones = _18_

Page 119

Numbers 19 Through 39

Directions: Complete the problems.

Example:

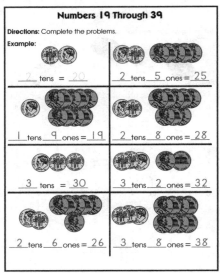

_2_ tens = _20_

_2_ tens _5_ ones = _25_

_1_ tens _9_ ones = _19_

_2_ tens _8_ ones = _28_

_3_ tens = _30_

_3_ tens _2_ ones = _32_

_2_ tens _6_ ones = _26_

_3_ tens _8_ ones = _38_

Page 120

Numbers 40 Through 99

Directions: Complete the problems.

Example:

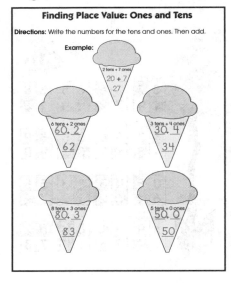

_4_ tens = _40_

_4_ tens _2_ ones = _42_

_5_ tens _6_ ones = _56_

_6_ tens _5_ ones = _65_

_7_ tens = _70_

_7_ tens _9_ ones = _79_

_8_ tens _7_ ones = _87_

_9_ tens _3_ ones = _93_

Page 121

Numbers 40 Through 99

Directions: Complete the problems.

Example:

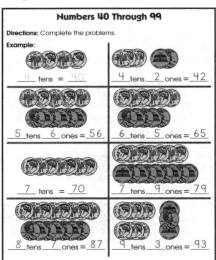

_4_ tens _5_ ones = _45_

_4_ tens _3_ ones = _43_

_5_ tens = _50_

_5_ tens _8_ ones = _58_

_6_ tens _6_ ones = _66_

_7_ tens _2_ ones = _72_

_8_ tens = _80_

_9_ tens _9_ ones = _99_

Page 122

Numbers Through 99

Directions: Complete the problems.

Example:

4 tens 6 ones = _46_   2 tens 1 one = _21_

1 ten 2 ones = _12_   5 tens 7 ones = _57_

3 tens 7 ones = _37_   1 ten 9 ones = _19_

2 tens 4 ones = _24_   8 tens 8 ones = _88_

9 tens = _90_   6 tens 7 ones = _67_

6 tens = _60_   7 tens 2 ones = _72_

5 tens 3 ones = _53_   9 tens 5 ones = _95_

7 tens 8 ones = _78_   4 tens 1 one = _41_

1 ten 1 one = _11_   3 tens 4 ones = _34_

8 tens 4 ones = _84_   6 tens 6 ones = _66_

3 tens 5 ones = _35_   8 tens 9 ones = _89_

4 tens 9 ones = _49_   2 tens = _20_

9 tens 6 ones = _96_   5 tens = _50_

Page 123

Hundreds, Tens, and Ones

Directions: Count the groups of crayons. Write the number of hundreds, tens, and ones.

Example:

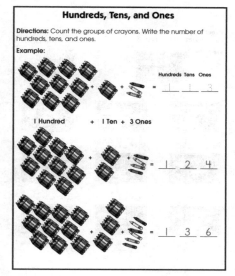

Hundreds Tens Ones

1 1 3

I Hundred + 1 Ten + 3 Ones

= 1 2 4

= 1 3 6

Page 124

What Big Numbers!

Directions: Write each number.

Example:

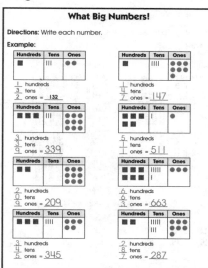

Hundreds	Tens	Ones
■	|||	●●

1 hundreds
3 tens
2 ones = 132

Hundreds	Tens	Ones
■	||||	●●●●●

1 hundreds
4 tens
7 ones = 147

Hundreds	Tens	Ones
■■■	|||	●●●●●●●●●

3 hundreds
3 tens
9 ones = 339

Hundreds	Tens	Ones
■■■■■			●

5 hundreds
1 tens
1 ones = 511

Hundreds	Tens	Ones
■■		●●●●●●●●●

2 hundreds
0 tens
9 ones = 209

Hundreds	Tens	Ones
■■■■■■	|||||	●●●

6 hundreds
6 tens
3 ones = 663

Hundreds	Tens	Ones
■■■	||||	●●●●●

3 hundreds
4 tens
5 ones = 345

Hundreds	Tens	Ones
■■	|||||||	●●●●●●●

2 hundreds
8 tens
7 ones = 287

Page 125

Count 'Em Up!

Directions: Look at the example. Then, write the missing numbers in the blanks.

Example:

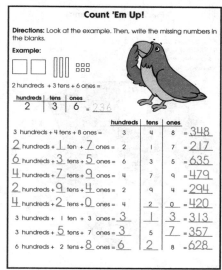

2 hundreds + 3 tens + 6 ones =

hundreds	tens	ones
2	3	6	= 236

		hundreds	tens	ones	
3 hundreds + 4 tens + 8 ones =		3	4	8	= 348
2 hundreds + 1 ten + 7 ones =		2	1	7	= 217
6 hundreds + 3 tens + 5 ones =		6	3	5	= 635
4 hundreds + 7 tens + 9 ones =		4	7	9	= 479
2 hundreds + 9 tens + 4 ones =		2	9	4	= 294
4 hundreds + 2 tens + 0 ones =		4	2	0	= 420
3 hundreds + 1 ten + 3 ones =		3	1	3	= 313
3 hundreds + 5 tens + 7 ones =		3	5	7	= 357
6 hundreds + 2 tens + 8 ones =		6	2	8	= 628

Page 126

Up, Up, and Away

Directions: Use the code to color the balloons. If the answer has:

7 hundreds, color it red.
6 hundreds, color it **green**.
5 hundreds, color it orange.
8 tens, color it yellow.
3 ones, color it brown.

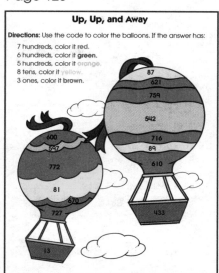

87
621
759
542
716
89
610
600
597
772
81
670
727
433
13

Page 127

Place Value: Thousands

Directions: Study the example. Write the missing numbers.

Example:

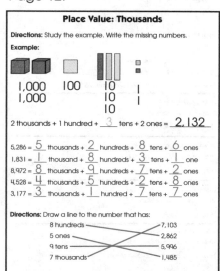

1,000   100   10   1
1,000   10   1
              10

2 thousands + 1 hundred + _3_ tens + 2 ones = _2,132_

5,286 = _5_ thousands + _2_ hundreds + _8_ tens + _6_ ones
1,831 = _1_ thousand + _8_ hundreds + _3_ tens + _1_ one
8,972 = _8_ thousands + _9_ hundreds + _7_ tens + _2_ ones
4,528 = _4_ thousands + _5_ hundreds + _2_ tens + _8_ ones
3,177 = _3_ thousands + _1_ hundred + _7_ tens + _7_ ones

Directions: Draw a line to the number that has:

8 hundreds —— 7,103
5 ones —— 2,862
9 tens —— 5,996
7 thousands —— 1,485

Page 128

Place Value: Thousands

6, 4 3 1

thousands hundreds tens ones

Directions: Tell which number is in each place.

☆ Thousands place:
2,456   4,621   3,456
2   4   3

☆ Tens place:
4,286   1,234   5,678
8   3   7

☆ Hundreds place:
6,321   3,210   7,871
3   2   8

☆ Ones place:
5,432   6,531   9,980
2   1   0

Page 129

Place Value: Thousands

Directions: Use the code to color the fan.

If the answer has:
9 thousands, color it pink.
6 thousands, color it green.
5 hundreds, color it orange.

8 tens, color it red.
3 ones, color it blue.

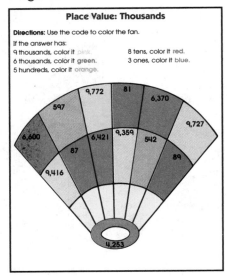

9,772 81 6,370
597 9,727
6,600 6,421 9,359 542
87 89
9,416
4,253

Page 130

2-Digit Addition

Directions: Study the example. Follow the steps to add.

Example:
33
+41

Step 1: Add the ones.

tens	ones
3	3
+4	1
	4

tens	ones
4	2
+2	4
6	6

Step 2: Add the tens.

tens	ones
3	3
+4	1
7	4

tens	ones
5	0
+4	7
9	7

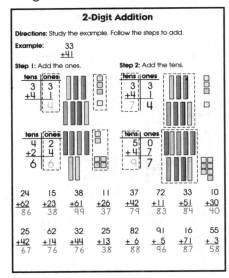

24	15	38	11	37	72	33	10
+62	+23	+61	+26	+42	+11	+51	+30
86	38	99	37	79	83	84	40

25	62	32	25	82	91	16	55
+42	+14	+44	+13	+6	+5	+71	+3
67	76	76	38	88	96	87	58

Page 131

2-Digit Addition

Directions: Add the total points scored in each game. Remember to add **ones** first and **tens** second.

Example:

HOME 22 VISITOR 17 Total 39

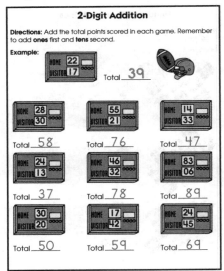

HOME 28 VISITOR 30 Total 58
HOME 55 VISITOR 21 Total 76
HOME 14 VISITOR 33 Total 47

HOME 24 VISITOR 13 Total 37
HOME 46 VISITOR 32 Total 78
HOME 83 VISITOR 06 Total 89

HOME 30 VISITOR 20 Total 50
HOME 17 VISITOR 42 Total 59
HOME 24 VISITOR 45 Total 69

Page 132

Adding Tens

3 tens	30	6 tens	60
+ 4 tens	+40	+ 2 tens	+20
7 tens	70	8 tens	80

Directions: Add.

2 tens	20	6 tens	60
+ 4 tens	+40	+ 2 tens	+20
6 tens	60	8 tens	80

20	10	40	30	50
+20	+50	+20	+40	+30
40	60	60	70	80

30	60	20	70	10
+20	+10	+50	+10	+10
50	70	70	80	20

10	40	80	60	20
+20	+40	+10	+30	+60
30	80	90	90	80

70	40	30	50	30
+20	+10	+10	+40	+30
90	50	40	90	60

Page 133

Problem Solving

Directions: Solve each problem.

Example:

There are 20 men in the plane.
30 women get in the plane.
How many men and women are in the plane?

20
+30
50

Jill buys 10 apples.
Carol buys 20 apples.
How many apples in all?

10
+20
30

There are 30 ears of corn in one pile.
There are 50 ears of corn in another pile.
How many ears of corn in all?

30
+50
80

Henry cut 40 pieces of wood.
Art cut 20 pieces of wood.
How many pieces of wood were cut?

40
+20
60

Adolpho had 60 baseball cards.
Maria had 30 baseball cards.
How many baseball cards in all?

60
+30
90

Page 134

Picture This

Directions: Add the ones, then the tens in each problem. Then, write the sum in the blank.

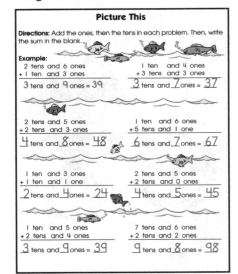

Example:

2 tens and 6 ones
+ 1 ten and 3 ones
3 tens and 9 ones = 39

1 ten and 4 ones
+ 3 tens and 3 ones
3 tens and 7 ones = 37

2 tens and 5 ones
+ 2 tens and 3 ones
4 tens and 8 ones = 48

1 ten and 6 ones
+ 5 tens and 1 one
6 tens and 7 ones = 67

1 ten and 3 ones
+ 1 ten and 1 one
2 tens and 4 ones = 24

2 tens and 5 ones
+ 2 tens and 0 ones
4 tens and 5 ones = 45

1 ten and 5 ones
+ 2 tens and 4 ones
3 tens and 9 ones = 39

7 tens and 6 ones
+ 2 tens and 2 ones
9 tens and 8 ones = 98

Page 135

Digital Addition

Add the ones.
tens	ones
2	4
+3	2
	6

Then, add the tens.
tens	ones
2	4
+3	2
5	6

Directions: Solve the addition problems below.

tens	ones
1	7
+2	1
3	8

tens	ones
3	4
+5	2
8	6

tens	ones
	5
+6	2
6	7

tens	ones
	6
+5	2
5	8

tens	ones
2	0
+4	0
6	0

tens	ones
5	1
+	8
5	9

tens	ones
7	2
+1	7
8	9

tens	ones
4	7
+2	1
6	8

tens	ones
2	5
+6	2
8	7

tens	ones
4	2
+2	4
6	6

tens	ones
8	3
+1	4
9	7

tens	ones
3	2
+2	5
5	7

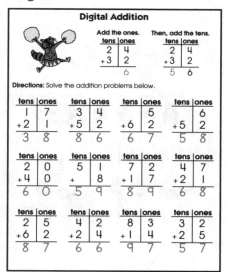

Page 136

Circus Fun

Directions: Add to solve the problems. Add the ones first. Then, add the tens.

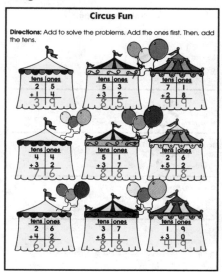

tens	ones
2	5
+1	4
3	9

tens	ones
5	3
+3	2
8	5

tens	ones
7	1
+2	8
9	9

tens	ones
4	4
+3	2
7	6

tens	ones
5	1
+3	7
8	8

tens	ones
2	6
+5	2
7	8

tens	ones
2	6
+4	2
6	8

tens	ones
3	7
+5	1
8	8

tens	ones
1	9
+3	0
4	9

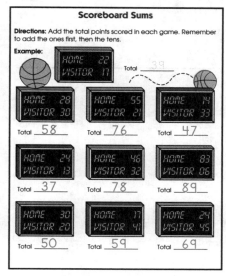

Page 137

Scoreboard Sums

Directions: Add the total points scored in each game. Remember to add the ones first, then the tens.

Example:

HOME 22
VISITOR 17
Total 39

HOME 28
VISITOR 30
Total 58

HOME 55
VISITOR 21
Total 76

HOME 14
VISITOR 33
Total 47

HOME 24
VISITOR 13
Total 37

HOME 46
VISITOR 32
Total 78

HOME 83
VISITOR 06
Total 89

HOME 30
VISITOR 20
Total 50

HOME 17
VISITOR 41
Total 59

HOME 24
VISITOR 45
Total 69

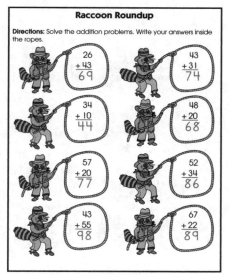

Page 138

Raccoon Roundup

Directions: Solve the addition problems. Write your answers inside the ropes.

26 + 43 = 69

43 + 31 = 74

34 + 10 = 44

48 + 20 = 68

57 + 20 = 77

52 + 34 = 86

43 + 55 = 98

67 + 22 = 89

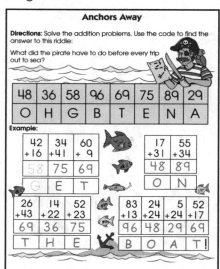

Page 139

Anchors Away

Directions: Solve the addition problems. Use the code to find the answer to this riddle.

What did the pirate have to do before every trip out to sea?

48	36	58	96	69	75	89	29
O	H	G	B	B	T	E	N	A

Example:

42 +16	34 +41	60 + 9
58	75	69
G	E	T

17 +31	55 +34
48	89
O	N

26 +43	14 +22	52 +23
69	36	75
T	H	E

83 +13	24 +24	5 +24	52 +17
96	48	29	69
B	O	A	T!

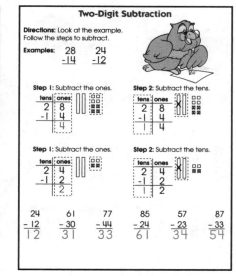

Page 140

Two-Digit Subtraction

Directions: Look at the example. Follow the steps to subtract.

Examples:
```
 28      24
-14     -12
```

Step 1: Subtract the ones.
tens	ones
2	8
-1	4
	4

Step 2: Subtract the tens.
tens	ones
2	8
-1	4
1	4

Step 1: Subtract the ones.
tens	ones
2	4
-1	2
	2

Step 2: Subtract the tens.
tens	ones
2	4
-1	2
1	2

```
 24      61      77      85      57      87
-12     -30     -44     -24     -23     -33
 12      31      33      61      34      54
```

Page 141

Subtracting Tens

Examples:

6 tens	60	8 tens	80
− 3 tens	− 30	− 2 tens	− 20
3 tens	30	6 tens	60

Directions: Subtract.

7 tens	70	4 tens	40
− 5 tens	− 50	− 2 tens	− 20
2 tens	20	2 tens	20

50	60	20	80	40
− 30	− 20	− 10	− 40	− 40
20	40	10	40	0

90	80	70	30	50
− 50	− 20	− 30	− 20	− 40
40	60	40	10	10

60	40	80	90	70
− 30	− 10	− 30	− 20	− 50
30	30	50	70	20

80	90	70	60	50
− 70	− 80	− 40	− 40	− 20
10	10	30	20	30

Page 142

Problem Solving

Directions: Solve each problem.

Example:

Mr. Cobb counts 70 ✏s.
He sells 30 ✏s.
How many ✏s are left?

70
− 30
40

Keith has 20 🔨s.
Leon has 10 🔨s.
How many more 🔨s does Keith have than Leon?

20
− 10
10

Tina plants 60 🌷s.
Melody plants 30 🌷s.
How many more 🌷s did Tina plant than Melody?

60
− 30
30

Link has 80 ⚫s.
Jessica has 50 ⚫s.
How many more ⚫s does Link have than Jessica?

80
− 50
30

Maranda hits 40 ⚾s.
Harold hits 30 ⚾s.
How many more ⚾s does Maranda hit than Harold?

40
− 30
10

Page 143

All Aboard

Directions: Count the tens and ones and write the numbers. Then, subtract to solve the problems.

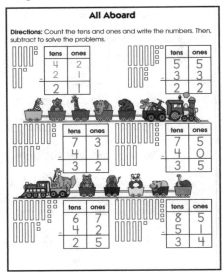

tens	ones
4	2
2	1
2	1

tens	ones
5	5
3	3
2	2

tens	ones
7	3
4	1
3	2

tens	ones
7	5
4	0
3	5

tens	ones
6	7
4	2
2	5

tens	ones
8	5
5	1
3	4

Page 144

Cookie Mania

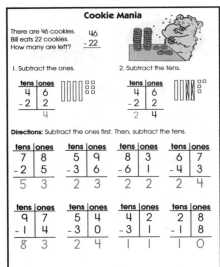

There are 46 cookies.
Bill eats 22 cookies.
How many are left?

46
− 22

1. Subtract the ones.

tens	ones
4	6
− 2	2
	4

2. Subtract the tens.

tens	ones
4	6
− 2	2
2	4

Directions: Subtract the ones first. Then, subtract the tens.

tens	ones
7	8
− 2	5
5	3

tens	ones
5	9
− 3	6
2	3

tens	ones
8	3
− 6	1
2	2

tens	ones
6	7
− 4	3
2	4

tens	ones
9	7
− 1	4
8	3

tens	ones
5	4
− 3	0
2	4

tens	ones
4	2
− 3	1
1	1

tens	ones
2	8
− 1	8
1	0

Page 145

Cookie Craze!

Directions: Subtract to solve the problems. Circle the answers. Color the cookies with answers greater than 30.

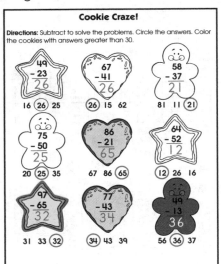

49
− 23
26

16 **26** 25

67
− 41
26

26 15 62

58
− 37
21

81 11 **21**

75
− 50
25

20 **25** 35

86
− 21
65

67 86 **65**

64
− 52
12

12 26 16

97
− 65
32

31 33 **32**

77
− 43
34

34 43 39

49
− 13
36

56 **36** 37

Page 146

How's Your Pitch?

Directions: Solve the subtraction problems. Write each answer.

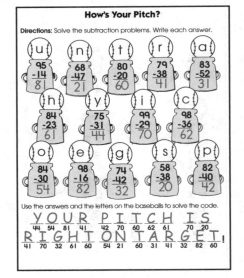

u	n	t	r	a
95	68	80	79	83
−14	−47	−20	−38	−52
81	21	60	41	31

h	y	i	c	
84	75	99	98	
−23	−31	−29	−36	
61	44	70	62	

o	e	g	s	p
84	98	74	58	82
−30	−16	−42	−38	−40
54	82	32	20	42

Use the answers and the letters on the baseballs to solve the code.

Y O U R   P I T C H   I S
44 54 81 41   42 70 60 62 61   70 20
R I G H T O N T A R G E T !
41 70 32 61 60   54 21   60 31 41 32 82 60

Page 147

Prehistoric Problems

Directions: Solve the subtraction problems. Use the code to color the picture.

Code:
25 = blue   57 = green
31 = yellow   14 = orange
21 = brown   11 = red

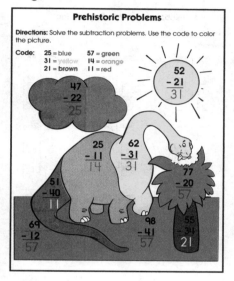

$$\begin{array}{r} 52 \\ -21 \\ \hline 31 \end{array}$$

$$\begin{array}{r} 47 \\ -22 \\ \hline 25 \end{array}$$

$$\begin{array}{r} 25 \\ -11 \\ \hline 14 \end{array}$$

$$\begin{array}{r} 62 \\ -31 \\ \hline 31 \end{array}$$

$$\begin{array}{r} 77 \\ -20 \\ \hline 57 \end{array}$$

$$\begin{array}{r} 51 \\ -40 \\ \hline 11 \end{array}$$

$$\begin{array}{r} 98 \\ -41 \\ \hline 57 \end{array}$$

$$\begin{array}{r} 55 \\ -34 \\ \hline 21 \end{array}$$

$$\begin{array}{r} 69 \\ -12 \\ \hline 57 \end{array}$$

Page 148

2-Digit Addition: Regrouping

Addition is "putting together" or adding two or more numbers to find the sum. Regrouping is using **ten ones** to form **one ten, ten tens** to form **one 100, fifteen ones** to form **one ten** and **five ones**, and so on.

Directions: Study the examples. Follow the steps to add.

Example:
$$\begin{array}{r} 14 \\ +8 \end{array}$$

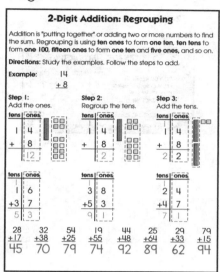

Step 1: Add the ones.

tens	ones
1	4
+	8
1	2

Step 2: Regroup the tens.

tens	ones
1	4
+	8
	2

Step 3: Add the tens.

tens	ones
1	4
+	8
2	2

tens	ones
1	6
+3	7
5	3

tens	ones
3	8
+5	3
9	1

tens	ones
2	4
+4	7
7	1

$$\begin{array}{r} 28 \\ +17 \\ \hline 45 \end{array} \quad \begin{array}{r} 32 \\ +38 \\ \hline 70 \end{array} \quad \begin{array}{r} 54 \\ +25 \\ \hline 79 \end{array} \quad \begin{array}{r} 19 \\ +55 \\ \hline 74 \end{array} \quad \begin{array}{r} 44 \\ +48 \\ \hline 92 \end{array} \quad \begin{array}{r} 25 \\ +64 \\ \hline 89 \end{array} \quad \begin{array}{r} 29 \\ +33 \\ \hline 62 \end{array} \quad \begin{array}{r} 79 \\ +15 \\ \hline 94 \end{array}$$

Page 149

2-Digit Addition: Regrouping

Directions: Add the total points scored in the game. Remember to add the ones, regroup, and then add the tens.

Example:

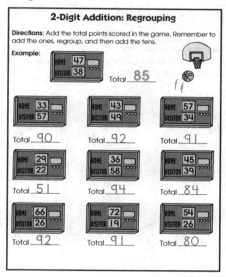

HOME 47 VISITOR 38   Total 85

HOME 33 VISITOR 57   Total 90
HOME 43 VISITOR 49   Total 92
HOME 57 VISITOR 34   Total 91

HOME 29 VISITOR 22   Total 51
HOME 36 VISITOR 58   Total 94
HOME 45 VISITOR 39   Total 84

HOME 66 VISITOR 26   Total 92
HOME 72 VISITOR 19   Total 91
HOME 54 VISITOR 26   Total 80

Page 150

2-Digit Addition

Directions: Add the ones.   Rename 15 as 10 + 5.   Add the tens.

$$\begin{array}{r} 56 \\ +29 \end{array} \qquad \begin{array}{r} 6 \\ +9 \\ \hline 15 \text{ or } 10+5 \end{array} \Rightarrow \begin{array}{r} 1 \\ 56 \\ +29 \\ \hline 5 \end{array} \Rightarrow \begin{array}{r} 1 \\ 56 \\ +29 \\ \hline 85 \end{array}$$

Directions: Add the ones.   Rename 12 as 10 + 2.   Add the tens.

$$\begin{array}{r} 47 \\ +35 \end{array} \qquad \begin{array}{r} 7 \\ +5 \\ \hline 12 \text{ or } 10+2 \end{array} \Rightarrow \begin{array}{r} 1 \\ 47 \\ +35 \\ \hline 2 \end{array} \Rightarrow \begin{array}{r} 1 \\ 47 \\ +35 \\ \hline 82 \end{array}$$

Directions: Add.

Examples:

$$\begin{array}{r} 45 \\ +28 \\ \hline 73 \end{array} \quad \begin{array}{r} 13 \\ +19 \\ \hline 32 \end{array} \quad \begin{array}{r} 48 \\ +35 \\ \hline 83 \end{array} \quad \begin{array}{r} 69 \\ +18 \\ \hline 87 \end{array} \quad \begin{array}{r} 54 \\ +39 \\ \hline 93 \end{array}$$

$$\begin{array}{r} 44 \\ +17 \\ \hline 61 \end{array} \quad \begin{array}{r} 37 \\ +18 \\ \hline 55 \end{array} \quad \begin{array}{r} 28 \\ +36 \\ \hline 64 \end{array} \quad \begin{array}{r} 73 \\ +18 \\ \hline 91 \end{array} \quad \begin{array}{r} 66 \\ +29 \\ \hline 95 \end{array}$$

$$\begin{array}{r} 52 \\ +39 \\ \hline 91 \end{array} \quad \begin{array}{r} 38 \\ +47 \\ \hline 85 \end{array} \quad \begin{array}{r} 64 \\ +18 \\ \hline 82 \end{array} \quad \begin{array}{r} 29 \\ +45 \\ \hline 74 \end{array} \quad \begin{array}{r} 75 \\ +17 \\ \hline 92 \end{array}$$

Page 151

2-Digit Addition

Directions: Add the ones.   Rename 11 as 10 + 1.   Add the tens.

$$\begin{array}{r} 38 \\ +43 \end{array} \qquad \begin{array}{r} 8 \\ +3 \\ \hline 11 \text{ or } 10+1 \end{array} \Rightarrow \begin{array}{r} 1 \\ 38 \\ +43 \\ \hline 1 \end{array} \Rightarrow \begin{array}{r} 1 \\ 38 \\ +43 \\ \hline 81 \end{array}$$

Directions: Add.

Example:

$$\begin{array}{r} 17 \\ +34 \\ \hline 51 \end{array} \quad \begin{array}{r} 26 \\ +47 \\ \hline 73 \end{array} \quad \begin{array}{r} 47 \\ +35 \\ \hline 82 \end{array} \quad \begin{array}{r} 68 \\ +24 \\ \hline 92 \end{array} \quad \begin{array}{r} 37 \\ +28 \\ \hline 65 \end{array}$$

$$\begin{array}{r} 29 \\ +48 \\ \hline 77 \end{array} \quad \begin{array}{r} 58 \\ +27 \\ \hline 85 \end{array} \quad \begin{array}{r} 69 \\ +17 \\ \hline 86 \end{array} \quad \begin{array}{r} 78 \\ +13 \\ \hline 91 \end{array} \quad \begin{array}{r} 19 \\ +44 \\ \hline 63 \end{array}$$

$$\begin{array}{r} 55 \\ +28 \\ \hline 83 \end{array} \quad \begin{array}{r} 27 \\ +35 \\ \hline 62 \end{array} \quad \begin{array}{r} 39 \\ +52 \\ \hline 91 \end{array} \quad \begin{array}{r} 57 \\ +27 \\ \hline 84 \end{array} \quad \begin{array}{r} 38 \\ +36 \\ \hline 74 \end{array}$$

$$\begin{array}{r} 49 \\ +43 \\ \hline 92 \end{array} \quad \begin{array}{r} 65 \\ +18 \\ \hline 83 \end{array} \quad \begin{array}{r} 23 \\ +18 \\ \hline 41 \end{array} \quad \begin{array}{r} 64 \\ +18 \\ \hline 82 \end{array} \quad \begin{array}{r} 46 \\ +39 \\ \hline 85 \end{array}$$

$$\begin{array}{r} 54 \\ +27 \\ \hline 81 \end{array} \quad \begin{array}{r} 38 \\ +44 \\ \hline 82 \end{array} \quad \begin{array}{r} 66 \\ +26 \\ \hline 92 \end{array} \quad \begin{array}{r} 28 \\ +34 \\ \hline 62 \end{array} \quad \begin{array}{r} 19 \\ +56 \\ \hline 75 \end{array}$$

Page 152

Problem Solving

Directions: Solve each problem.

Example:
16 boys ride their bikes to school.
18 girls ride their bikes to school.
How many bikes are ridden to school?

$$\begin{array}{r} 1 \\ 16 \\ +18 \\ \hline 34 \end{array}$$

Dad reads 26 pages.
Mike reads 37 pages.
How many pages did Dad and Mike read?

$$\begin{array}{r} 26 \\ +37 \\ \hline 63 \end{array}$$

Tiffany counts 46 stars.
Mike counts 39 stars.
How many stars did they count?

$$\begin{array}{r} 46 \\ +39 \\ \hline 85 \end{array}$$

Mom has 29 golf balls.
Dad has 43 golf balls.
How many golf balls do they have?

$$\begin{array}{r} 29 \\ +43 \\ \hline 72 \end{array}$$

Vicki ran in 26 races.
Kay ran in 14 races.
How many races did they run?

$$\begin{array}{r} 26 \\ +14 \\ \hline 40 \end{array}$$

2-Digit Subtraction: Regrouping

Subtraction is "taking away" or subtracting one number from another to find the difference. Regrouping is using **one ten** to form **ten ones**, **one 100** to form **ten tens**, and so on.

Directions: Study the examples. Follow the steps to subtract.

Example: 37
       −19

Step 1: Regroup. **Step 2:** Subtract the ones. **Step 3:** Subtract the tens.

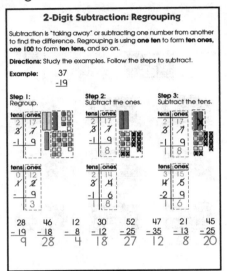

28	46	12	30	52	47	21	45
−19	−18	−8	−12	−25	−35	−13	−25
9	28	4	18	27	12	8	20

2-Digit Subtraction: Regrouping

Directions: Study the steps for subtracting. Solve the problems using the steps.

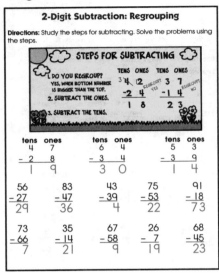

tens ones	tens ones	tens ones
4 7	6 4	5 3
− 2 8	− 3 4	− 3 9
1 9	3 0	1 4

56	83	43	75	91
−27	−47	−39	−53	−18
29	36	4	22	73

73	35	67	26	68
−66	−14	−58	−7	−45
7	21	9	19	23

Subtraction With Regrouping

Directions: Use manipulatives to find the difference.

Example:

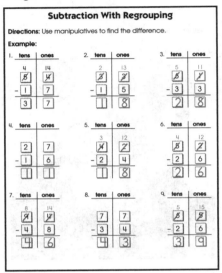

1. tens ones	2. tens ones	3. tens ones
4 14	2 13	5 11
8 4	3 3	6 1
− 1 7	− 1 5	− 3 3
3 7	1 8	2 8

4. tens ones	5. tens ones	6. tens ones
2 7	3 12	4 12
	4 2	5 2
− 1 6	− 2 4	− 2 6
1 1	1 8	2 6

7. tens ones	8. tens ones	9. tens ones
8 14	7 7	5 15
9 4		6 5
− 4 8	− 3 4	− 2 6
4 6	4 3	3 9

Subtraction With Regrouping

Directions: Subtract to find the difference. Regroup as needed. Color the spaces with differences of:

10–19 = red   50–59 = brown   30–39 = green
40–49 = yellow   20–29 = blue   60–69 = orange

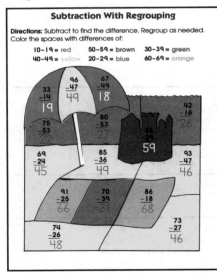

96 −47 = 49
67 −49 = 18
33 −14 = 19
42 −16 = 26
75 −53 = 22
80 −53 = 27
85 −25 = 59
69 −24 = 45
85 −36 = 49
93 −47 = 46
91 −25 = 66
70 −39 = 31
86 −18 = 68
74 −26 = 48
73 −27 = 46

2-Digit Subtraction

Directions: Rename 53 as 4 tens and 13 ones.

4 13
53   Subtract the ones.   Subtract the tens.
−26

Rename 45 as 3 tens and 15 ones.

3 15
45
−18

Directions: Subtract.

Examples:

5 13	6 14	47	52	64
63	74	−28	−26	−36
−28	−39	19	26	28
35	35			

84	93	71	26	67
−47	−56	−23	−18	−48
37	37	48	8	19

44	53	82	94	55
−28	−37	−46	−66	−39
16	16	36	28	16

86	34	54	73	86
−58	−18	−29	−59	−69
28	16	25	14	17

2-Digit Subtraction

Directions: Rename 73 as 6 tens and 13 ones.

6 13
73   Subtract the ones.   Subtract the tens.
−48

Directions: Subtract.

Example:

5 13	83	74	94	62
63	−45	−29	−48	−25
−48	38	45	46	37
15				

45	33	24	86	72
−27	−24	−8	−37	−48
18	9	6	49	24

36	26	43	63	93
−17	−18	−19	−48	−18
19	8	24	15	75

82	73	95	57	41
−26	−28	−69	−38	−25
56	45	26	19	16

54	61	91	81	32
−18	−34	−37	−44	−15
36	27	54	37	17

Problem Solving

Directions: Solve each problem.

Example:
Dad cooks 23 potatoes.
He uses 19 potatoes in the potato salad.
How many potatoes are left?

$$\begin{array}{r} 1\,13 \\ \cancel{2}\cancel{3} \\ -\ 19 \\ \hline 4 \end{array}$$

Susan draws 32 butterflies.
She colored 15 of them brown.
How many butterflies does she have left to color?

$$\begin{array}{r} 32 \\ -15 \\ \hline 17 \end{array}$$

A book has 66 pages.
Pedro reads 39 pages.
How many pages are left to read?

$$\begin{array}{r} 66 \\ -39 \\ \hline 27 \end{array}$$

Jerry picks up 34 sea shells.
He puts 15 of them in a box.
How many does he have left?

$$\begin{array}{r} 34 \\ -15 \\ \hline 19 \end{array}$$

Beth buys 72 sheets of paper.
She uses 44 sheets for her school work.
How many sheets of paper are left?

$$\begin{array}{r} 72 \\ -44 \\ \hline 28 \end{array}$$

Addition and Subtraction Review

Directions: Add.

4	8	9	7	5	6
+9	+6	+8	+6	+7	+5
13	14	17	13	12	11

9	5	7	9	8	7
+6	+8	+4	+9	+7	+9
15	13	11	18	15	16

30	20	45	52	60	83
+40	+30	+23	+23	+25	+15
70	50	68	75	85	98

Directions: Subtract.

16	15	13	12	11	17
-7	-9	-4	-7	-9	-8
9	6	9	5	2	9

18	17	16	15	4	16
-9	-9	-8	-8	-7	-9
9	8	8	7	7	7

40	60	85	73	96	54
-30	-10	-23	-41	-43	-44
10	50	62	32	53	10

Addition and Subtraction Review

Directions: Add.

4	9	5	6	7	9
+8	+2	+9	+6	+5	+4
12	11	14	12	12	13

8	7	3	7	6	6
+8	+6	+9	+7	+9	+5
16	13	12	14	15	11

40	50	75	66	47	34
+20	+30	+20	+31	+51	+23
60	80	95	97	98	57

Directions: Subtract.

17	15	12	13	14	16
-9	-6	-3	-7	-6	-8
8	9	9	6	8	8

15	14	13	15	12	11
-7	-9	-6	-7	-9	-8
8	5	7	8	3	3

30	50	65	87	75	66
-10	-30	-30	-34	-23	-43
20	20	35	53	52	23

Review: 2-Digit Addition

Directions: Add the ones.   Rename 12 as 10 + 2.   Add the tens.

$$\begin{array}{r} 64 \\ +28 \end{array} \qquad \begin{array}{r} 4 \\ +8 \\ \hline 12\ \text{or}\ 10+2 \end{array} \rightarrow \begin{array}{r} 1 \\ 64 \\ +28 \\ \hline 2 \end{array} \rightarrow \begin{array}{r} 1 \\ 64 \\ +28 \\ \hline 92 \end{array}$$

Directions: Add.

Example:

28	34	25	46	54
+19	+49	+16	+29	+39
47	83	41	75	93

16	64	58	39	34
+39	+28	+24	+17	+19
55	92	82	56	53

57	14	37	61	29
+39	+48	+39	+19	+44
96	62	76	80	73

17	39	44	25	18
+35	+14	+37	+49	+18
52	53	81	74	36

26	39	14	65	59
+48	+27	+27	+25	+18
74	66	41	90	77

Review: 2-Digit Addition

Directions: Add.

36	14	57	44	33
+55	+28	+38	+48	+29
91	42	95	92	62

23	27	68	23	42
+18	+27	+25	+19	+19
41	54	93	42	61

56	49	38	36	49
+28	+27	+49	+18	+24
84	76	87	54	73

18	51	74	35	52
+54	+39	+17	+28	+19
72	90	91	63	71

48	25	39	29	54
+26	+28	+33	+44	+27
74	53	72	73	81

Problem Solving

Directions: Solve each problem.

Example:
Simon sees 36 birds flying.
Julie sees 28 birds flying.
How many birds do they see flying?

$$\begin{array}{r} 36 \\ +28 \\ \hline 64 \end{array}$$

Brandon ran the race in 35 seconds.
Ryan ran the race in 28 seconds.
How many seconds did they run?

$$\begin{array}{r} 35 \\ +28 \\ \hline 63 \end{array}$$

Tom has 63 nickels.
Connie has 29 nickels.
How many nickels do they have?

$$\begin{array}{r} 63 \\ +29 \\ \hline 92 \end{array}$$

Pam sees 48 monkeys at the zoo.
Brenda sees 35 different monkeys.
How many monkeys did they see?

$$\begin{array}{r} 48 \\ +35 \\ \hline 83 \end{array}$$

There are 29 cows in one pen.
There are 47 cows in the other pen.
How many cows in all?

$$\begin{array}{r} 29 \\ +47 \\ \hline 76 \end{array}$$

Page 166

Keep on Truckin'

Directions: Write each sum. Connect the sums of 83 to make a road for the truck.

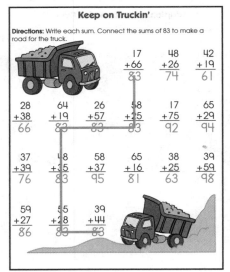

	17 +66 = 83	48 +26 = 74	42 +19 = 61

| 28 +38 = 66 | 64 +19 = 83 | 26 +57 = 83 | 58 +25 = 83 | 17 +75 = 92 | 65 +29 = 94 |

| 37 +39 = 76 | 48 +35 = 83 | 58 +37 = 95 | 65 +16 = 81 | 38 +25 = 63 | 39 +59 = 98 |

| 59 +27 = 86 | 55 +28 = 83 | 39 +44 = 83 |

Page 167

Shoot for the Stars

Directions: Add the total points scored in the game. Remember to add the ones first and regroup. Then, add the tens.

Example:

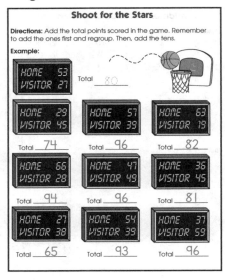

HOME 53 VISITOR 27 Total 80

HOME 29 VISITOR 45 Total 74

HOME 57 VISITOR 39 Total 96

HOME 63 VISITOR 19 Total 82

HOME 66 VISITOR 28 Total 94

HOME 47 VISITOR 49 Total 96

HOME 36 VISITOR 45 Total 81

HOME 27 VISITOR 38 Total 65

HOME 54 VISITOR 39 Total 93

HOME 37 VISITOR 59 Total 96

Page 168

Review: 2-Digit Subtraction

Directions: Rename 61 as 5 tens and 11 ones.

$$\begin{array}{r} 61 \\ -43 \end{array}$$

Subtract the ones.

Subtract the tens.

Directions: Subtract.

Example:
$$\begin{array}{r} 3\,17 \\ \cancel{47} \\ -28 \\ \hline 19 \end{array}$$

73 -48 = 25	84 -66 = 18	95 -18 = 77	64 -29 = 35

| 56 -38 = 18 | 31 -15 = 16 | 25 -17 = 8 | 33 -19 = 14 | 46 -29 = 17 |

| 93 -64 = 29 | 82 -55 = 27 | 72 -14 = 58 | 45 -28 = 17 | 61 -23 = 38 |

| 51 -44 = 7 | 62 -48 = 14 | 37 -19 = 18 | 50 -32 = 18 | 83 -47 = 36 |

| 92 -73 = 19 | 82 -75 = 7 | 76 -38 = 38 | 47 -29 = 18 | 74 -39 = 35 |

Page 169

Review: 2-Digit Subtraction

Directions: Add.

| 85 -16 = 69 | 93 -48 = 45 | 72 -35 = 37 | 63 -27 = 36 | 43 -38 = 5 |

| 56 -29 = 27 | 75 -49 = 26 | 84 -38 = 46 | 91 -65 = 26 | 37 -18 = 19 |

| 21 -14 = 7 | 35 -18 = 17 | 42 -29 = 13 | 72 -47 = 25 | 81 -54 = 27 |

| 64 -38 = 26 | 53 -28 = 25 | 94 -57 = 37 | 48 -39 = 9 | 23 -18 = 5 |

| 74 -58 = 16 | 83 -36 = 47 | 62 -26 = 36 | 54 -28 = 26 | 32 -17 = 15 |

Page 170

Go "Fore" It!

Directions: Add or subtract using regrouping.

tens	ones
2	15
3	5
-2	7
	8

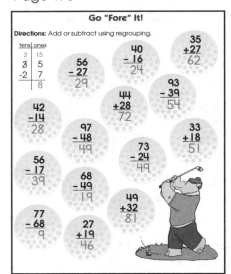

35 +27 = 62

40 -16 = 24

56 -27 = 29

93 -39 = 54

44 +28 = 72

42 -14 = 28

97 -48 = 49

33 +18 = 51

73 -24 = 49

56 -17 = 39

68 -49 = 19

49 +32 = 81

77 -68 = 9

27 +19 = 46

Page 171

Monster Math

Directions: Add or subtract using regrouping.

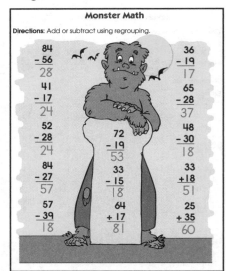

| 84 -56 = 28 | | 36 -19 = 17 |

| 41 -17 = 24 | | 65 -28 = 37 |

| 52 -28 = 24 | 72 -19 = 53 | 48 -30 = 18 |

| 84 -27 = 57 | 33 -15 = 18 | 33 +18 = 51 |

| 57 -39 = 18 | 64 +17 = 81 | 25 +35 = 60 |

Page 172

Adding Hundreds

Examples:

5 hundreds	500		4 hundreds	400
+ 3 hundreds	+ 300		+ 5 hundreds	+ 500
8 hundreds	800		9 hundreds	900

Directions: Add.

3 hundreds	300		6 hundreds	600
+ 1 hundreds	+ 100		+ 2 hundreds	+ 200
4 hundreds	400		8 hundreds	800

200	100	600	400
+ 200	+ 700	+ 300	+ 500
400	800	900	900

300	800	400	700
+ 400	+ 100	+ 400	+ 200
700	900	800	900

500	100	500	300
+ 100	+ 600	+ 200	+ 200
600	700	700	500

300	400	300	200
+ 300	+ 200	+ 500	+ 100
600	600	800	300

Page 173

Problem Solving

Directions: Solve each problem.

Example:

Ria packed 300 boxes.
Melvin packed 200 boxes.
How many boxes did Ria and Melvin pack?
+ 300 / 200 / 500

Santo typed 500 letters.
Hale typed 400 letters.
How many letters did they type?
500 + 400 / 900

Paula used 100 paper clips.
Milton used 600 paper clips.
How many paper clips did they use?
100 + 600 / 700

The grocery store sold 400 red apples.
The grocery store also sold 100 yellow apples.
How many apples did the grocery store sell in all?
400 + 100 / 500

Miles worked 200 days.
Julia worked 500 days.
How many days did they work?
200 + 500 / 700

Page 174

3-Digit Addition

245		245		245
+ 253		+ 253		+ 253
8		98		498

Directions: Add.

Example:

745		623
+ 23		+ 156
768		779

Add the ones.
Add the tens.
Add the hundreds.

415	566	373	160
+ 342	+ 33	+ 221	+ 334
757	599	594	494

835	642	287	723
+ 42	+ 251	+ 412	+ 45
877	893	699	768

133	454	314	654
+ 522	+ 324	+ 602	+ 235
655	778	916	889

Page 175

Problem Solving

Directions: Solve each problem.

Example:

Gene collected 342 rocks.
Lester collected 201 rocks.
How many rocks did they collect?
342 + 201 / 543

Tina jumped the rope 403 times.
Henry jumped the rope 426 times.
How many times did they jump?
403 + 426 / 829

There are 210 people wearing blue hats.
There are 432 people wearing red hats.
How many hats in all?
210 + 432 / 642

Asta used 135 paper plates.
Clyde used 143 paper plates.
How many paper plates did they use in all?
135 + 143 / 278

Aunt Mary had 536 dollars.
Uncle Lewis had 423 dollars.
How many dollars did they have in all?
536 + 423 / 959

Page 176

Problem Solving

Directions: Solve each problem.

There are 236 boys in school.
There are 250 girls in school.
How many boys and girls are in school?
236 + 250 / 486

Mary saw 131 cars.
Marvin saw 268 trucks.
How many cars and trucks did they see in all?
131 + 268 / 399

Jack has 427 pennies.
Jill has 370 pennies.
How many pennies do they have in all?
427 + 370 / 797

There are 582 red apples.
There are 206 yellow apples.
How many apples are there in all?
582 + 206 / 788

Ann found 122 shells.
Pedro found 76 shells.
How many shells did they find?
122 + 76 / 198

Page 177

Subtracting Hundreds

8 hundreds	800		6 hundreds	600
- 3 hundreds	- 300		- 2 hundreds	- 200
5 hundreds	500		4 hundreds	400

Directions: Subtract.

Example:

9 hundreds	900		3 hundreds	300
- 7 hundreds	- 700		- 1 hundreds	- 100
2 hundreds	200		2 hundreds	200

700	500	900	800
- 300	- 400	- 400	- 500
400	100	500	300

600	300	500	400
- 500	- 200	- 100	- 200
100	100	400	200

900	800	600	500
- 100	- 400	- 200	- 300
800	400	400	200

400	700	800	900
- 100	- 600	- 200	- 600
300	100	600	300

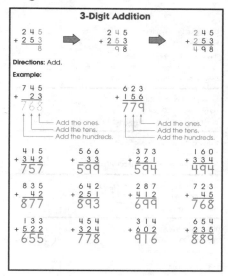

Page 178

Problem Solving

Directions: Solve each problem.

Example:

There were 400 apples in a box.
Jesse took 100 apples from the box.
How many apples are still in the box?

$$\begin{array}{r} 400 \\ -100 \\ \hline 300 \end{array}$$

Tommy bought 300 golf balls.
He gave Irene 200 golf balls.
How many golf balls does he have left?

$$\begin{array}{r} 300 \\ -200 \\ \hline 100 \end{array}$$

The black horse ran 900 feet.
The brown horse ran 700 feet.
How many more feet did the black horse run?

$$\begin{array}{r} 900 \\ -700 \\ \hline 200 \end{array}$$

The paint store has 800 gallons of paint.
It sells 300 gallons of paint.
How many gallons of paint are left?

$$\begin{array}{r} 800 \\ -300 \\ \hline 500 \end{array}$$

There are 700 children.
There are 200 boys.
How many girls are there?

$$\begin{array}{r} 700 \\ -200 \\ \hline 500 \end{array}$$

Page 179

3-Digit Subtraction

Directions: Subtract the ones.

$$\begin{array}{r} 746 \\ -424 \\ \hline 2 \end{array}$$

Subtract the tens.

$$\begin{array}{r} 746 \\ -424 \\ \hline 22 \end{array}$$

Subtract the hundreds.

$$\begin{array}{r} 746 \\ -424 \\ \hline 322 \end{array}$$

Directions: Add.

Example:

$$\begin{array}{r} 879 \\ -46 \\ \hline 833 \end{array}$$

Subtract the ones.
Subtract the tens.
Subtract the hundreds.

$$\begin{array}{r} 586 \\ -142 \\ \hline 444 \end{array}$$

Subtract the ones.
Subtract the tens.
Subtract the hundreds.

$\begin{array}{r} 635 \\ -423 \\ \hline 212 \end{array}$	$\begin{array}{r} 478 \\ -241 \\ \hline 237 \end{array}$	$\begin{array}{r} 338 \\ -27 \\ \hline 311 \end{array}$	$\begin{array}{r} 957 \\ -734 \\ \hline 223 \end{array}$
$\begin{array}{r} 297 \\ -145 \\ \hline 152 \end{array}$	$\begin{array}{r} 846 \\ -325 \\ \hline 521 \end{array}$	$\begin{array}{r} 769 \\ -514 \\ \hline 255 \end{array}$	$\begin{array}{r} 653 \\ -142 \\ \hline 511 \end{array}$
$\begin{array}{r} 569 \\ -333 \\ \hline 236 \end{array}$	$\begin{array}{r} 365 \\ -213 \\ \hline 152 \end{array}$	$\begin{array}{r} 818 \\ -618 \\ \hline 200 \end{array}$	$\begin{array}{r} 936 \\ -424 \\ \hline 512 \end{array}$

Page 180

Problem Solving

Directions: Solve each problem.

Example:

The grocery store buys 568 cans of beans.
It sells 345 cans of beans.
How many cans of beans are left?

$$\begin{array}{r} 568 \\ -345 \\ \hline 223 \end{array}$$

The cooler holds 732 gallons of milk.
It has 412 gallons of milk in it.
How many more gallons of milk
will it take to fill the cooler?

$$\begin{array}{r} 732 \\ -412 \\ \hline 320 \end{array}$$

Ann does 635 push-ups.
Carl does 421 push-ups.
How many more push-ups does Ann do?

$$\begin{array}{r} 635 \\ -421 \\ \hline 214 \end{array}$$

Kurt has 386 pennies.
Neal has 32 pennies.
How many more pennies does Kurt have?

$$\begin{array}{r} 386 \\ -32 \\ \hline 354 \end{array}$$

It takes 874 nails to build a tree house.
Jillian has 532 nails.
How many more nails does she need?

$$\begin{array}{r} 874 \\ -532 \\ \hline 342 \end{array}$$

Page 181

Problem Solving

Directions: Solve each problem.

Example:

There were 787 bales of hay.
Glenda fed the cows 535 bales.
How many bales of hay are left?

$$\begin{array}{r} 787 \\ -535 \\ \hline 252 \end{array}$$

There are 673 bolts in a box.
Maria took 341 bolts out of the box.
How many bolts are left in the box?

$$\begin{array}{r} 673 \\ -341 \\ \hline 332 \end{array}$$

The secretary types 459 letters.
138 of the letters were mailed.
How many letters are left?

$$\begin{array}{r} 459 \\ -138 \\ \hline 321 \end{array}$$

Mr. Jones had 569 dollars.
He spent 203 dollars.
How many dollars does he have left?

$$\begin{array}{r} 569 \\ -203 \\ \hline 366 \end{array}$$

There are 342 riding horses in the rodeo.
There are 132 bucking horses in the rodeo.
How many more riding horses are there?

$$\begin{array}{r} 342 \\ -132 \\ \hline 210 \end{array}$$

Page 182

Review: Addition and Subtraction

Directions: Add.

$\begin{array}{r} 124 \\ +323 \\ \hline 447 \end{array}$	$\begin{array}{r} 520 \\ +407 \\ \hline 927 \end{array}$	$\begin{array}{r} 739 \\ +150 \\ \hline 889 \end{array}$	$\begin{array}{r} 861 \\ +6 \\ \hline 867 \end{array}$

Directions: Subtract.

$\begin{array}{r} 900 \\ -600 \\ \hline 300 \end{array}$	$\begin{array}{r} 800 \\ -200 \\ \hline 600 \end{array}$	$\begin{array}{r} 974 \\ -564 \\ \hline 410 \end{array}$	$\begin{array}{r} 508 \\ -7 \\ \hline 501 \end{array}$
$\begin{array}{r} 728 \\ -326 \\ \hline 402 \end{array}$	$\begin{array}{r} 657 \\ -45 \\ \hline 612 \end{array}$	$\begin{array}{r} 894 \\ -464 \\ \hline 430 \end{array}$	$\begin{array}{r} 596 \\ -352 \\ \hline 244 \end{array}$

Directions: Solve each problem.

There are 275 nails in a box.
123 nails are taken out of the box.
How many nails are still in the box?

$$\begin{array}{r} 275 \\ -123 \\ \hline 152 \end{array}$$

Gerald peeled 212 apples.
Anna peeled 84 apples.
How many apples did they peel in all?

$$\begin{array}{r} 212 \\ +84 \\ \hline 296 \end{array}$$

Page 183

Review: 3-Digit Addition

Directions: Add.

Examples:

$\begin{array}{r} 340 \\ +225 \\ \hline 565 \end{array}$	$\begin{array}{r} 754 \\ +32 \\ \hline 786 \end{array}$	$\begin{array}{r} 826 \\ +3 \\ \hline 829 \end{array}$	$\begin{array}{r} 632 \\ +322 \\ \hline 954 \end{array}$
$\begin{array}{r} 198 \\ +200 \\ \hline 398 \end{array}$	$\begin{array}{r} 456 \\ +31 \\ \hline 487 \end{array}$	$\begin{array}{r} 541 \\ +333 \\ \hline 874 \end{array}$	$\begin{array}{r} 273 \\ +415 \\ \hline 688 \end{array}$
$\begin{array}{r} 900 \\ +34 \\ \hline 934 \end{array}$	$\begin{array}{r} 847 \\ +131 \\ \hline 978 \end{array}$	$\begin{array}{r} 721 \\ +176 \\ \hline 897 \end{array}$	$\begin{array}{r} 402 \\ +383 \\ \hline 785 \end{array}$
$\begin{array}{r} 156 \\ +423 \\ \hline 579 \end{array}$	$\begin{array}{r} 644 \\ +251 \\ \hline 895 \end{array}$	$\begin{array}{r} 215 \\ +542 \\ \hline 757 \end{array}$	$\begin{array}{r} 372 \\ +417 \\ \hline 789 \end{array}$
$\begin{array}{r} 518 \\ +351 \\ \hline 869 \end{array}$	$\begin{array}{r} 783 \\ +5 \\ \hline 788 \end{array}$	$\begin{array}{r} 684 \\ +14 \\ \hline 698 \end{array}$	$\begin{array}{r} 710 \\ +260 \\ \hline 970 \end{array}$

Page 184

Review: 3-Digit Subtraction

Directions: Subtract.

Example:

856	432	598	769
- 352	- 21	- 416	- 345
504	411	182	424

319	954	275	643
- 6	- 731	- 3	- 313
313	223	272	330

775	834	942	478
- 261	- 12	- 111	- 324
514	822	831	154

562	444	385	754
- 431	- 212	- 152	- 3
131	232	233	751

868	943	689	577
- 234	- 843	- 417	- 37
634	100	272	540

Page 185

Multiplication

Multiplication is a short way to find the sum of adding the same number a certain amount of times. For example, 7 x 4 = 28 instead of 7 + 7 + 7 + 7 = 28.

Directions: Study the example. Solve the problems.

Example:
3 + 3 + 3 = 9
3 threes = 9
3 x 3 = 9

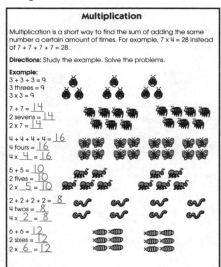

7 + 7 = 14
2 sevens = 14
2 x 7 = 14

4 + 4 + 4 + 4 = 16
4 fours = 16
4 x 4 = 16

5 + 5 = 10
2 fives = 10
2 x 5 = 10

2 + 2 + 2 + 2 = 8
4 twos = 8
4 x 2 = 8

6 + 6 = 12
2 sixes = 12
2 x 6 = 12

Page 186

Multiplication

Multiplication is repeated addition.

Directions: Draw a picture for each problem. Then, write the missing numbers.

Example:
Draw 2 groups of three apples.

3 + 3 = 6
or 2 x 3 = 6

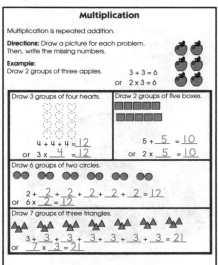

Draw 3 groups of four hearts.

4 + 4 + 4 = 12
or 3 x 4 = 12

Draw 2 groups of five boxes.

5 + 5 = 10
or 2 x 5 = 10

Draw 6 groups of two circles.

2 + 2 + 2 + 2 + 2 + 2 = 12
or 6 x 2 = 12

Draw 7 groups of three triangles.

3 + 3 + 3 + 3 + 3 + 3 + 3 = 21
or 7 x 3 = 21

Page 187

Multiplication

Directions: Study the example. Draw the groups and write the total.

Example: 3 x 2
2 + 2 + 2 = 6

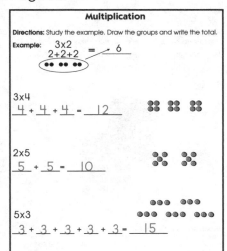

3 x 4
4 + 4 + 4 = 12

2 x 5
5 + 5 = 10

5 x 3
3 + 3 + 3 + 3 + 3 = 15

Page 188

Multiplication

Directions: Solve the problems.

9 + 9 = 18
2 nines = 18
2 x 9 = 18

7 + 7 = 14
2 sevens = 14
2 x 7 = 14

Multiplication saves time.
It's faster than addition!

4 + 4 + 4 + 4 = 16
4 fours = 16
4 x 4 = 16

8 + 8 + 8 + 8 + 8 = 40
5 eights = 40
5 x 8 = 40

5 + 5 + 5 = 15
3 fives = 15
3 x 5 = 15

9 + 9 = 18
2 nines = 18
2 x 9 = 18

6 + 6 + 6 = 18
3 sixes = 18
3 x 6 = 18

3 + 3 = 6
2 threes = 6
2 x 3 = 6

7 + 7 + 7 + 7 = 28
4 sevens = 28
4 x 7 = 28

2 + 2 = 4
2 twos = 4
2 x 2 = 4

Page 189

Multiplication

Directions: Use the code to color the fish.

If the answer is:

6, color it red.

8, color it yellow.

12, color it orange.

15, color it green.

16, color it blue.

18, color it purple.

27, color it brown.

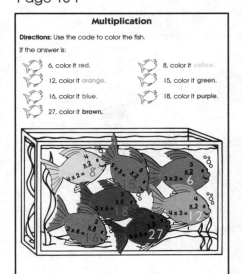

Page 190

Multiplication

Directions: Use the code to color the rainbow.

If the answer is:

6, color it **green**.   16, color it pink.   25, color it orange.

8, color it **purple**.   18, color it white.   27, color it blue.

9, color it **red**.   21, color it **brown**.

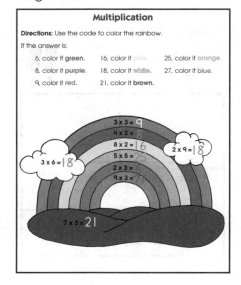

3 x 3 = 9
4 x 2 = 8
8 x 2 = 16
5 x 5 = 25
2 x 3 = 6
9 x 3 = 27
3 x 6 = 18
2 x 9 = 18
7 x 3 = 21

Page 191

Problem Solving

Directions: Tell if you add, subtract, or multiply. Then, write the answers. Hints: "In all" means to add. "Left" means to subtract. Groups with the same number in each means to multiply.

Example:

There are 6 red birds and 7 blue birds.
How many birds in all?

   add   13 birds

The pet store had 25 goldfish, but 10 were sold.
How many goldfish are left?

subtract 15 goldfish

There are 5 cages of bunnies. There are two bunnies in each cage.
How many bunnies are there in the store?

multiply 10 bunnies

The store had 18 puppies this morning. It sold 7 puppies today.
How many puppies are left?

subtract 11 puppies

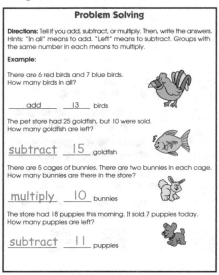

Page 192

Problem Solving

Directions: Tell if you add, subtract, or multiply. Then, write the answers.

There were 12 frogs sitting
on a log by a pond, but
3 frogs hopped away.
How many frogs were left?

subtract 9 frogs

There are 9 flowers growing by the pond. Each flower has 2 leaves.
How many leaves are there?

multiply 18 leaves

A tree had 7 squirrels playing in it. Then, 8 more came along.
How many squirrels are there in all?

  add   15 squirrels

There were 27 birds living in the trees around the pond,
but 9 flew away.
How many birds are left?

subtract 18 birds

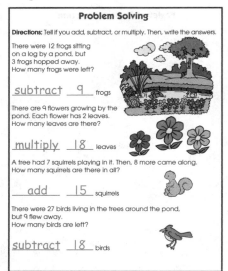

Page 193

Circle

A **circle** is a shape that is round. This is a circle: ○

Directions: Find the circles and draw squares around them.

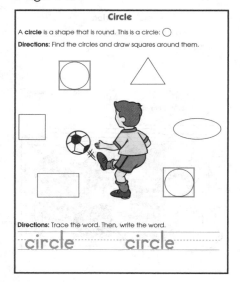

Directions: Trace the word. Then, write the word.

circle   circle

Page 194

Square

A **square** is a shape with four corners and four sides of the same length. This is a square: □

Directions: Find the squares and draw circles around them.

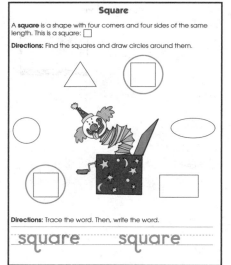

Directions: Trace the word. Then, write the word.

square   square

Page 195

Rectangle

A **rectangle** is a shape with four corners and four sides. The sides opposite each other are the same length. This is a rectangle: ▭

Directions: Find the rectangles and draw circles around them.

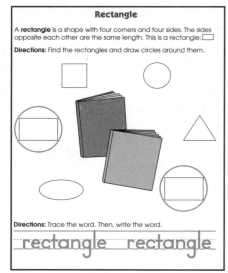

Directions: Trace the word. Then, write the word.

rectangle   rectangle

Page 196

Triangle

A **triangle** is a shape with three corners and three sides. This is a triangle: △

Directions: Find the triangles and draw circles around them.

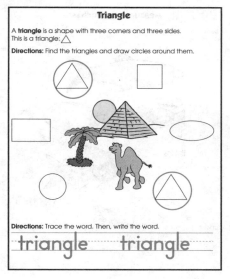

Directions: Trace the word. Then, write the word.

triangle triangle

Page 197

Oval and Diamond

An **oval** is egg-shaped. This is an oval: ◯

A **diamond** is a shape with four sides of the same length. Its corners form points at the top, sides, and bottom. This is a diamond: ◇

Directions: Find the ovals. Color them **red**. Find the diamonds. Color them **blue**.

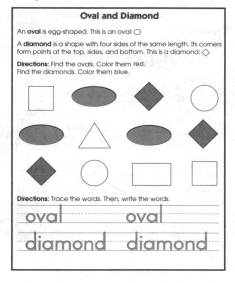

Directions: Trace the words. Then, write the words.

oval oval

diamond diamond

Page 198

Geometry

Geometry is mathematics that has to do with lines and shapes.

Directions: Color the shapes.

Color the triangles **blue**.
Color the circles **red**.
Color the squares **green**.
Color the rectangles **pink**.

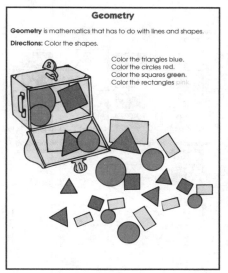

Page 199

Geometry

Directions: Draw a line from the word to the shape.

Use a **red** line for circles.   Use a **yellow** line for rectangles.
Use a **blue** line for squares.   Use a **green** line for triangles.

Circle   Square   Triangle   Rectangle

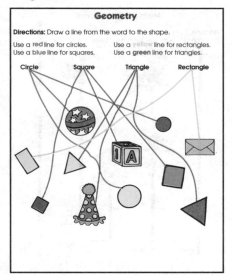

Page 200

Shapes

Robbie the robot and his pal Roger are made of many different-shaped objects. Look at all the shapes on their bodies. Then, follow the directions below.

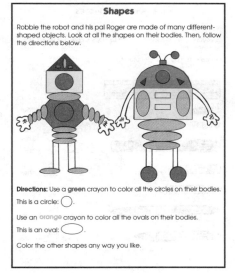

Directions: Use a **green** crayon to color all the circles on their bodies.

This is a circle: ◯.

Use an **orange** crayon to color all the ovals on their bodies.

This is an oval: ◯.

Color the other shapes any way you like.

Page 201

Shapes

Directions: Some shapes have sides. How many sides does each shape below have? Write the number of sides inside each shape.

4	4	3
square	rectangle	triangle

Directions: Help Robbie get to his space car by tracing the path that has only squares, rectangles, and triangles.

Hint: You may want to draw an **X** on all the other shapes. This will help you see the path more clearly.

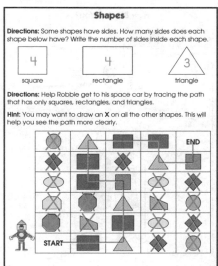

Page 202

Shapes

Directions: Look at the grid below. All the shapes have straight sides, like a square.

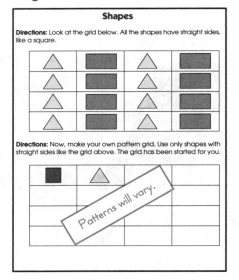

Directions: Now, make your own pattern grid. Use only shapes with straight sides like the grid above. The grid has been started for you.

Patterns will vary.

Page 203

Measurement: Inches

Directions: Cut out the ruler. Measure each object to the nearest inch.

2 inches

3 inches

1 inches

Directions: Measure objects around your house. Write the measurement to the nearest inch.

can of soup _____ inches
pen
toothbrush
paper clip
small toy

Answers will vary.

cut out

8 7 6 5 4 3 2 1

Page 205

Measurement: Inches

Directions: Use the ruler from pg. 203 to measure the fish to the nearest inch.

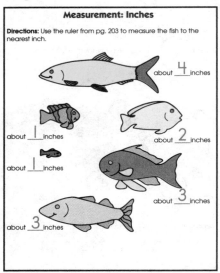

about 4 inches

about 1 inches

about 2 inches

about 1 inches

about 3 inches

about 3 inches

Page 206

How Big Are You?

Directions: How big are you? **Estimate,** or guess, how long some of your body parts are. Write your estimates below. Then, have a friend use an inch ruler to measure you. Write the numbers below. How close were your estimates?

Height Estimate _____ Inches _____

Arm Span Estimate _____ Inches _____

Arm Length Estimate _____ Inches _____

Leg Length Estimate _____ Inches _____

Foot Length Estimate _____ Inches _____

Answers will vary.

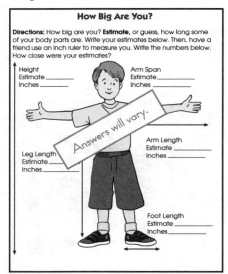

Page 207

Measurement: Inches

An **inch** is a unit of length in the standard measurement system.

Directions: Use the ruler on pg. 203 to measure each object to the nearest inch.

Example: The paper clip is about 1 inch long.

1 inch

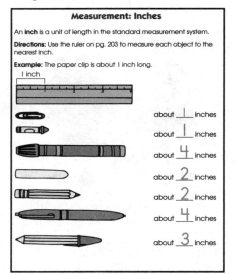

about 1 inches

about 1 inches

about 4 inches

about 2 inches

about 2 inches

about 4 inches

about 3 inches

Page 208

Measuring Monkeys

Directions: Use the inch ruler on pg. 203 to measure the length of each rope. Write the answer in each blank.

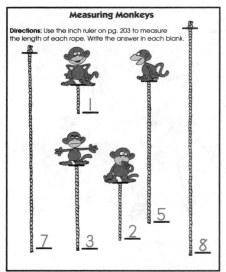

1

5

7   3   2   8

Page 209

Measurement: Centimeters

A **centimeter** is a unit of length in the metric system. There are 2.54 centimeters in an inch.

Directions: Use a centimeter ruler to measure the crayons to the nearest centimeter.

Example: The first crayon is about 7 centimeters long.

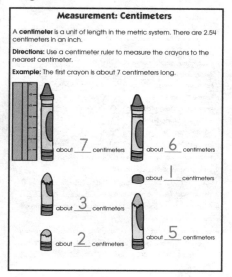

about __7__ centimeters   about __6__ centimeters

about __1__ centimeters

about __3__ centimeters   about __5__ centimeters

about __2__ centimeters

Page 210

Measurement: Centimeters

Directions: The giraffe is about 8 centimeters high. How many centimeters (cm) high are the trees? Write your answers in the blanks.

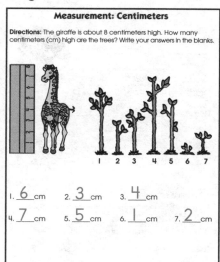

1. __6__ cm   2. __3__ cm   3. __4__ cm

4. __7__ cm   5. __5__ cm   6. __1__ cm   7. __2__ cm

Page 211

Measuring in Centimeters

Directions: Use a centimeter ruler to find the height or the length of the objects below. Write the answer in each blank.

Example:

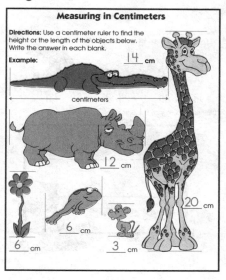

__14__ cm

centimeters

__12__ cm

__20__ cm

__6__ cm

__3__ cm

__6__ cm

Page 212

Trip to the Watering Hole

Directions: Use a centimeter ruler to measure the distance each animal has to travel to reach the watering hole. Write the answer in each blank.

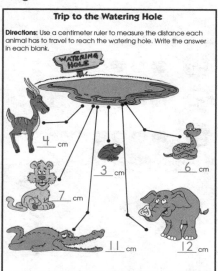

__4__ cm

__3__ cm

__6__ cm

__7__ cm

__11__ cm

__12__ cm

Page 213

Centimeter Sharpening

Directions: Use a centimeter ruler to measure each pencil. Subtract to find how many centimeters were lost when sharpening each pencil.

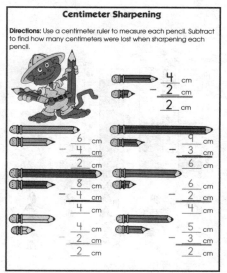

$$\begin{array}{r} 4 \text{ cm} \\ -\ 2 \text{ cm} \\ \hline 2 \text{ cm} \end{array}$$

$$\begin{array}{r} 6 \text{ cm} \\ -\ 4 \text{ cm} \\ \hline 2 \text{ cm} \end{array}$$

$$\begin{array}{r} 9 \text{ cm} \\ -\ 3 \text{ cm} \\ \hline 6 \text{ cm} \end{array}$$

$$\begin{array}{r} 8 \text{ cm} \\ -\ 4 \text{ cm} \\ \hline 4 \text{ cm} \end{array}$$

$$\begin{array}{r} 6 \text{ cm} \\ -\ 2 \text{ cm} \\ \hline 4 \text{ cm} \end{array}$$

$$\begin{array}{r} 4 \text{ cm} \\ -\ 2 \text{ cm} \\ \hline 2 \text{ cm} \end{array}$$

$$\begin{array}{r} 5 \text{ cm} \\ -\ 3 \text{ cm} \\ \hline 2 \text{ cm} \end{array}$$

Page 214

Good Morning

Directions: Make your own bar graph. List 5 kinds of cereal on the graph below. Ask 5 people to vote for one cereal. Record the votes on the graph by coloring in 1 space for each vote. Use the information to answer the questions.

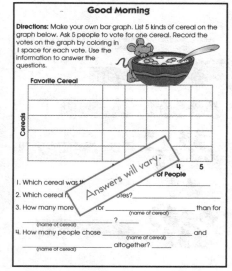

Favorite Cereal

Cereals

Number of People

   4   5

1. Which cereal was the _____

2. Which cereal had _____ votes?

3. How many more _____ for _____ (name of cereal) than for _____ (name of cereal) ?

4. How many people chose _____ (name of cereal) and _____ (name of cereal) altogether? _____

Answers will vary.

Page 215

Jungle Weather

Directions: The pictures show the weather for one month. Count the number of sunny, cloudy, and rainy days.

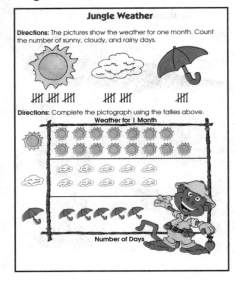

Directions: Complete the pictograph using the tallies above.

Weather for 1 Month

Number of Days

Page 216

What a Meal!

Directions: Use the pictograph to complete each sentence below.

= 2 worms

Grace Goldfish	
Willie Walleye	
Calvin Catfish	
Benny Bluegill	
Beth Bass	
Patty Perch	

1. __Benny__ got the fewest worms.
2. __Beth__ got the most worms.
3. __Grace__ and __Calvin__ got the same number of worms.
4. Benny and Patty together caught the same number of worms as __Willie__.
5. Write the number of worms that each fish ate.

| 8 | 10 | 8 | 4 | 12 | 6 |
| Grace | Willie | Calvin | Benny | Beth | Patty |

Page 217

"Play Ball"

Directions: Eight baseball teams have just completed their season. Each team played eight games. Use this pictograph to answer the questions below.

= 1 win

Washington Wiggle Worms	
Jersey Jaguars	
Pittsburgh Pandas	
Tampa Toucans	
Kansas City Centipedes	
Lansing Lightning Bugs	
Houston Hornets	
Memphis Monkeys	

1. How many games did the Memphis Monkeys lose? __7__
2. Which teams tied for last place? __Lansing Lightning Bugs__ and __Memphis Monkeys__
3. Which team won the most games? __Jersey Jaguars__
4. How many more games did the Washington Wiggle Worms win than the Tampa Toucans? __4__
5. Which four teams' total number of games won equal the Jersey Jaguars' number of games won? __Kansas City Centipedes, Lansing Lightning Bugs, Houston Hornets, Memphis Monkeys__

Page 218

Graphs

A **graph** is a drawing that shows information about numbers.

Directions: Count the apples in each row. Color the boxes to show how many apples have bites taken out of them.

Example:

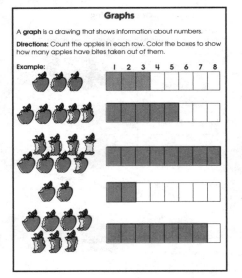

Page 219

Graphs

Directions: Count the banana peels in each column. Color the boxes to show how many bananas have been eaten by the monkeys.

Example:

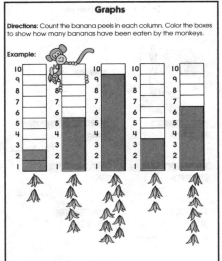

Page 220

Graphs

Directions: Count the fish. Color the bowls to make a graph that shows the number of fish.

Directions: Use your fishbowl graphs to find the answers to the following questions. Draw a line to the correct bowl.

The most fish

The fewest fish

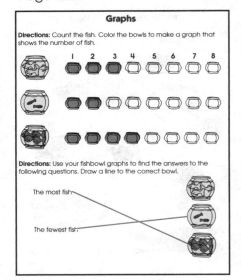

Page 221

Treasure Quest

Directions: Read the directions. Draw the pictures where they belong on the grid. Start at 0 and go . . .

over 2, up 5. Draw a

over 9, up 3. Draw a

over 8, up 6. Draw a

over 5, up 2. Draw a

over 1, up 7. Draw a

over 7, up 1. Draw a

over 6, up 4. Draw a

over 2, up 3. Draw a

over 3, up 1. Draw a

over 4, up 6. Draw a

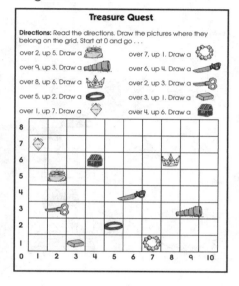

Page 222

Let's Get Things in Order!

Directions: Help Mrs. Brown pick flowers in her garden. The flowers she wants are listed in the chart. Use the descriptions to color the flowers in her garden.

		Color it:
1st row	6th flower	red
2nd row	4th flower	blue
3rd row	1st flower	yellow
4th row	9th flower	pink
5th row	10th flower	orange
6th row	2nd flower	green
7th row	5th flower	black
8th row	7th flower	grey
9th row	8th flower	purple
10th row	3rd flower	brown

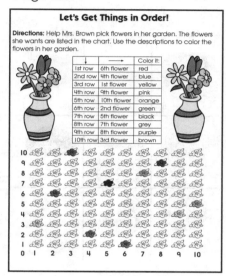

Page 223

Whole and Half

A **fraction** is a number that names part of a whole, such as $\frac{1}{2}$.

Directions: Color half of each thing.

Example: whole apple   half an apple

Page 224

One Third

$\frac{1}{1}$ part is blue.

The $\boxed{3}$ parts are the same size.

$\boxed{\frac{1}{3}}$ of the inside is blue.

Directions: Complete the fraction statements.

Example:

$\frac{1}{3}$ part is blue.
$\frac{3}{3}$ parts are the same size.
$\frac{1}{3}$ of the inside is blue.

$\frac{1}{3}$ part is blue.
$\frac{3}{3}$ parts are the same size.
$\frac{1}{3}$ of the inside is blue.

$\frac{1}{3}$ part is blue.
$\frac{3}{3}$ parts are the same size.
$\frac{1}{3}$ of the inside is blue.

$\frac{1}{3}$ part is blue.
$\frac{3}{3}$ parts are the same size.
$\frac{1}{3}$ of the inside is blue.

$\frac{1}{3}$ of the inside is blue.

$\frac{1}{3}$ of the inside is blue.

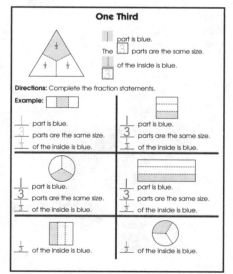

Page 225

One Fourth

$\frac{1}{1}$ part is blue.

The $\boxed{4}$ parts are the same size.

$\boxed{\frac{1}{4}}$ of the inside is blue.

Directions: Complete the fraction statements.

Example:

$\frac{1}{4}$ part is blue.
$\frac{4}{4}$ parts are the same size.
$\frac{1}{4}$ of the inside is blue.

$\frac{1}{4}$ part is blue.
$\frac{4}{4}$ parts are the same size.
$\frac{1}{4}$ of the inside is blue.

$\frac{1}{4}$ part is blue.
$\frac{4}{4}$ parts are the same size.
$\frac{1}{4}$ of the inside is blue.

$\frac{1}{4}$ part is blue.
$\frac{4}{4}$ parts are the same size.
$\frac{1}{4}$ of the inside is blue.

$\frac{1}{4}$ of the inside is blue.

$\frac{1}{4}$ of the inside is blue.

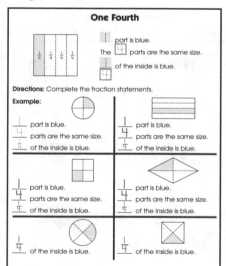

Page 226

Thirds and Fourths

Directions: Each shape has **3** equal parts. Color one section, or $\frac{1}{3}$, of each shape.

Directions: Each shape has **4** equal parts. Color one section, or $\frac{1}{4}$, of each shape.

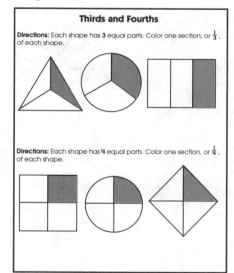

Page 227

Fractions: Half, Third, Fourth

Directions: Color the correct fraction of each shape.

Examples:

shaded part 1
equal parts 2
$\frac{1}{2}$ (one-half)

shaded part 1
equal parts 3
$\frac{1}{3}$ (one-third)

shaded part 1
equal parts 4
$\frac{1}{4}$ (one-fourth)

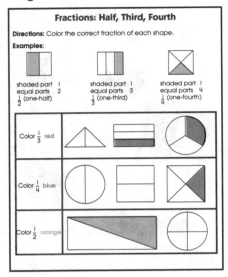

Color $\frac{1}{3}$ red

Color $\frac{1}{4}$ blue

Color $\frac{1}{2}$ orange

Page 228

Fraction Food

Directions: Count the equal parts. Circle the fraction that names one of the parts.

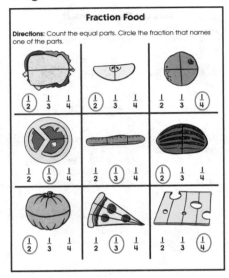

Page 229

Shaded Shapes

Directions: Draw a line to match each fraction with its correct shape.

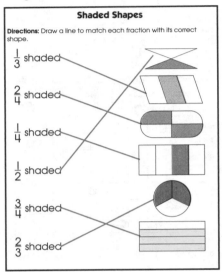

$\frac{1}{3}$ shaded

$\frac{2}{4}$ shaded

$\frac{1}{4}$ shaded

$\frac{1}{2}$ shaded

$\frac{3}{4}$ shaded

$\frac{2}{3}$ shaded

Page 230

Mean Monster's Diet

Directions: Help Mean Monster choose the right piece of food.

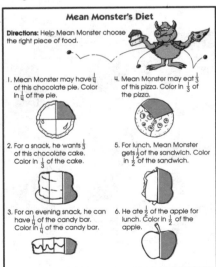

1. Mean Monster may have $\frac{1}{4}$ of this chocolate pie. Color in $\frac{1}{4}$ of the pie.

2. For a snack, he wants $\frac{1}{3}$ of this chocolate cake. Color in $\frac{1}{3}$ of the cake.

3. For an evening snack, he can have $\frac{1}{4}$ of the candy bar. Color in $\frac{1}{4}$ of the candy bar.

4. Mean Monster may eat $\frac{1}{3}$ of this pizza. Color in $\frac{1}{3}$ of the pizza.

5. For lunch, Mean Monster gets $\frac{1}{2}$ of the sandwich. Color in $\frac{1}{2}$ of the sandwich.

6. He ate $\frac{1}{2}$ of the apple for lunch. Color in $\frac{1}{2}$ of the apple.

Page 231

Fractions: Half, Third, Fourth

Directions: Study the examples. Circle the fraction that shows the shaded part. Then, circle the fraction that shows the white part.

Examples:

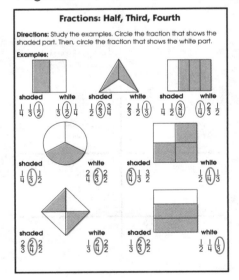

Page 232

Fractions

One morning, Mrs. Murky asks her class:

"Which would you rather have, $\frac{1}{2}$ of a candy bar or $\frac{2}{4}$ of a candy bar?"

Directions: Which would you rather have? Explain your answer.

$\frac{1}{2}$ and $\frac{2}{4}$ are the same amount.

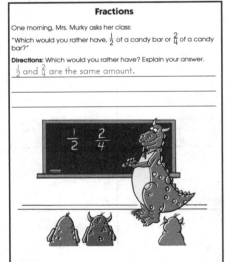

Page 233

Fractions

Directions: Rodney, Jed, and Ursula had a pizza party. They ordered I large fish-eye pizza and I large toadstool pizza. Draw lines through the pizzas to divide them equally into slices. Color the pizza slices in 3 colors, I for each monster, to show how many slices each monster gets.

Answers will vary.

How many slices will each monster get? _____

Page 235

Writing the Time

An hour is sixty minutes long. It takes an hour for the BIG HAND to go around the clock. When the BIG HAND is on 12, and the little hand points to a number, that is the hour!

Directions: The **BIG HAND** is on the **12**. Color it red. The **little hand** is on the **8**. Color it blue.

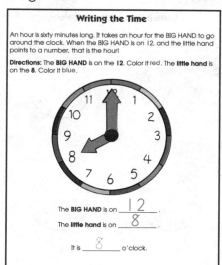

The **BIG HAND** is on __12__.

The **little hand** is on __8__.

It is __8__ o'clock.

Page 236

Writing the Time

Directions: Color the little hour hand red. Fill in the blanks.

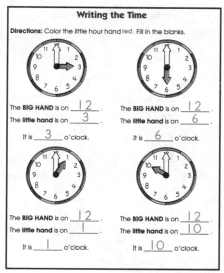

The **BIG HAND** is on __12__.
The **little hand** is on __3__.
It is __3__ o'clock.

The **BIG HAND** is on __12__.
The **little hand** is on __6__.
It is __6__ o'clock.

The **BIG HAND** is on __12__.
The **little hand** is on __1__.
It is __1__ o'clock.

The **BIG HAND** is on __12__.
The **little hand** is on __10__.
It is __10__ o'clock.

Page 237

Practice

Directions: What is the time?

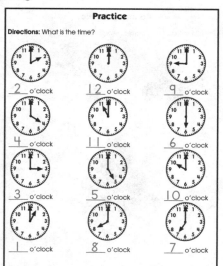

__2__ o'clock   __12__ o'clock   __9__ o'clock

__4__ o'clock   __11__ o'clock   __6__ o'clock

__3__ o'clock   __5__ o'clock   __10__ o'clock

__1__ o'clock   __8__ o'clock   __7__ o'clock

Page 238

Matching Digital and Face Clocks

Long ago, there were only wind-up clocks. Today, we also have electric and battery clocks. We may soon have solar clocks!

Directions: Match the digital and face clocks that show the same time.

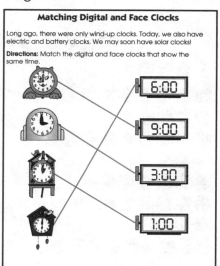

Page 239

Writing Time on the Half-Hour

Directions: Write the times.

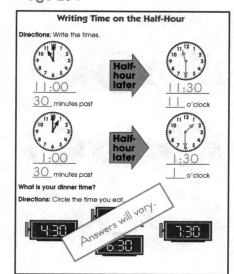

__11:00__
__30__ minutes past

Half-hour later →

__11:30__
__11__ o'clock

__1:00__
__30__ minutes past

Half-hour later →

__1:30__
__1__ o'clock

What is your dinner time?
Directions: Circle the time you eat.

Answers will vary.

4:30   7:30   6:30

Page 240

Writing Time on the Half-Hour

Directions: What time is it?

half past _2:30_

half past _9:30_

half past _4:30_

half past _12:30_

half past _11:30_

half past _1:30_

Page 242

Writing Time on the Half-Hour

Directions: Draw the hands. Write the times.

5:15

_15_ minutes after
_5_ o'clock

10:15

_15_ minutes after
_10_ o'clock

2:15

_15_ minutes after
_2_ o'clock

9:15

_15_ minutes after
_9_ o'clock

Page 243

Time to the Minute Intervals: Introduction

Each **number** on the clock face stands for **5 minutes**.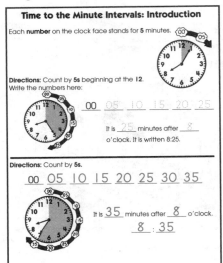

Directions: Count by **5s** beginning at the **12**.
Write the numbers here:

_00_ _05_ _10_ _15_ _20_ _25_

It is _25_ minutes after _8_
o'clock. It is written 8:25.

Directions: Count by **5s.**

_00_ _05_ _10_ _15_ _20_ _25_ _30_ _35_

It is _35_ minutes after _8_ o'clock.

_8_ : _35_

Page 244

Drawing the Minute Hand

Directions: Draw the hands on these fish clocks.

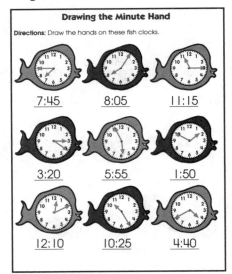

_7:45_   _8:05_   _11:15_

_3:20_   _5:55_   _1:50_

_12:10_   _10:25_   _4:40_

Page 245

Counting Pennies

Directions: Count the pennies.
How many cents?

Example:

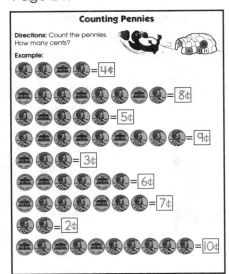

= _4¢_

= _8¢_

= _5¢_

= _9¢_

= _3¢_

= _6¢_

= _7¢_

= _2¢_

= _10¢_

Page 246

Counting Pennies

Directions: Count the pennies in each triangle.

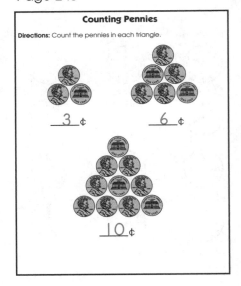

_3_ ¢

_6_ ¢

_10_ ¢

Page 247

Nickels: Introduction

Directions: Look at the two sides of a nickel. Color the nickels silver.

front   back

__1__ nickel = __5__ pennies

__1__ nickel = __5__ cents

__1__ nickel = __5__ ¢

Directions: Write the number of cents in a nickel.

5¢ = __1__ ¢ + __1__ ¢ + __1__ ¢ + __1__ ¢ + __1__ ¢

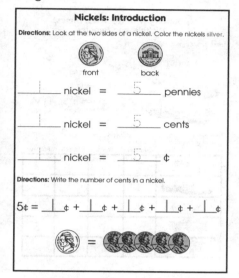

Page 248

Nickels: Counting by Fives

Directions: Count the nickels by 5s. Write the amount.

Example: 5 cents = 1 nickel

[15]¢   [10]¢

Count __5__ __10__ __15__.   Count __5__ __10__.

[25]¢   [35]¢

Count __5__ __10__ __15__   Count __5__ __10__ __15__ __20__
__20__ __25__.   __25__ __30__ __35__.

[20]¢   [30]¢

Count __5__ __10__ __15__   Count __5__ __10__ __15__
__20__.   __20__ __25__ __30__.

Page 249

Dimes: Introduction

A dime is small, but quite strong. It can buy more than a penny or a nickel.

front   back

Directions: Each side of a dime is different. It has ridges on its edge. Color the dime silver.

Directions: Write the number of cents in a dime.

__1__ dime = __10__ pennies

__1__ dime = __10__ cents

__1__ dime = __10__ ¢

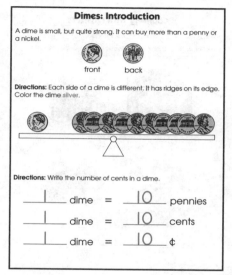

Page 250

Dimes: Counting by Tens

Directions: Count by 10s. Write the number. Circle the group with more.

__30__ ¢   or   __10__ ¢

__40__ ¢   or   __30__ ¢

__50__ ¢   or   __90__ ¢

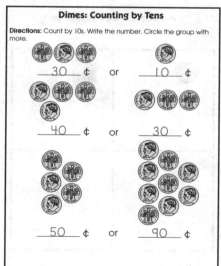

Page 251

Counting With Dimes, Nickels, and Pennies

Directions: Count the money. Start with the dime. Write the amount.

1.   __12__ ¢

2.   __16__ ¢

3. Circle the answer.
    Who has more money?

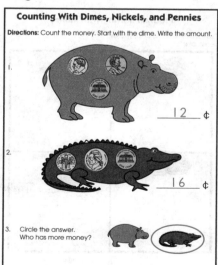

Page 252

Quarters: Introduction

Our first president, George Washington, is on the front. The American eagle is on the back.

front   back

Directions: Write the number of cents in a quarter.

__1__ quarter = __25__ pennies

__1__ quarter = __25__ cents

__1__ quarter = __25__ ¢

Directions: Count these nickels by 5s. Is this another way to make 25¢?

(yes)   no

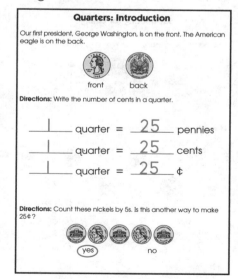

Page 253

Counting With Quarters

These are some machines that use quarters.

Directions: Color each machine you have to put quarters into. Circle the number of quarters you need.

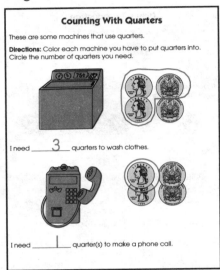

I need ___3___ quarters to wash clothes.

I need ___1___ quarter(s) to make a phone call.

Page 254

Counting With Quarters, Dimes, Nickels, and Pennies

Directions: Match the money with the amount.

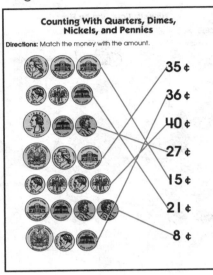

35 ¢
36 ¢
40 ¢
27 ¢
15 ¢
21 ¢
8 ¢

Page 255

Counting With Quarters, Dimes, Nickels, and Pennies

Here are things to buy for your hair.

Directions: How many of each coin do you need? Write 1, 2, 3, or 4.

	Quarters	Dimes	Nickels	Pennies
(earring)	1		1	2
(brush)	1	1		
(headband)	1			4
(bow)			1	3
(comb)		2		

Page 256

Subtracting for Change

Adam wanted to know how much change he would have left when he bought things. He made this picture to help him subtract.

```
  4 dimes          40 ¢
- 1 dime         - 10 ¢
  3 dimes          30 ¢
```

Directions: Cross out and subtract.

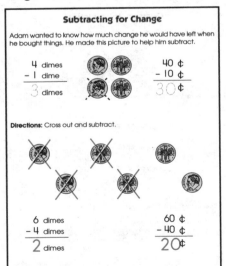

```
  6 dimes          60 ¢
- 4 dimes        - 40 ¢
  2 dimes          20 ¢
```

Page 257

Problem-Solving With Money

Directions: Draw the coins you use. Write the number of coins on each blank.

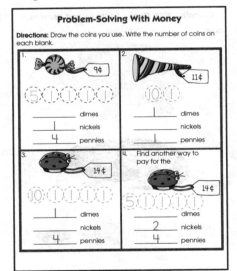

1. 9¢
(5)(1)(1)(1)(1)
___ dimes
_1_ nickels
_4_ pennies

2. 11¢
(10)(1)
_1_ dimes
___ nickels
_1_ pennies

3. 14¢
(10)(1)(1)(1)(1)
_1_ dimes
___ nickels
_4_ pennies

4. Find another way to pay for the 14¢
(5)(1)(1)(1)(1)
___ dimes
_2_ nickels
_4_ pennies

Page 258

Problem-Solving With Money

Directions: Draw the coins you use. Write the number of coins on each blank.

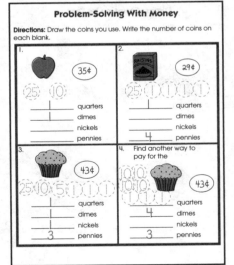

1. 35¢
(25)(10)
_1_ quarters
_1_ dimes
___ nickels
___ pennies

2. 29¢
(25)(1)(1)(1)(1)
_1_ quarters
___ dimes
___ nickels
_4_ pennies

3. 43¢
(25)(10)(5)(1)(1)(1)
_1_ quarters
_1_ dimes
_1_ nickels
_3_ pennies

4. Find another way to pay for the 43¢
(10)(10)(10)(1)(1)(1)
___ quarters
_4_ dimes
___ nickels
_3_ pennies

Page 259

Making Exact Amounts of Money: Two Ways to Pay

Directions: Find two ways to pay. Show what coins you use.

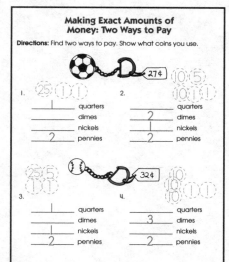

27¢

1.
1	quarters
	dimes
	nickels
2	pennies

2.
	quarters
2	dimes
1	nickels
2	pennies

32¢

3.
1	quarters
	dimes
1	nickels
2	pennies

4.
	quarters
3	dimes
	nickels
2	pennies

Page 260

Making Exact Amounts of Money: Two Ways to Pay

Directions: Find two ways to pay. Show what coins you use.

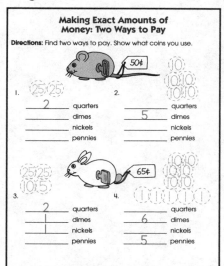

50¢

1.
2	quarters
	dimes
	nickels
	pennies

2.
	quarters
5	dimes
	nickels
	pennies

65¢

3.
2	quarters
1	dimes
1	nickels
	pennies

4.
	quarters
6	dimes
	nickels
5	pennies

Page 261

Making Exact Amounts of Money: How Much More?

Directions: Count the coins. Find out how much more money you need to pay the exact amount.

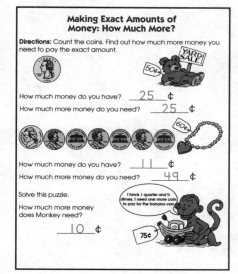

How much money do you have? __25__ ¢

How much more money do you need? __25__ ¢

How much money do you have? __11__ ¢

How much more money do you need? __49__ ¢

Solve this puzzle.

How much more money does Monkey need?

__10__ ¢

I have 1 quarter and 4 dimes. I need one more coin to pay for the banana-van.

75¢

This page was
intentionally left blank.

Test Practice

About the Tests

What Are Standardized Achievement Tests?

Achievement tests measure what children know in particular subject areas such as reading, language arts, and mathematics. They do not measure your child's intelligence or ability to learn.

When tests are standardized, or *normed*, children's test results are compared with those of a specific group who have taken the test, usually at the same age or grade.

Standardized achievement tests measure what children around the country are learning. The test makers survey popular textbook series, as well as state curriculum frameworks and other professional sources, to determine what content is covered widely.

Because of variations in state frameworks and textbook series, as well as grade ranges on some test levels, the tests may cover some material that children have not yet learned. This is especially true if the test is offered early in the school year. However, test scores are compared to those of other children who take the test at the same time of year, so your child will not be at a disadvantage if his or her class has not covered specific material yet.

Different School Districts, Different Tests

There are many flexible options for districts when offering standardized tests. Many school districts choose not to give the full test battery, but select certain content and scoring options. For example, many schools may test only in the areas of reading and mathematics. Similarly, a state or district may use one test for certain grades and another test for other grades. These decisions are often based on

the amount of time and money a district wishes to spend on test administration. Some states choose to develop their own statewide assessment tests.

On pages 310 and 311 you will find information about these five widely used standardized achievement tests:

- California Achievement Test (CAT)
- Terra Nova/CTBS
- Iowa Test of Basic Skills (ITBS)
- Stanford Achievement Test (SAT9)
- Metropolitan Achievement Test (MAT)

However, this section contains strategies and practice questions for use with a variety of tests. Even if your state does not give one of the five tests listed above, your child will benefit from doing the practice questions in this section. If you're unsure about which test your child takes, contact your local school district to find out which tests are given.

Types of Test Questions

Traditionally, standardized achievement tests have used only multiple-choice questions. Today, many tests may include constructed response (short answer) and extended response (essay) questions as well.

In addition, many tests include questions that tap students' higher-order thinking skills. Instead of simple recall questions, such as identifying a date in history, questions may require students to make comparisons and contrasts or analyze results, among other skills.

What the Tests Measure

These tests do not measure your child's level of intelligence, but they do show how well your child

knows material that he or she has learned and that is also covered on the tests. It's important to remember that some tests cover content that is not taught in your child's school or grade. In other instances, depending on when in the year the test is given, your child may not yet have covered the material.

If the test reports you receive show that your child needs improvement in one or more skill areas, you may want to seek help from your child's teacher and find out how you can work with your child to improve his or her skills.

California Achievement Test (CAT/5)

What Is the California Achievement Test?

The *California Achievement Test* is a standardized achievement test battery that is widely used with elementary through high school students.

Parts of the Test

The *CAT* includes tests in the following content areas:

Reading
- Word Analysis
- Vocabulary
- Comprehension

Spelling

Language Arts
- Language Mechanics
- Language Usage

Mathematics

Science

Social Studies

Your child may take some or all of these subtests if your district uses the *California Achievement Test*.

Terra Nova/CTBS (Comprehensive Tests of Basic Skills)

What Is the Terra Nova/CTBS?

The *Terra Nova/Comprehensive Tests of Basic Skills* is a standardized achievement test battery used in elementary through high school grades.

While many of the test questions on the T*erra Nova* are in the traditional multiple choice form, your child may take parts of the *Terra Nova* that include some open-ended questions (constructed-response items).

Parts of the Test

Your child may take some or all of the following subtests if your district uses the *Terra Nova/CTBS*:

Reading/Language Arts
Mathematics
Science
Social Studies

Supplementary tests include:
- Word Analysis
- Vocabulary
- Language Mechanics
- Spelling
- Mathematics Computation

Critical thinking skills may also be tested.

Iowa Test of Basic Skills (ITBS)

What Is the ITBS?

The *Iowa Test of Basic Skills* is a standardized achievement test battery used in elementary through high school grades.

Parts of the Test

Your child may take some or all of these subtests if your district uses the *ITBS*, also known as the *Iowa*:

Reading
- Vocabulary
- Reading Comprehension

Language Arts
- Spelling
- Capitalization
- Punctuation
- Usage and Expression

Math
- Concepts/Estimate
- Problems/Data Interpretation

Social Studies

Science

Sources of Information

Stanford Achievement Test (SAT9)

What Is the Stanford Achievement Test?

The *Stanford Achievement Test, Ninth Edition (SAT9)* is a standardized achievement test battery used in elementary through high school grades.

Note that the *Stanford Achievement Test (SAT9)* is a different test from the *SAT* used by high school students for college admissions.

While many of the test questions on the *SAT9* are in traditional multiple choice form, your child may take parts of the *SAT9* that include some open-ended questions (constructed-response items).

Parts of the Test

Your child may take some or all of these subtests if your district uses the *Stanford Achievement Test*:

Reading
- Vocabulary
- Reading Comprehension

Mathematics
- Problem Solving
- Procedures

Language Arts

Spelling

Study Skills

Listening
Critical thinking skills may also be tested.

Metropolitan Achievement Test (MAT7 and MAT8)

What Is the Metropolitan Achievement Test?

The *Metropolitan Achievement Test* is a standardized achievement test battery used in elementary through high school grades.

Parts of the Test

Your child may take some or all of these subtests if your district uses the *Metropolitan Achievement Test*:

Reading
- Vocabulary
- Reading Comprehension

Math
- Concepts and Problem Solving
- Computation

Language Arts
- Pre-writing
- Composing
- Editing

Science

Social Studies

Research Skills

Thinking Skills

Spelling

Statewide Assessments

Today the majority of states give statewide assessments. In some cases these tests are known as *high-stakes assessments*. This means that students must score at a certain level in order to be promoted. Some states use minimum competency or proficiency tests. Often these tests measure more basic skills than other types of statewide assessments.

Statewide assessments are generally linked to state curriculum frameworks. Frameworks provide a blueprint, or outline, to ensure that teachers are covering the same curriculum topics as other teachers in the same grade level in the state. In some states, standardized achievement tests (such as the five described in this section) are used in connection with statewide assessments.

When Statewide Assessments Are Given

Statewide assessments may not be given at every grade level. Generally, they are offered at one or more grades in elementary school, middle school, and high school. Many states test at grades 4, 8, and 10.

State-by-State Information

You can find information about statewide assessments and curriculum frameworks at your state Department of Education Web site. To find the address for your individual state, go to www.ed.gov, click on Topics A–Z, and then click on State Departments of Education. You will find a list of all the state departments of education, mailing addresses, and Web sites.

How to Help Your Child Prepare for Standardized Testing

Preparing All Year Round

Perhaps the most valuable way you can help your child prepare for standardized achievement tests is by providing enriching experiences. Keep in mind also that test results for younger children are not as reliable as for older students. If a child is hungry, tired, or upset, this may result in a poor test score. Here are some tips on how you can help your child do his or her best on standardized tests.

Read aloud with your child. Reading aloud helps develop vocabulary and fosters a positive attitude toward reading. Reading together is one of the most effective ways you can help your child succeed in school.

Share experiences. Baking cookies together, planting a garden, or making a map of your neighborhood are examples of activities that help build skills that are measured on the tests, such as sequencing and following directions.

Become informed about your state's testing procedures. Ask about or watch for announcements of meetings that explain about standardized tests and statewide assessments in your school district. Talk to your child's teacher about your child's individual performance on these state tests during a parent-teacher conference.

Help your child know what to expect. Read and discuss with your child the test-taking tips in this book. Your child can prepare by working through a couple of strategies a day so that no practice session takes too long.

Help your child with his or her regular school assignments. Set up a quiet study area for homework. Supply this area with pencils, paper, markers, a calculator, a ruler, a dictionary, scissors, glue, and so on. Check your child's homework and offer to help if he or she gets stuck. But remember, it's your child's homework, not yours. If you help too much, your child will not benefit from the activity.

Keep in regular contact with your child's teacher. Attend parent-teacher conferences, school functions, PTA or PTO meetings, and school board meetings. This will help you get to know the educators in your district and the families of your child's classmates.

Learn to use computers as an educational resource. If you do not have a computer and Internet access at home, try your local library.

Remember—simply getting your child comfortable with testing procedures and helping him or her know what to expect can improve test scores!

Getting Ready for the Big Day

There are lots of things you can do on or immediately before test day to improve your child's chances of testing success. What's more, these strategies will help your child prepare him- or herself for school tests, too, and promote general study skills that can last a lifetime.

Provide a good breakfast on test day. Instead of sugar cereal, which provides immediate but not long-term energy, have your child eat a breakfast with protein or complex carbohydrates, such as an egg, whole grain cereal or toast, or a banana-yogurt shake.

Assure your child that he or she is not expected to know all of the answers on the test. Explain that other children in higher grades may take the same test, and that the test may measure things your child has not yet learned in school. Help your child understand that you expect him or her to put forth a good effort—and that this is enough. Your child should not try to cram for these tests. Also avoid threats or bribes; these put undue pressure on children and may interfere with their best performance.

Promote a good night's sleep. A good night's sleep before the test is essential. Try not to overstress the importance of the test. This may cause your child to lose sleep because of anxiety. Doing some exercise after school and having a quiet evening routine will help your child sleep well the night before the test.

Keep the mood light and offer encouragement. To provide a break on test days, do something fun and special after school—take a walk around the neighborhood, play a game, read a favorite book, or prepare a special snack together. These activities keep your child's mood light—even if the testing sessions have been difficult—and show how much you appreciate your child's effort.

Taking Standardized Tests

What You Need to Know About Taking Tests
You can get better at taking tests. Here are some tips.

Do your schoolwork. Study in school. Do your homework all the time. These things will help you in school and on any tests you take. Learn new things a little at a time. Then you will remember them better when you see them on a test.

Feel your best. One way you can do your best on tests and in school is to make sure your body is ready. Get a good night's sleep. Eat a healthy breakfast.

One more thing: Wear comfortable clothes. You can also wear your lucky shirt or your favorite color on test day. It can't hurt. It may even make you feel better about the test.

Be ready for the test. Do practice questions. Learn about the different kinds of questions. Books like this one will help you.

Follow the test directions. Listen carefully to the directions your teacher gives. Read all instructions carefully. Watch out for words such as *not*, *none*, *never*, *all*, and *always*. These words can change the meaning of the directions. You may want to circle words like these. This will help you keep them in mind as you answer the questions.

Look carefully at each page before you start. Do reading tests in a special order. First, read the directions. Read the questions next. This way you will know what to look for as you read. Then read the story. Last, read the story again quickly. Skim it to find the best answer.

On math tests, look at the labels on graphs and charts. Think about what the graph or chart shows. You will often need to draw conclusions about the information to answer some questions.

Use your time wisely. Many tests have time limits. Look at the clock when the test starts. Figure out when you need to stop. When you begin, look over the whole thing. Do the easy parts first. Go back and do the hard parts last. Make sure you do not spend too much time on any one part. This way, if you run out of time, you still have completed much of the test.

Fill in the answer circles the right way. Fill in the whole circle. Make your pencil mark dark, but not so dark that it goes through the paper! Be sure you pick just one answer for each question. If you pick two answers, both will be marked as wrong.

Use context clues to figure out hard questions. You may come across a word or an idea you don't understand. First, try to say it in your own words. Then use context clues— the words in the sentences nearby— to help you figure out its meaning.

Sometimes it's good to guess. Here's what to do. Each question may have four or five answer choices. You may know that two answers are wrong, but you are not sure about the rest. Then make your best guess. If you are not sure about any of the answers, skip it. Do not guess. Tests like these take away extra points for wrong answers. So it is better to leave them blank.

Check your work. You may finish the test before the time is up. Then you can go back and check your answers. Make sure you answered each question you could. Also, make sure that you filled in only one answer circle for each question. Erase any extra marks on the page.

Finally—stay calm! Take time to relax before the test. One good way to relax is to get some exercise. Stretch, shake out your fingers, and wiggle your toes. Take a few slow, deep breaths. Then picture yourself doing a great job!

Skills Checklists

Do you need more practice in math? Find out. Use the checklists below. Read each sentence. Is it true for you? Put a check next to it. Then look at the unchecked sentences. These are the skills you need to review.

Keep in mind that if you are using these checklists in the middle of the school year, you may not have learned some skills yet. Talk to your teacher or a parent if you need help with a new skill.

Numeration

☐ I can read numbers to 1000.

☐ I can count objects to 1000.

☐ I can compare numbers.

☐ I can count on by 2s, 3s, 4s, 5s, and 10s.

☐ I understand place value to the hundreds place.

☐ I can put numbers in order.

☐ I can complete number patterns.

Addition, Subtraction, and Multiplication

☐ I know addition and subtraction facts to 18.

☐ I can add and subtract two- and three-digit numbers with regrouping.

☐ I can multiply one-digit numbers by 2, 3, 4, 5, and 10.

☐ I can write and solve number sentences.

Problem Solving

☐ When I do number problems, I read the directions carefully.

☐ When I do word problems, I read the problem carefully.

☐ I look for words that tell whether I must add or subtract to solve the problem.

Time, Measurement, Money, and Geometry

☐ I can use charts and graphs.

☐ I can understand a calendar.

☐ I can tell time on both kinds of clocks.

☐ I can use basic measuring tools.

☐ I can compare and measure lengths.

☐ I understand how much coins are worth.

☐ I know the basic shapes.

☐ I can match and complete shape patterns.

☐ I can find lines of symmetry.

☐ I understand basic fractions.

Getting Ready All Year

You can do better in school and on tests if you know how to study and make good use of your time. Here are some tips.

Make it easy to get your homework done. Set up a place in which to do it each day. Choose a place that is quiet. Get the things you need, such as pencils, paper, and markers. Put them in your homework place.

Homework Log and Weekly Calendar Make your own homework log. Or copy the one on pages 320–321 of this section. Write down your homework each day. Also list other things you have to do, such as sports practice or music lessons. Then you won't forget easily.

Do your homework right away. Do it soon after you get home from school. Give yourself a lot of time. Then you won't be too tired to do it later on.

Get help if you need it. If you need help, just ask. Call a friend. Or ask a family member. If they cannot help you, ask your teacher the next day.

Figure out how you learn best. Some people learn best by listening, others by looking. Some learn best by doing something with their hands or moving around. Some children like to work in groups. And some are very happy working alone.

Think about your favorite parts of school. Are you good in art, mathematics, or maybe gym? Your favorite class may be a clue to how you learn best. Try to figure it out. Then use it to study and learn better.

Practice, practice, practice! The best way to get better is by practicing a lot. You may have trouble in a school subject. Do some extra work in that subject. It can give you just the boost you need.

Homework Log
and Weekly Schedule

	MONDAY	TUESDAY	WEDNESDAY
MATHEMATICS			
READING			
LANGUAGE ARTS			
OTHER			

for the week of _____

THURSDAY	FRIDAY	SATURDAY/SUNDAY	
$\begin{array}{r} 2 \\ +3 \\ \hline 5 \end{array}$		MATH	MATHEMATICS
			READING
			LANGUAGE ARTS
			OTHER

Everyone in school has to take tests. This book will help you get ready for them. Ask a family member to help you.

The best way to get ready for tests is to do your best in school. You can also learn about the kinds of questions that will be on them. That is what this book is about. It will help you know what to do on the day of the test.

You will learn about the questions that will be on the test. You will get questions on which to practice. You will get hints for how to answer the questions.

In this section, there is a Practice Test and Final Test for Grade 2. These tests look like the ones you take in school. There is also a list of answers to help you check your answers.

If you practice, you will be all ready on test day.

Math Questions

On some tests, you will have to answer math questions. Some of these questions will tell a story or show pictures.

EXAMPLE

Look at the picture. Which number sentence shows how many treats there are in all?

○　1 + 2 + 1

○　4 + 6

○　3 + 2 + 1

When you answer math questions on a test:

• Look at the picture. Read all the choices. Then mark your answer.

• Look for important words and numbers.

• Draw pictures or write numbers on scratch paper.

• Look for clue words like *in all, more, less, left,* and *equal.*

Testing It Out

Look at the sample question more closely.

Think: I see 3 groups of treats. The number sentence should have 3 numbers. The first sentence has 3 numbers. But it does not match the pictures. The next sentence only has 2 numbers. They are also too big. The last sentence matches the picture. There are 3 cookies, 2 lollipops, and 1 candy bar.

Math Questions Practice

Directions: Fill in the circle next to the answer that matches the picture.

1

- ○ 39 cents
- ○ 40 cents
- ○ 50 cents

2

- ○ 13 books
- ○ 11 books
- ○ 14 books

Directions: Use scratch paper to work out your answer.
Then fill in the circle next to the right number.

3

$$\begin{array}{r} 26 \\ + 7 \end{array}$$

- ○ 33
- ○ 36
- ○ 39

4

$$\begin{array}{r} 11 \\ 21 \\ + 32 \end{array}$$

- ○ 34
- ○ 54
- ○ 64

Using a Graph

You will have to read a graph to answer some questions.

EXAMPLE

Who read the same amount of books?

○ Barbara and Tom

○ Sue and Barbara

○ Sammy and Sue

When answering graph questions:

• Read the question carefully.

• Look for clue words such as *most, least, same, more*, and *less*.

• You don't always need to count. Try to see how much of each column or row is filled in.

Testing It Out

Now look at the sample question more closely.

Think: Barbara read 2 books and Tom only read 1. Sue read 2 books and Barbara read 2 books. That is the same number. Sammy read 3 books and Sue read 2. The answer is Sue and Barbara.

Using a Graph Practice

Directions: The graph shows how many children get to school by bus, car, train, bike, and walking. Look at the graph. Then fill in the circle next to your answer.

1 How do most children get to school?

○ Bus

○ Car

○ Train

○ Bike

○ Walk

2 How many children walk to school?

○ 10

○ 15

○ 20

3 Do more children ride in cars or on the train?

○ Car

○ Train

Grade 2 Introduction to Practice Test and Final Test

The rest of this book is made up of two tests. On page 328, you will find Grade 2 Math Practice Test. On page 336, you will find Grade 2 Math Final Test. These tests will give you a chance to put the tips you have learned to work.

Here are some things to remember as you take these tests:

• Read and listen carefully to all the directions.

• Be sure you understand all the directions before you begin.

• Ask an adult questions about the directions if you do not understand them.

• Work as quickly as you can during each test.

• Using a pencil, make sure to fill in only one little answer circle for each question. Don't mark outside the circle. If you change an answer, be sure to erase your first mark completely.

• If you're not sure about an answer, you can guess.

• Use the tips you have learned whenever you can.

• It is OK to be a little nervous. You may even do better.

• When you complete all the lessons in this book, you will be on your way to test success!

Mathematics Practice Test

Lesson 1 Mathematics Skills

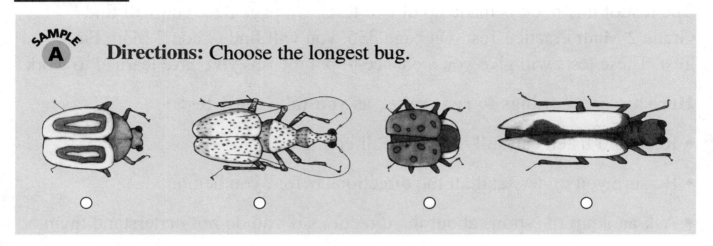

SAMPLE A **Directions:** Choose the longest bug.

Listen carefully while you look at the problem and all the answer choices.

Listen for key words and numbers.

Mark the right answer as soon as you know which one it is. Then get ready for the next item.

GO

1 **What number is shown on the place value chart?**

36   360   306   63
○   ○   ○   ○

---

2 **Find the shape that is one-third shaded.**

  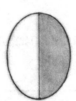 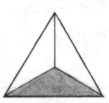

Shape 1   Shape 2   Shape 3   Shape 4
○   ○   ○   ○

---

3 **Which number sentence can be used to show the total number of books?**

○ $4 + 2 = \square$ ○ $2 + 2 + 2 + 2 = \square$

○ $4 + 4 + 4 + 4 = \square$ ○ $4 + 4 = \square$

GO

4 **Which tool would students use to measure a pint of water from the stream?**

hanging scale ○

tape measure ○

measuring cup ○

thermometer ○

---

5 **Pablo has two quarters, one dime, and three nickels. How much money does he have in all?**

75¢ ○

65¢ ○

60¢ ○

70¢ ○

GO

6 **Which child is third from the lifeguard?**

Ann	Tom	Reg	Beth
○	○	○	○

7 **Which squares contain numbers that are all less than 19?**

○ 7 15 10 18   ○ 18 6 23 65

○ 91 20 32 57   ○ 12 81 17 44

8 **Which answer choice names a shape not in the circle?**

○ cone   ○ box
○ can   ○ ball

9 **Which number is missing from the pattern?**

3 5 7 ... 11 13

6	8	9	10
○	○	○	○

GO

Name _____

Directions: The students in Mr. Naldo's class are having a Math Fair. One of the games is a number wheel. The chart shows how many times the spinner landed on each number after 20 spins. Use the chart to do numbers 10 and 11.

Number	1	2	3
Spins	Жll	lll	Жll Жll ll

10   **How many times did the spinner land on the number 3?**

3   5   7   12
○   ○   ○   ○

---

11   **Which spinner looks most like the one the students are using?**

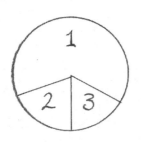 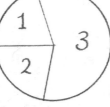 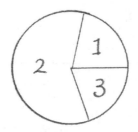  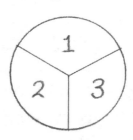

spinner 1   spinner 2   spinner 3   spinner 4
○   ○   ○   ○

STOP

Name _____

Lesson 2 Review

SAMPLE A **Directions:** A train left the station at 9:30. It arrived in Sharon Hill twenty minutes later. Which clock shows the time the train arrived?

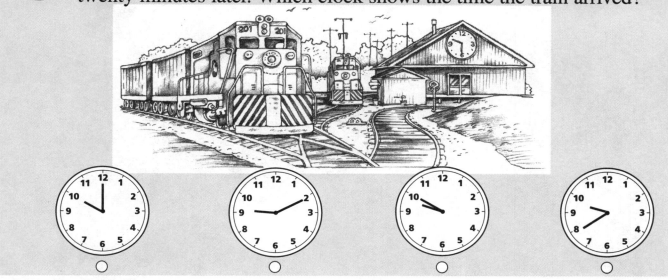

○   ○   ○   ○

1   **Four planes are on the ground at the airport. Two more planes land. How many planes are on the ground all together?**

○ 8

○ 6

○ 7

○ 2

2   **Find the calendar that has thirty-one days.**

	June							September							October							November					

June

S	M	T	W	T	F	S
					1	2	3
4	5	6	7	8	9	10
11	12	13	14	15	16	17
18	19	20	21	22	23	24
25	26	27	28	29	30	

September

S	M	T	W	T	F	S
					1	2
3	4	5	6	7	8	9
10	11	12	13	14	15	16
17	18	19	20	21	22	23
24	25	26	27	28	29	30

October

S	M	T	W	T	F	S
1	2	3	4	5	6	7
8	9	10	11	12	13	14
15	16	17	18	19	20	21
22	23	24	25	26	27	28
29	30	31				

November

S	M	T	W	T	F	S
				1	2	3	4
5	6	7	8	9	10	11
12	13	14	15	16	17	18
19	20	21	22	23	24	25
26	27	28	29	30		

June   September   October   November

○   ○   ○   ○

GO

Directions: The bar graph shows how many fish are in a pond at a school's nature center. Use the graph to do numbers 3–5 on the next page.

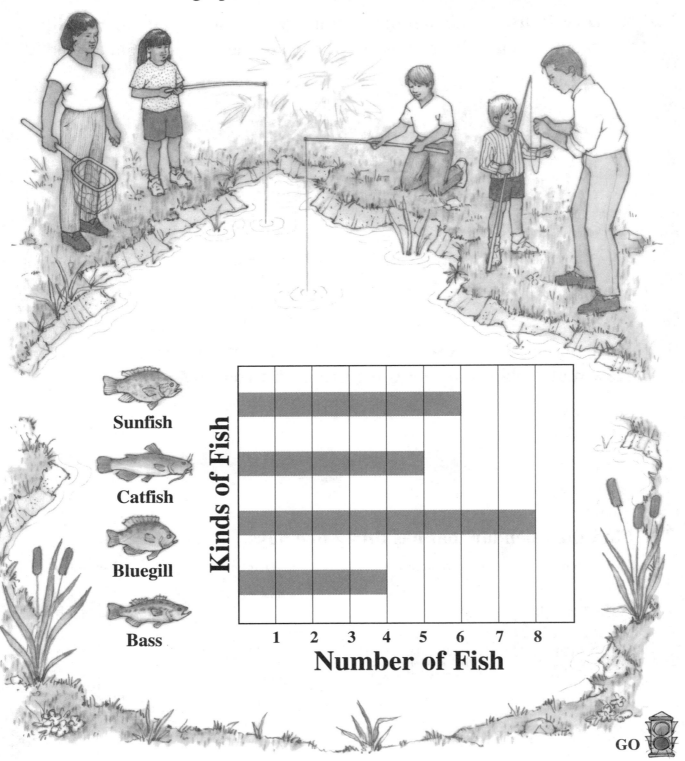

Sunfish

Catfish

Bluegill

Bass

Kinds of Fish

1 2 3 4 5 6 7 8

Number of Fish

GO

3 Look at the graph. What kind of fish are there fewest of in the pond?

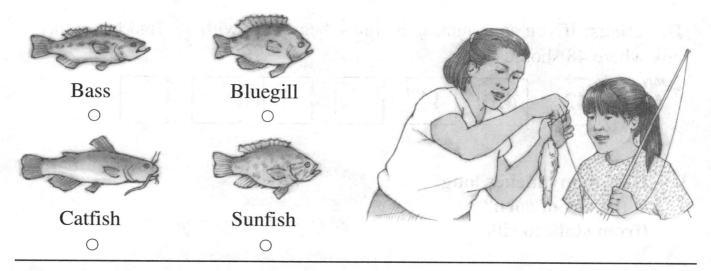

Bass ○

Bluegill ○

Catfish ○

Sunfish ○

4 The average weight of the sunfish in the pond is six ounces. How much do the sunfish in the pond weigh all together? One pound equals 16 ounces.

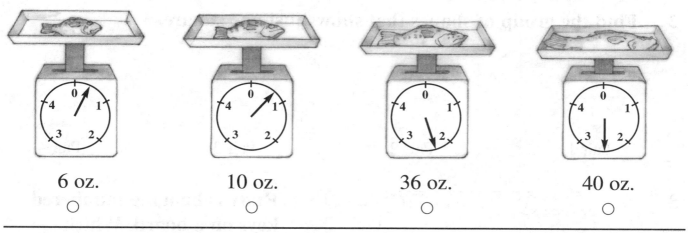

6 oz. ○

10 oz. ○

36 oz. ○

40 oz. ○

5 Nadia counted eight of this kind of fish in the pond. What kind of fish did she count?

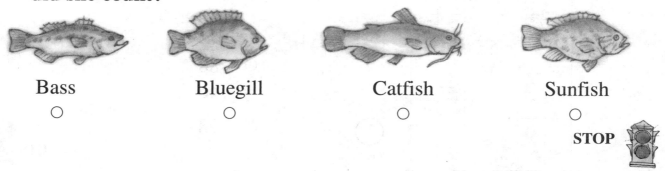

Bass ○

Bluegill ○

Catfish ○

Sunfish ○

STOP

 Name _____

Mathematics Final Test

Directions: If you are counting by ones, beginning with 42, find the empty box where 48 should be.

SAMPLE
A | **42** | **43** | **44** | | | | |
○ ○ ○ ○

1 **How many inches long is the ear of corn?** (from stalk to silk)

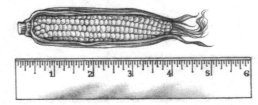

6 inches   5 inches   4 inches   3 inches
○   ○   ○   ○

2 **Find the group of shapes that shows just one square.**

Pair 1   Pair 2   Pair 3   Pair 4
○   ○   ○   ○

3

Rudy is hanging numbered keys on a board. Which numbered key should go in the box that is circled?

○   77
○   88
○   89
○   98

 GO

4 Which coin can be removed from the second group so both groups have the same amount of money?

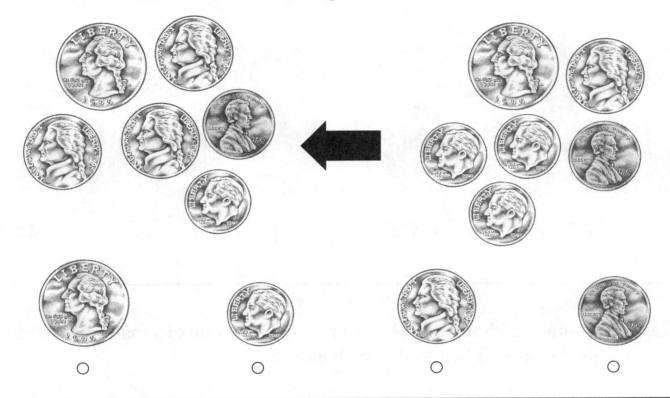

○   ○   ○   ○

---

5 Find the fraction that tells what part of the set is circles.

○ $\dfrac{5}{8}$

○ $\dfrac{3}{8}$

○ $\dfrac{3}{5}$

○ $\dfrac{1}{5}$

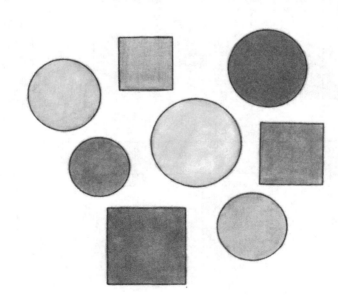

GO

 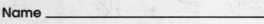

6   **Which number should the missing address be?**

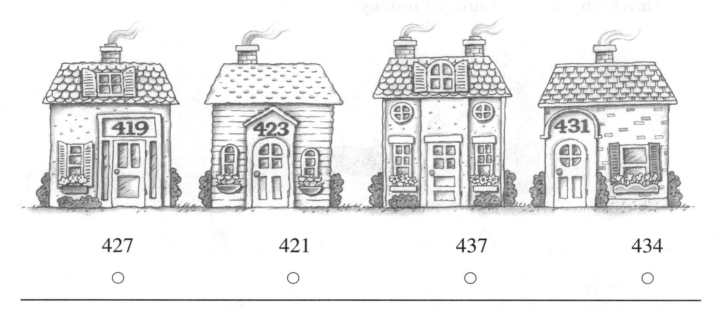

419   423   431

427   421   437   434

○   ○   ○   ○

---

7   **Toshi made a shape on his geoboard. Paula wants to make the same shape. What will her geoboard look like?**

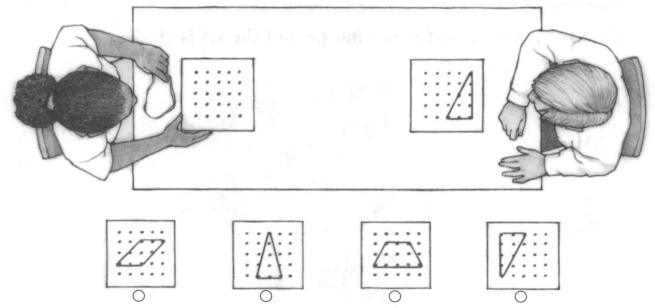

○   ○   ○   ○

GO

8 **Elle saw that some t-shirts on a clothes line formed a pattern. If the pattern continued, which pair of the t-shirts would come next?**

○   ○   ○   ○

9

Cliff counted 3 [hawk].

Georgia counted 9 [hawk].

Cliff counted 3 hawks on bird watch day. Georgia counted 9 hawks. Which number sentence could be used to find how many hawks they counted in all?

$9 - 3 = \square$ $3 + \square = 9$ $3 + 9 = \square$ $9 - \square = 3$
○   ○   ○   ○

STOP

Grade 2 Answer Key

Page 324
1. 40 cents
2. 14 books
3. 33
4. 64

Page 326
1. bus
2. 15
3. train

Page 328
A. last picture

Page 329
1. 360
2. Shape 4
3. 2 + 2 + 2 + 2 =

Page 330
4. measuring cup
5. 75 cents

Page 331
6. Beth
7. 7 15 10 18
8. box
9. 9

Page 332
10. 12
11. spinner 2

Page 333
A. third picture
1. 6
2. October

Page 335
3. Bass
4. 36 oz.
5. Bluegill

Page 336
A. last box
1. 5 inches
2. Pair 4
3. 88

Page 337
4. second picture (dime)
5. 5/8

Page 338
6. 427
7. last picture

Page 339
8. first pair
9. 3 + 9 =

Grade 2 Record Your Scores

After you have completed and checked each test, record your scores below. Do not count your answers for the sample questions.

Practice Test

Mathematics Skills
Number of Questions: 11   Number Correct _____

Review

Number of Questions: 5   Number Correct _____

Final Test

Mathematics
Number of Questions: 9   Number Correct _____

This page was
intentionally left blank.

Tangram Activities

Directions: Cut apart the seven pattern pieces in the back of this book. Then, follow the directions on each of the tangram activity pages.

A. Cover this shape with one piece.

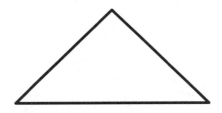

B. Cover this shape with one piece.
   Then, cover it with two pieces.

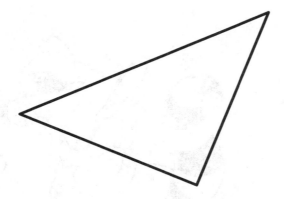

A. Cover this shape with one piece.

B. Cover this shape with three pieces.

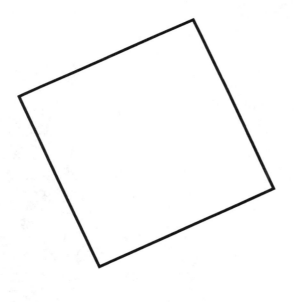

Match the shapes.

Match the shapes.

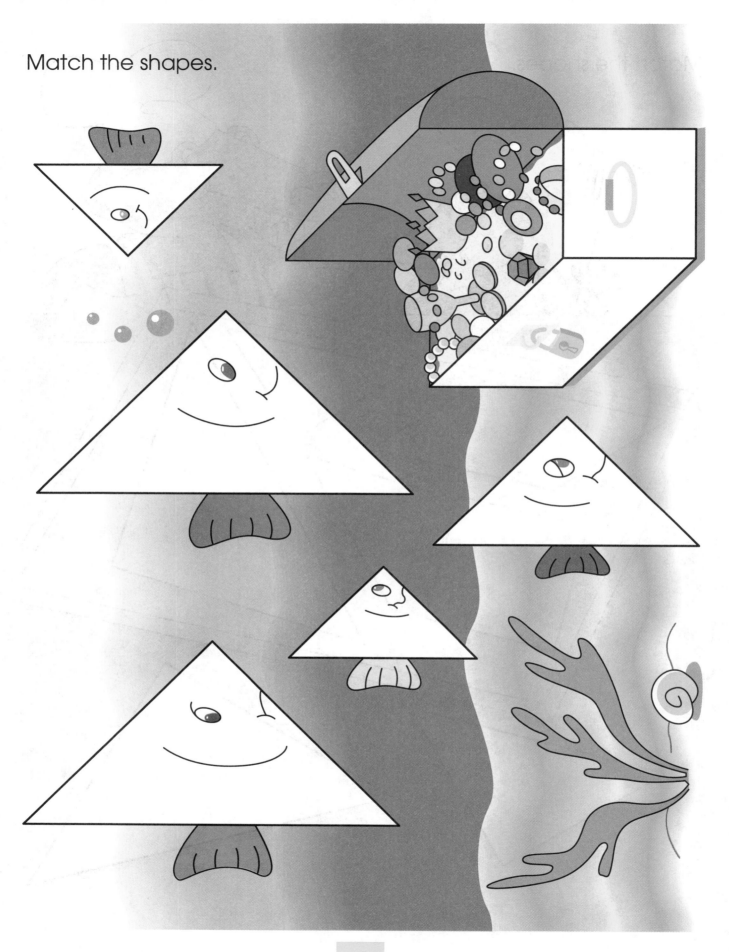

346

Match the shapes.

Match the shapes.

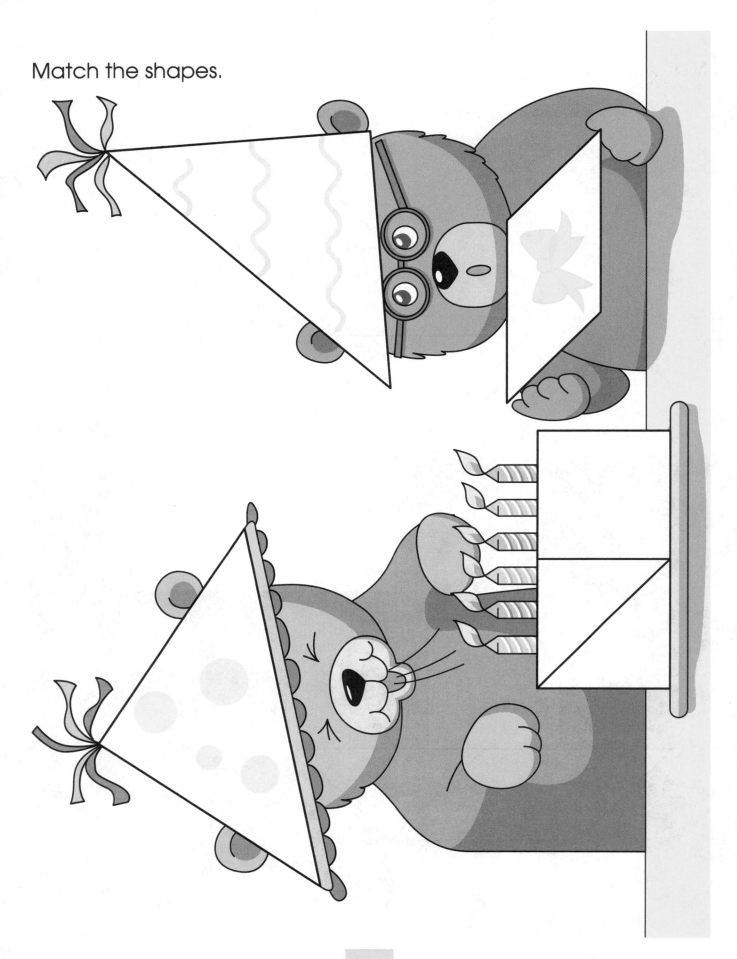

348

Match the shapes.

Match the shapes.

Match the shapes.

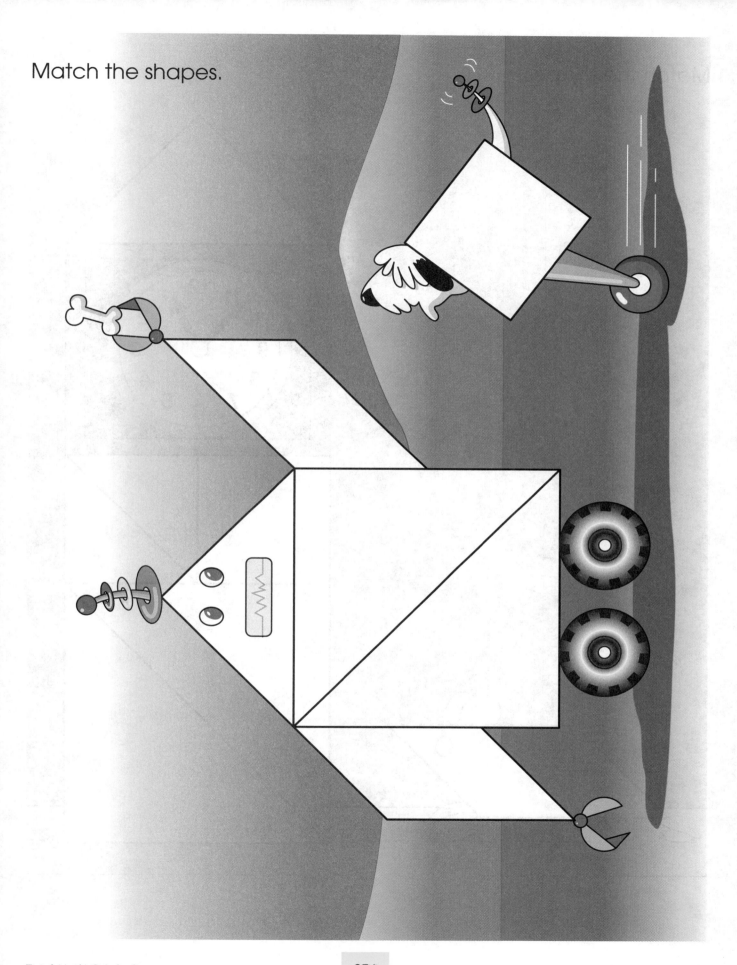

Match the shapes.

Tangram Pieces

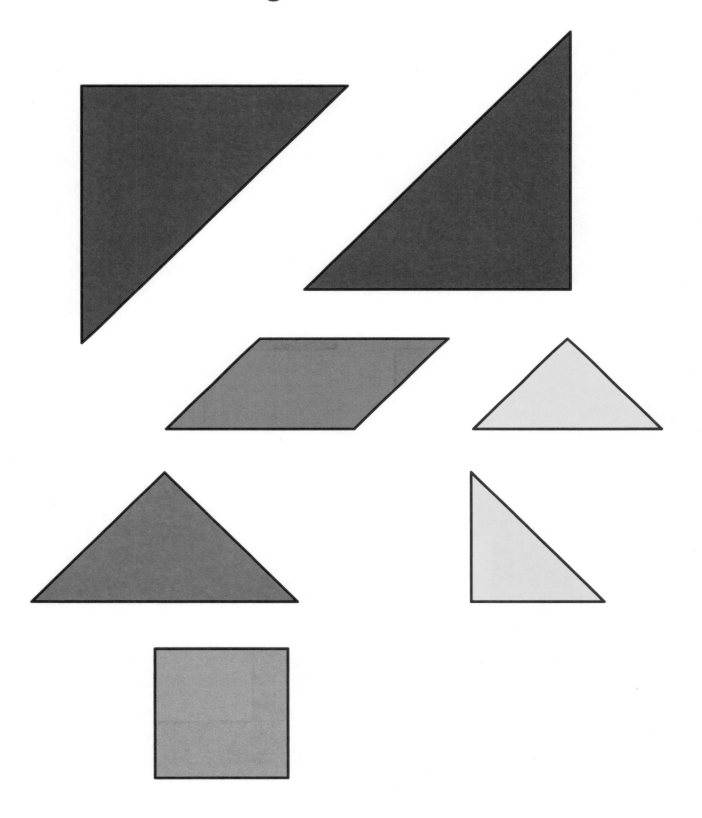

GRADE 2

How to Add

Hundreds	Tens	Ones

1. Add the ones.
Regroup if necessary.

$9 + 5 = 14$

2. Add the tens.
Regroup if necessary.

$30 + 80 + 10 = 120$

3. Add the hundreds.

$400 + 100 + 100 = 600$

$$
\begin{array}{r}
4\ 3\ 9 \\
+\ 1\ 8\ 5 \\
\hline
6\ 2\ 4
\end{array}
$$